MODERN TEACHING OF SOCIAL STUDIES

MODERN TEACHING OF SOCIAL STUDIES

[Strictly According to the UGC Syllabus for B.Ed. Course]

By

NAYYAR SHAMSI

ANMOL PUBLICATIONS PVT. LTD.
NEW DELHI - 110 002 (INDIA)

ANMOL PUBLICATIONS PVT. LTD.
4374/4B, Ansari Road, Daryaganj
New Delhi - 110 002
Ph.: 23261597, 23278000
Visit us at: www.anmolpublications.com

Modern Teaching of Social Studies

First Published, 2004

ISBN 81-261-2027-4

PRINTED IN INDIA

Published by J.L. Kumar for Anmol Publications Pvt. Ltd., New Delhi - 110 002 and Printed at Mehra Offset Press, Delhi.

Contents

Preface

Education is a vast discipline and Teachers' Training is a vital part of it. The responsibilities of the educationists and educators are focused on the task of providing better training to the future teachers for their better learning and proper development. Needless to say that this responsibility can only be exercised, if the trainers are equipped with the required knowledge of the subject concerned. That's why it becomes essential for making adequate provisions for each course to the student-teachers or teacher trainees. The present series is designed for providing a solid workable base for all course-papers. It has been prepared strictly according to the syllabus of the B.Ed class, prescribed by the UGC for different universities.

No doubt, there are so many other books on the subject, available in the market, written by worthy authors. However, every writer has his or her own style and way of presentation. The present work also has its own features and characteristics.

In preparation of this series of texts, the editor had to refer to the works of other authors and information sources. The editor feels a deep sense of gratitude for incorporating their ideas in the text. Hopefully, this series would serve as a 'ready to refer' tool for all teachers, teacher-students and others.

—Editor

1

The Subject

With a view to implement the directions contained in the NPE 1986, the NCERT organised a number of meetings and group discussions and prepared a model national curriculum in 1988. Thereafter it issued guidelines and syllabi in 1989. Extracts from these on Social Sciences are given below.

Wider Goals

The child, at this stage, could be initiated into the study of India's past in all its major aspects such as social, cultural and scientific development. He should also be helped to appreciate diversities in ways of living and interdependence of various regions of India and the world. He should also know the civic and political institutions and understand contemporary social and economic issues and problems. Social skills and civic competencies and a national perspective would, thus, equip him to participate in the task of social and economic reconstruction.

The study of Social Sciences at the Upper Primary stage may comprise the study of History, Geography, Civics and contemporary issues and problems. The various components of the content drawn from different subjects of Social Sciences should be seen as interrelated.

Historical Background

The purpose of teaching/learning History may, very broadly be seen as widening the horizons. No one would disagree with the view that parochialism is not a good thing and that for a proper understanding of one's immediate present also, it is necessary to see it in its wider context of space as well as time. In terms of space, it means that one should see one's immediate spatial environment in the context of the wider world. In terms of time, it means to see the present age among other ages. The present cannot be understood independently and in isolation of what has gone before. History is a continuous process, of which the present is a part which is linked to the past and, hence, can be understood only as a part of that process. Thus, the context of time, that is of history, is crucial to an understanding of the present. No major problem can be seen and understood apart from its historical context. The study of history also shows that the world of man is not stationary but is subject to constant and continuous movement, change and development. It helps in understanding contemporary processes of change, of movement as well as of continuity. By making us aware of the variety and diversity in humanity as well as of unity, and of change, it makes for a less narrow-minded personality and promotes independence of judgment and an attitude of appreciation of contemporary process of change.

History was, for long, misused to legitimize and sanctify the status quo, including the most illegitimate authority and the most oppressive social systems. Imperialists have used it to promote ideas of national chauvinism and 'racial' superiority and to justify their wars of conquest in terms of fulfilling their 'national destiny'. Pernicious uses, in the same way, have often been made in India to promote obscurantism. It is useful to be aware of these misuses while framing the objectives and content outline of the syllabi in history.

The content of history at the school stage also needs some clarification. Although, keeping in view the conceptual level of pupils at different stages, some simplification of historical knowledge is necessary, it should not mean merely presentation of scattered bits of information about events and personalities of the past with a lot of simple, moral judgements thrown in. It may comprise major events and developments in the life of man from the earliest times with a locus on the sequence of changes in society in all its aspects. It should deepen the child's awareness and understanding of the society in which he/she lives, from his/her immediate environment to the country and to the world as a whole.

Initial Level

At the Primary Stage, some elements of historical knowledge form a part of 'a composite area of instruction' called Environmental Studies (Social Studies). The main aim of the historical component, at this stage, is to introduce the pupil to certain elements of man's past, to give him/her general 'feel' of chronology and of the vast span of time during which human beings have lived and worked and those aspects of recent history which would promote a better understanding of the present. It may comprise an introduction to the remains of the past in the form of monuments and cultural objects and elements in the child's immediate environment and elsewhere, events and inventions of the past which had a deep impact on the life of man, and of personalities, Indian and non-Indian, from various periods, who made significant contributions to the culture and civilization of India and of the world. The treatment of these content areas may be in the form of stories, imaginative but without any myth-making, or simple narratives. The syllabus may also include, in a simple form, the story of the struggle for freedom.

Teaching Objectives

History may be introduced as a separate subject as a part of the Social Sciences from Class VI. The general objectives of teaching History from Class VI to Class X, as a part of general education, may be as follows:

1. To develop an understanding of the evolution of human societies and civilizations in general and of Indian society and civilization in particular;

2. To develop an understanding of the processes through which human societies have changed and evolved;
3. To develop an understanding of the integrated nature of historical development and of the homogeneity of civilization;
4. To inculcate an appreciation of the contribution of different peoples to the progress of mankind as a whole;
5. To develop an appreciation of the growth of various components of Indian culture and legitimate pride in the achievements of the Indian people in different periods and in different parts of the country;
6. To develop a historical perspective for understanding contemporary India and the contemporary processes of change;
7. To develop an integrated view of Indian history and civilization and of human civilization as a whole:
8. To develop a spirit ot enquiry and the ability to think critically and creatively and to differentiate between the obsolescent and the dying and the living and the emerging; and
9. To develop a critical appreciation of the past so that the pupil's personality is free from parochialism, irrational prejudices, bigotry, communalism and every kind of chauvinism and is imbued with a rational, scientific and forward-looking outlook.

The Ingredients

For the realization of these objectives, it is necessary to introduce the child a systematic study, appropriate to the school stage, of Indian history and of human civilization from the earliest to the modern times.

While determining the stage-wise, class-wise distribution of various content areas, it may be necessary to keep in view the necessity of promoting a systematic understanding of the subject and avoiding unnecessary repetitions. The concentric method generally suffers from both these defects. It may also be kept in view that for many students, the Upper Primary Stage is the terminal stage of formal schooling. Also, a proper understanding of historical developments requires some degree of geographical knowledge. Keeping these considerations in view, it is suggested that two broadly systematic courses be developed, one dealing with the history of India and the second with the history of civilization. The first may be introduced at the Upper Primary Stage but it may also include a general perspective of world civilization. The second may be introduced at the Secondary Stage and it may include historical development of India as a part of world historical development and may also give adequate importance to those aspects and developments in Indian history that have a close bearing on the understanding of contemporary India such as the freedom movement.

The distribution of the content in Indian history may follow the usual division into ancient, medieval and modern India which may be introduced in Classes VI, VII and VIII respectively.

India's cultural heritage and India's freedom struggle may be important components of the syllabus at all stages, viz. Primary, Upper Primary and Secondary. A proper understanding of these areas is crucial to promoting an understanding of contemporary India and an appreciation of the value and ideals which are basic to India's nationhood. In the selection of content for these areas, it is necessary to focus attention on the contributions of all parts of the country and to present an overall picture of the country as a whole.

The Traditions

What should be the place of local history in this framework? The term 'Local History' is understood differently by different people. It may mean promoting an awareness of the historical and cultural remains found in the child's immediate environment. The term has also been used to mean the history of a region or State, presenting the region or State as having a distinct and independent historical identity, traced back to the earliest times. Establishing the historical distinctiveness of a region corresponding to the present political boundaries of a State is often unhistorical and overlooks the historical interconnections of that region with other parts of the country. Introducing this kind of local history at the school stage has the danger of promoting parochialism and regional cultural chauvinism. This is not to suggest a diminishing of the importance of historical developments in the region, but only to emphasize the need to study local developments in the broader country-wide context. It may be desirable to avoid regional histories at the school stage as separate courses of study and to include the details of developments in the region in any period in the general context of Indian history in that period. For example, while dealing with the history of India in any particular period or aspect, more details about developments in one's region or State could be given. Alternatively, for each period of Indian history, a separate section on developments in one's region/State could be added.

A very important use of local history can be made in the form of independent, individual and group project work involving the study of past events and developments in the locality, local monuments and other remains of the past, etc. This would help promote the ability to do independent work and develop a sense of the past and interest in the work of preservation of the cultural remains of the past.

Second Level

The History component of the course in Social Sciences at this stage, as suggested earlier, may consist of a general introduction to Indian history from prehistoric times to the emergence of India as an independent nation, alongwith a broad perspective of world history. The emphasis in this course may be on social and economic conditions and various aspects of culture, including science and technology, in different parts of the country, in different periods of history, besides giving a broad idea of political developments. While, obviously, it is neither necessary nor possible to give a continuous chronological account of every development in every part of the country, it is essential that historical development of all parts of the country is covered. The main focus may be on providing a broad all-India view, including the main regional trends. While this is important in dealing with political developments which provide a broad framework of chronology, it is even more important in the teaching/learning of cultural development. Promotion of knowledge and understanding of India's cultural heritage is a major objective of teaching/learning. The emphasis in dealing with this area should be on the study of the growth of various components of culture in different parts of the country, along with their mutual interactions, in different periods of history. Some of the existing shortcomings to be avoided are that it is monolithic, that it had any one region of the country as its main centre and that it emerged in isolation and in a fully developed form in any particular period of history. While the neglect of regional trends needs to be avoided, it is also necessary to avoid giving an exclusive and chauvinistic emphasis to regional trends and treating them in isolation.

Specific Objectives

1. To develop an understanding and appreciation of the dynamics of the ethnic diversity of India;
2. To promote an understanding of the major stages in the evolution of Indian society through the ages;
3. To develop an appreciation of the growth of various components of Indian culture in different parts of the country in different periods;
4. To develop a critical appreciation of the past so that the pupil's personality is free from irrational prejudices and bigotry, parochialism and communalism, and is imbued with a scientific and forward-looking outlook;
5. To develop an appreciation of India's cultural heritage and its composite nature, of its richness and variety, and of the processes through which it has developed;
6. To develop the ability to study contemporary problems of Indian society in their historical perspective;

7. To develop an understanding of the processes of change so that an appreciation of the aspiration for change to establish a just social order is inculcated;
8. To promote the study of the historical development of India in relation to and in the perspective of the history of mankind as a whole;
9. To deepen knowledge about and understanding of India's freedom struggle and of the values and ideals that it represented; and
10. To develop an awareness of the necessity of and participation in the work of preservation of historical remains.

Adequate attention should be paid to the aspects of change and development. The teaching should be free from communal, parochial and other types of prejudices and should aim at the cultivation of a broad humanistic outlook.

The class-wise organization of the syllabus may be as follows: history of ancient India in Class VI, medieval India in Class VII and modern India in Class VIII.

The major component of the syllabus for Class VIII comprises the study of the struggle for freedom. The secular character of the struggle, participation by the people from all communities and all parts of the country, and different facets and phases of the struggle should be stressed in the teaching/learning process. The study of the freedom movement should provide the historical perspective for the understanding of contemporary India and of the basic framework of the goals and policies of independent India's national development.

Some part of the school time allotted to the teaching of history should be devoted to practical activities and project work, to be done outside the classroom, in the library, and outside the school. These may consist of studying local monuments and participation in the work of their preservation, studying local cultural traditions, folk-lore and other aspects of culture and preparing museum kits on these, working on projects relating to art and culture in different parts of the country, use of some elementary source materials, studying the place names of historical sites and places and identifying their location, and preparation of historical maps. Practical activities and projects should be devised which may be taken up by individual students, groups of students, or by the class as a whole. Adequate attention should be paid to practical activities and project work so that the pupil is helped to progress from being a passive recipient to an active participant in the teaching/learning process. This is also essential to promote the growth of the pupil's ability to learn on his/her own.

The Curriculum

Class VI Ancient India

Unit I: Introduction

How and Why We Study the Past. How and why we know about the past, sources for reconstructing the past, sources for studying Indian history: Written records, literary sources, archaeological and other remains, oral traditions; their relative importance—Importance of studying the past for understanding the present—Importance of Critical attitude.

Geographical and Ethnographical Features of India

(a) Physical divisions of India: Main physical features—mountainous regions—river valleys—forests—coastal areas.

(b) Ecology and human habitations.

(c) The commercial routes and lines of communications that existed in ancient times.

(d) Ethnic composition, intermingling of ethnic groups, etc.

(e) The distribution of the major language groups in India.

(f) The continuance of some tribal groups and cultures in different parts of the country.

Pre-historic Cultures of India

(a) The evolution of man's life on earth – Old Stone Age – Man as a food-gatherer – Old Stone Age tools. Belief – Nomadic life; Discovery and use of fire.

(b) Man takes to farming, change from nomadic to settled life – Pottery – Invention of the wheel – Domestication of animals – Improved tools. Clothing – Some important sites of Stone Age in India.

Unit II: The Harappan Culture

(a) Transition to urban civilisation – First civilisations in Mesopotamia, Egypt, etc. Evidence found in different parts of India.

(b) The extent of Harappan culture – Major sites – Chronology.

(c) The layout of the city – houses – roads – public conveniences (baths) – drainage.

(d) Life of the people – social divisions – food, clothing, ornaments, religious beliefs.

(e) Agriculture, trade and commerce – arts and crafts – use of metals.

(f) Script.

(g) Contacts with contemporary civilizations. (h) Decline of the culture.

Unit III: New Cultural Patterns in India (1500 B.C. 600 B.C.)

(a) Chalcolithic cultures in India.

(b) Iron Age cultures – Megaliths and Painted Grey Ware.

(c) The advent of the Indo-Aryan speaking people, their settlement in Sapta Sindhu area – beginnings of contacts with the other areas and cultures – their economy – social and political organization – religion and literature in the early Vedic Age.

(d) The movement of the Indo-Aryan speaking people to other part of India—Madhya Desa, Eastern India and Western India—Material life in the later Vedic Age—Religion—Sacrifices—Beginnings of social stratification—Political Changes—Monarchy in North India—Megalithic cultures in peninsular India.

Unit IV: India from the Rise of Magadha to the Mauryan Empire

(a) Socio-economic changes—Emergence of towns, trade and commerce—Beginning of coinage—Arts and Crafts—Wider use of iron.

(b) Political systems—Monarchies and tribal politics in north India— conflicts.

(c) New religious movements—Mahavira and the Buddha—their teachings—other sects.

(d) Iranians and Greeks—Invasions—their impact.

(e) Rise and Growth of Mauryan Empire: Polity Administration—Social and Economic life—Religion (with special reference to Ashoka)—Art and culture—Relations with Tamil States—Their echo in Sangam literature.

Unit V: India during the period 200 B.C. to 300 A.D.

(a) The decline of the Mauryas—the rise of Greeks, Sakas and Kushanas in the north and the Satavahanas in the south—their mutual relations. The Sangam Age.

(b) Economic activities—growth of commercial contacts with the western world, South-East Asia and China—Deve-lopment of crafts and guilds—coinage.

(c) Social and religious life—Revival of Brahmanical religion and the birth of Mahayana—Spread of Buddhism in and outside India.

(d) Art and literature—various schools—Prakrit and Sanskrit languages and literature.

Unit VI: India from 300 A.D. to 800 A.D.

(a) A brief outline of the political history of the Guptas, Vakatakas, Pallavas, Chalukyas, and Vardhamanas.

(b) (i) Economic conditions of the people—land grants and extension of agriculture—trade—conditions of towns and cities.

(ii) The caste system—Position of women.

(iii) The general description of the condition of the people—Writings of Fahien and other travellers.

(iv) Religion—decline of Buddhism—Revival of Brahmanical religion.

(v) Art, Literature and Languages, Science and Technology— Medicine, astronomy and meta-llurgy.

(vi) Contacts with the outside world—Trade and cultural contacts with Christianity—Rise of Islam—Early contacts through Arab traders— Arab conquest of Sind—Migrations to South-East Asia.

Class VII Medieval India

Unit I: India and the World

Middle Ages, meaning of the term Medieval period in Indian history— Sources—Developments in West Asia in Medieval times—Arab Empire— Europe in medieval times—Feudalism—Turks—Mongols—Trade routes— Influence of developments in other parts of the world on India.

Unit II: India from 800 A.D. to 1200 A.D.

(a) General characteristics of this period.

(b) Political Fragmentation—Process of formation of new dynasties; the Pratiharas, Palas, Rashtrakutas, Cholas, Pandavas, Hoysalas and the Yadavas—Turkish invasions.

(c) Changes in the caste system – Proliferation of new castes and sub-castes.

(d) Religion – The emergence of the temple as an important institution – Formation of new religious sects and monastic orders.

(e) The importance of the village in socio-economic life – Guilds of traders and artisans.

(f) Birth of new languages, scripts and regional literature – Growth of new art styles.

Unit III: India from Early Thirteenth Century to Early Sixteenth Century

(a) The establishment of the Sultanate of Delhi and unification of northern India.

(b) Administration under the Sultanate with social reference to Alauddin Khalji and Mohammad Tughlaq.

  (i) The emergence of Iqta system.

  (ii) Military nature of the Turkish rule.

  (iii) Economic life – organization and production in Royal Karkhanas

  (iv) Public works under the Sultans.

(c) Disintegration of the Sultanate and rise of regional kingdoms:

  (i) Bahmani and Vijayanagar Kingdoms – Their conflicts.

  (ii) Regional Kingdoms in North India and South India.

(d) Developments in society and economy:

  (i) Social and economic conditions of the people.

  (ii) International Trade – Expansion of Trade with Europe and China

(e) Developments in culture:

(i) Evaluation of a Composite Indian Culture.

(ii) Art and Architecture: Tombs, Mosques, Temples, Forts—Bronze sculpture.

(iii) Growth of literature in the regional languages—Persian literature.

(iv) The Bhakti and Sufi movements—Religious reform movements in Deccan and South.

Unit IV: Advent of the Mughals and Europeans

(a) Coming of the Mughals—conflict with the Afghans—Bahmani and Vijayanagar Kingdoms, internal developments and their mutual conflicts.

(b) Developments in Europe—Renaissance—Voyages of discovery— Trade routes and articles of trade—European trade with India—Coming of the Portuguese—Influence of developments in other parts of the world on India.

Unit V: India under the Mughals

(a) The expansion of the Mughal empire from Akbar to Aurangzeb.

(b) Administration: Army, Mansabdars—Revenue system—Justice.

(c) Religious policy of the Mughals with special reference to Akbar's Din-i-Ilahi.'

(d) Social and economic conditions.

(e) Development of art, literature and architecture.

(f) Conditions in India outside the Mughal empire.

Unit VI: Disintegration of the Mughal Empire

(a) Decline of the Mughal Empire

(b) Weakening of the central authority and administration.

(c) Rise of independent and semi-independent States; Bengal, Awadh, Hyderabad, Marathas, Sikhs, etc.

(d) Foreign invasions: Nadir Shah – Ahmad Shah

Class VIII Modern India

Unit I: India and the Modern World

(a) Beginnings of modern age in Europe – colonization and the plunder of colonies.

(b) Rise of capitalism – The Industrial Revolution – Rise of Imperialism-Other major world developments in the 18lh, 19th and 20th centuries and their impact on India.

(c) The coming of Europeans to India – Early activities – Mutual conflicts – Local resistance to European powers.

Unit II: The Rise, Growth and Impact of British Rule in India

(a) The rise of British power in Bengal.

(b) Expansion of British Power

 (i) in the south

 (ii) in the north

 (iii) in central and western India

(c) The evolution of British administration

 (i) General administration

 (ii) The Revenue and Judicial Systems

(d) The impact of British rule in India

 (i) Impact on village economy

 (ii) Decline of indigenous trade and industry

 (iii) Beginnings of new education

 (iv) Transport and communications

Unit III: Revolts against British Rule

(a) Early revolts against British rule in different parts of the country.

(b) Revolt of 1857 – its causes, extent, nature and results.

Unit IV: British Policies and Administration in India after 1858

(a) British political, economic and social policies after 1858 – British Government and Princely States – Policy towards neighbouring countries.

(b) Constitutional developments between 1909 and 1917.

Unit V: Changes in Economy and Society

(a) Economic life: Agriculture – Commercial crops – Impoverishment of the peasantry – Rural Indebtedness – Famines – Development of irrigation – Transport – Railways – Plantations – Beginning of modern industries – Trade – Nature of industrial development – Economic conditions of the people – Emergence of new classes in Indian society.

(b) Social and Religious Reform Movements and Cultural Awakening:

Rise of new social classes – Education, its nature and influence – social and religious reform movements. Raja Rammohan Roy – Brahmo Samaj – Ishwarchandar Vidyasagar – Prarthana Samaj – Ramakrishna Mission Reform – Movements among Muslim – Veersalingam – Jotiba Phule and Sri Narayan Guru – Singh Sabha movement – Cultural awakening – Literature in modern Indian languages – Art – Science – Press – Influence of economic and social changes and of reform movements on the national consciousness of the people – Role of literature, art and press in promoting nationalism.

Unit VI: Rise of Indian Nationalism and Struggle for Freedom

(a) Emergence of Indian Nationalism: Factors and forces – Political associations – Formation of the Indian National

Congress – Main demands and methods of struggle in the early phase (1885 – 1905)

(b) Nationalist Movement from 1905 to 1918 – Rise of Extremism – Partition of Bengal – Boycott and Swadeshi – Swaraj as the objective – British Policy – Divide-and-rule – Revolutionary movement in India and abroad – Ghadar – Home Rule Movement – Lucknow Pact.

(c) Beginning of Mass Anti-Imperialist Movements – Emergence of Gandhiji and his role – Consequences of the First World War for India – Repressive measures – Jallianwala Bagh massacre – Khilafat Question – Khilafat and Non-Cooperation Movement – New methods of a struggle – Role of peasants and workers – Suspension of movement – Constructive Programme" and Swarajists.

(d) Revolutionary Movement: Revival of revolutionary activities in early 1920's – Bhagat Singh and his comrades – Surya Sen and revolutionary activities in Bengal – Assessment of the role of revolutionaries.

(e) Civil Disobedience Movement: Simon Commission and the revival of the mass movement – Adoption of Purna Swaraj Resolution – Dandi March – Civil Disobedience Movement – Repression – Round Table Conference – Resumption of Civil Disobedience Movement – Main features and trends in the movement.

(f) Communalism and the freedom movement – Movements of Depressed classes – Socialist ideas and movements – Workers' and peasants' movement – Indian Freedom Movement and the world – Freedom Movement in the Princely States.

(g) Government ot India Act of 1935 – Formation of provincial Ministries.

(h) Indian Freedom Movement during the Second World War – Individual Satyagraha – Cripps Mission – Quit India Movement – Azad Hind Fauj.

(i) Popular upsurge after the Second World War—Cabinet Mission— Demand for Pakistan—Interim Government and Constituent Assembly— Partition and Independence—Immediate tasks—Framing of the Constitution—Integration of Princely States—Liberation of French and Portuguese possession.

N.B.: The role of individual leaders may be mentioned in relation of specific movements and events.

Geographical Concept

Rationale and Objectives. Geography at the Lower Primary stage may form a part of the composite area of instruction called environmental studies. It should expose the child in his/her physical and socio-cultural environment in a graded manner. It say, thus, include the study of physical and cultural features as well as the Ire of the people in the immediate environment of the child i.e. his/her home and neighbourhood. Gradually, the child's mental horizon is extended to the study of these features in relatively distant places starting from his/ her State and country to the world at large.

At the Upper Primary Stage. Geography may be introduced as a separate subject under Social Sciences. The course in Geography at this stage, covering a period of three years, should be able to widen the perspective of the student through the study of life in different parts of the world. Elements of physical, economic/ regional, and practical geography should form an integral part of the course spreading over three years. These would help in developing a geographical perspective, so necessary to understand the complexities of the man-environment relationship in a global context and the interdependence of region/countries of the world. This framework should also help the student in understanding the problems of economic development of his/her own Country/State in the final year of this state.

The Geography course at this stage should have the following objectives:

1. to promote an understanding of the different elements of the physical environment which, in fact, affect man's ways of living:
2. to help the student realize that human beings everywhere try to make the best possible use of their environment, including gifts provided by nature to satisfy their needs;
3. to help the student appreciate the role of man, armed with science and technology, in developing the natural resources for raising the standard of living of the people;

   to help the student realize that man's interaction with the environment has resulted in environmental degradation, e.g. depletion of resources and population of the environment, threatening the very survival of mankind. Hence, there is an urgent need to use the resources of the environment wisely;
5. to help the student understand the variety of ways of living in different parts of the world and interdependence of regions/countries, leading ultimately to the promotion of international understanding;
6. to develop an appreciation of the value of cooperative effort at the local, national and world levels for developmental activities;
7. to help the pupil learn from the experiences of other peoples/nations and understand their relevance to India in developing its own resources;
8. to acquaint the student with the political map of the world, location of different countries, distribution of major resources and major economic products entering into international trade;
9. to develop an ability to use the tools of geography such as maps, globes, charts and photographs; and
10. to acquaint the student with elementary methods of study used by geographers such as field study/project work.

Selection and Organisation of Content Areas

The course in Geography, at this stage, should be developed after careful selection of material, keeping in view the following considerations:

(a) that Geography is being taught as a separate subject for the first time;

(b) that the children must be able to link up their basic knowledge of Geography, acquired through their lessons in Environmental Studies/Social Studies at the Lower Primary stage.

(c) that the child would acquire a basic knowledge and understanding of the geography of the world which would help him/her to understand the world better.

Thus, the major components of the Geography syllabus, at this stage, should include the following:

(i) Elementary principles of Physical Geography

(ii) Geography of the continents and selected countries

(iii) Geography of India and Geography of the state

(iv) Practical Geography

The principles of Physical Geography should include the study of the earth and solar system, the lithosphere, atmosphere, hydrosphere and biosphere. Instead of taking all the topics together in one class, they may be distributed over the entire stage. Their class-wise distribution should be done on the basis of the difficulty-level of the topic, broad area and its structural placement.

The age and the attainments of the pupils at this stage and the use that the majority of them would make of Geography in later life, preclude the study of world geography in terms of natural regions alone. In order to sake the children familiar with the world, an introductory study of continents and the study of a few countries representing some typical examples of natural regions and economic development patterns, should be spread over three years of the Upper Primary stage.

In Class VI, the study of the Southern Continents i.e. Africa, Australia, South America and Antarctica should be taken up because of the comparatively less complex nature of man-environment relationship. In Class VII, the continents of Europe and North America together with the USSR representing the comparatively more complex nature of man-environment relationship should be dealt with. It would provide the students an opportunity to compare the life of people in different parts of the world and assess the impact of scientific and technological advancements on their lives. In Class VIII, the geography if its neighbouring countries should be taken up.

In every continent only a few countries, typical of different natural regions, should be selected for detailed study. In the shrinking world of today it is with these political entities that we interact—culturally, socially, politically and economically. Considering the short span of time available for teaching Geography, it is not possible to study all the countries in detail. Hence, the selection of countries as case studies is a must. However, this selection should be done carefully so that they represent typical conditions of different natural regions. For example, while selecting countries from Africa, Zaire could be the best representation of the hot-wet forests of the equatorial type of climate. The study of the geography of the continents/ countries should centre around the following:

(a) location, size, shape and political divisions;

(b) physical features, drainage, climate and vegetation;

(c) natural resources of the country and their utilization:

  (i) soil, forests and wild-life, minerals, power and human resources;

  (ii) agriculture, industries, trade, transport and communication;

  (iii) economic development.

The Geography of India in detail, should be taken up at the terminal stage. It should include the study of physical features, climate, resources — both natural and human — of the country, and their utilization, trade, transport and communication. Having studied the geography of the world for two and a half years and having grown in maturity-level, the children would be in a much better position to understand their own country. It is suggested that the States following these guidelines may include the study of respective State alongwith the geography of India on the same lines. For maintaining a balance in the syllabus, the course content for 'Geography of India' should be reduced. However, it should be done by condensing the course rather than dropping topics altogether.

Like Physical Geography, the practical Geography course should also be spread over three years. It should be given due weightage. Besides having separate units in all three years, practical activities should form an integral part of all other units. This would help the children in Geography, representing geographical data through maps, sketches, models, charts, etc. and in acquainting themselves with the methods of study used for geographical studies.

Significant Factors

Some of the core curricular areas as mentioned in POA (Progra-mme of Action) such as protection of environment, inculcating scientific temper and small family norm have been integrated into the course content of Geography at appropriate places.

Learning Techniques

An inter-disciplinary approach should be followed in the teaching of Geography. Emphasis should be laid on concept formations and their development. Facts and figures should be used as supplementary and complementary to the basic concepts. They should not be used in isolation just for memorization. Audio-visual aids are of great importance in the teaching of Geography and they should be used liberally in the classroom. Geographical terms should be explained properly with the help of diagrams and suitable examples. Children should be encouraged to make observations and record their findings. They should be able to identify various geographical features.

Due care should be taken in developing geographical skills such as reading and interpreting maps, diagrams and pictures, locating places on maps, drawing simple maps and diagrams and collecting, processing and analysing geographical information.

It is, therefore, necessary that students are given enough opportunities to take up such activities which would help them in developing the necessary geographical skills and competencies. Some of these activities may be as follows:

Map Reading and Map Making

Students should be encouraged to:

(a) study a globe, atlas, wall map, maps given in newspapers, a local map;

(b) find the location of a given place or feature in a map;

(c) fill an outline map with given details;

(d) make a sketch and plan;

(e) draw simple diagrams such as line graphs.

Picture Reading

Activities in picture reading would help students collect geographical information from and through pictures. Such assignments may be based on illustrations given in textbooks, magazines, newspapers, charts, and so on. These assignments may be framed as the following:-

(a) observing given pictures and deriving information from them;

(b) matching pictures and places;

(c) identifying various land forms, both physical and cultural, from a given set of pictures such as a port and harbour; a hill and a mountain; a 'V' shaped valley and a 'U' shaped valley; an iceberg and a glacier; a hot-wet forest and a taiga forest; and a rural market and an urban shopping complex.

Maintaining a Record Book

Students should be encouraged to maintain a record book in the classroom in which news items of geographical interest such as daily weather, earthquakes, volcanic eruptions, floods, famines, cyclones, etc. may be collected and analyzed. These activities could be taken up collectively.

Project Work

Collection of geographical information and their presentation should form part of the project work. Any topic of geographical interest suitable to this age group may be selected for the purpose.

Class Discussion

A suitable geographical topic, having different dimensions, may be selected for the purpose. The class may be divided into a few groups, each selecting a particular aspect. The teacher may act as the moderator who will conduct the discussion and would present a summary in the end.

Field Trips

Field trips should be organized to provide an opportunity to students for direct observation. Hence, a place of geographical interest such as a forest, an industry, a power station, traffic junction, market place or a slum should be selected. Preparation of the visit should be made in advance. Each student should be clear about his/her task. The report, based on the field visit, should be prepared and discussed collectively with the help of the teacher.

Evaluation

Evaluation in Geography should be planned systematically to realize the objectives of teaching Geography to the maximum possible extent. For developing necessary skills in Geography, it is essential that little more weightage is given to this part. Besides map filling, map reading, picture reading, interpreting diagrams and project work should also form part of the evaluation. However, this should be done in a graded manner.

Syllabus

Class VI

Unit I: The Earth – Our Planet

1. The earth and the solar system
2. The rotation and revolution of the earth
3. Locating places on the earth by latitude and longitude
4. Four realms of the earth – the lithosphere, atmosphere, hydrosphere and biosphere
5. Globes and maps – their relative advantages and disadvantages

Unit II: Africa – Lands and Peoples

1. Land climate, vegetation and wild life
2. Natural resources and their utilization
3. The people
4. Zaire – Example of the equatorial lowland
5. Nigeria – Example of the Savanna
6. The Arab Republic of Egypt – the Nile Valley – Example of a developed region of the Sahara
7. South Africa – Example of the Veld and the Mediterranean lands

Unit III: South America – Land and Peoples

1. Land, climate, vegetation and wild life
2. Natural resources and their utilization
3. The people
4. Brazil and Argentina – Examples of equatorial hot-wet forest lands and temperate grasslands respectively.

Unit IV: Australia – Land and People

1. Land, climate, vegetation and wild life

2. Natural resources and their utilization
3. The people
4. Economic development

Unit V: Antarctica

1. Land, climate, natural vegetation and wild life
2. Exploration of the continent with special reference to the Indian expeditions

Unit VI: Practical Work: Map Reading

1. A sketch, a plan, and a map
2. Distance and direction on a map
3. Recognition of simple conventional signs and symbols

Class VII

Unit I: Atmosphere and Hydrosphere

1. The composition and layers of the atmosphere
2. The air and its changing temperature
3. Pressure and winds, major pressure and wind belts
4. Ocean waters and their circulation—waves, tides and currents.

Unit II: North America—Lands and Peoples

1. Land, climate, vegetation and wild life
2. Natural resources and their utilization
3. The people
4. Canada and the United Slates

Unit III: Europe—Lands and Peoples

1. Land, climate, vegetation and wild life
2. Natural resources and their utilization

3. The people
4. France, the United Kingdom, Federal Republic of Germany and German Democratic Republic

Unit IV: The Soviet Union—Lands and Peoples

1. Land, climate, vegetation and wild life
2. Natural resources and their utilization
5. The people
4. Economic development

Unit V: Practical Work—Studying the Weather and Night Sky

1. Understanding "today's weather"—temperature, rainfall, relative humidity and wind direction.
2. Observation and record keeping of weather conditions with the help of weather instruments.
3. Observation and keeping records of sunrise and sunset.
4. Identification of some stars and constellations in the night sky.

Class VIII

Unit I: Lithosphere and Land forms

1. The crust of the earth and major rock types
2. Interior of the earth
3. Earthquakes and volcanoes
4. Process of gradation and the agents of gradation
   (i) Weathering, formation and conservation of soil
   (ii) Running water
   (iii) Ground water
   (iv) Moving ice
   (v) Winds
   (vi) Sea waves

Unit II: Asia—Lands and Peoples

1. Land, climate, vegetation and wild life
2. Natural resources and their utilization
3. The people
4. Our neighbours—Pakistan, Nepal, Bhutan, Bangladesh, Burma and Sri Lanka
5. Malaysia and Indonesia
6. China and Japan

Unit III: India—Physical Setting

1. Relief features and drainage
2. Climate and vegetation

Unit IV: India—Natural Resources

1. Major natural resources, their distribution and utilization
   - (a) Soil
   - (b) Minerals—iron, coal, petroleum, bauxite and manganese
   - (c) forest and wild life
   - (d) water
2. Conservation of natural resources

Unit V: India—Human Resources

1. Population: density, distribution, growth rate and structure of population—sex composition, literacy, rural-urban ratio, employment, age-structure
2. Quality of life—economic and social development, health and nutrition

Unit VI: India—Economic Development

(a) Agriculture: Predominance of monsoon, irrigation projects, food production, Green Revolution.

(b) Industries: Development of industry, types of industries—heavy, small-scale and cottage; few important industries—iron and steel, textiles, sugar, oil refineries, heavy machinery and chemicals.

(c) Trade—internal and external.

(d) Transport and communications: Land, water and air transport; means of communication and their development.

Unit VII: Practical Work—Studying Local Maps

1. Studying local map—a city map or a country map
2. Observing land forms in the neighbourhood and locating them on a map

Civil Concept

Rationale and Objectives. The course in Civics at the Upper Primary stage is intended to promote well informed and intelligent citizens who have the ability to participate in the affairs of their community effectively. From this point of view, the course at this stage should aim mainly at imparting training in civic life. It should contain such socially imperative knowledge as would not only impart understanding of the civic processes but also provide training in the development of civic competencies which are essential to ensure citizens' participation in the task of social and economic reconstruction. In this context, it is equally important that Civics should include the study of the functioning of various civic and political institutions. Some practical aspects of citizenship education should also be incorporated from the point of view of adopting a functional approach.

Curriculum Aims

1. to provide the student with intelligent understanding of the various social responsibilities and civic processes;
2. to help the student understand our Constitution and the values enshrined in it;

3. to acquaint the student with the machinery of the government at different levels;
4. to make the student conscious of the contemporary social and economic problems and issues, instilling in him, thereby, a sense of responsibility to face them effectively;
5. to promote a feeling of Indianness among students;
6. to promote among students the feeling of oneness with the people and their institutions;
7. to inculcate in the student the values of egalitarianism, democracy, secularism and national integration; and
8. to develop in the student an understanding that there is a need for international peace and cooperation.

Choice of Spheres

In the primary stage, efforts are made to develop in the child an understanding that in his social environment there are a large number of people who work in different institutions and organisations, and who help us in many ways. They make our civic life comfortable. The child, at this stage, gets some idea about his rights and duties, and elementary information about government at the State and National levels. Some elements of international understanding are also introduced.

At the Upper Primary stage, the child's mental growth continues at a rapid rate. He now begins to show interest in governmental institutions and the various problems facing the country today.

The Civics course in Class VI may include civic life in the community, local government, how we can cooperate with local authorities, preservation of public property and what should be our role. Class VII may give some elementary understanding of the Indian Constitution and the functioning of the Government. For Class VIII, a course on contemporary problems and issues may be designed. The current social and economic problems facing the country and the problems relating to the environmental preservation, arms race and human rights are of topical interest for children. It is clear that the course on contemporary problems and issues for Class VIII will be an integrated course to which various social sciences can contribute significantly.

The National Policy on Education 1986, and the Programme of Action have listed various components of the common core. If the courses are designed on the lines suggested in the above paras, it would be possible to incorporate the following core components in the Syllabus at the Upper Primary stage:

1. Constitutional Obligations
2. Content Essential to Nurture National Identity
3. Egalitarianism, Democracy and Secularism
4. Equality of Sexes
5. Removal of Social Barriers
6. Observance of the Small Family Norm
7. Inculcation of the Scientific Temper
8. Preservation of Cultural Heritage
9. Environmental Preservation
10. Legacy of India's Freedom Movement

Significant Tasks

For each class, one unit on project work (practical activities) should be included. Under this unit, an opportunity should be provided to the student to develop abilities which are essential for an active citizen in India.

The expected learning, in behavioural terms, may be as follows:

Class VI

1. Identifying with the community and showing interest in its development.
2. Showing awareness of various problems facing the urban and rural governments, and showing interest in their solution.

3. Cooperating with the local administration in its proper and effective functioning.

Class VII

1. Showing respect for the Constitution and values enshrined in it.
2. Showing awareness of the fundamental rights and duties incorporated in the Constitution.
3. Obeying laws and rules.
4. Showing respect for our National Symbols.

Class VIII

1. Showing awareness of our National Goals viz. Democracy, Socialism, Secularism, National Integration and International Understanding.
2. Showing critical appreciation of contemporary social and economic problems and issues facing the country and the world.

The nature and scope of Civics require that an interdisciplinary approach be adopted for its teaching. The teaching of Civics has to play a vital role in the promotion of desirable attitudes and social behaviour in children. For this purpose, it is essential that the Civics curriculum is not confined to mere theoretical treatment in the classroom. Well planned programmes of activities should provide opportunities to children for continued participation in the desired practices over a sufficiently long period of time. Methods, which encourage student participation, such as seminars and group discussions, should be increasingly used. Children should be given opportunities for group activities such as organizing a youth Parliament, so as to share responsibility, to be considerate to others and to participate in decision making.

Study of contemporary events and problems forms a major component in the content of Civics and, therefore, use of cartoons and newspaper cuttings should prove very effective in the teaching of Civics.

The Examination

Development of abilities, attitudes and civic values should form a major part in Civics teaching. In spite of repeated emphasis on the teaching and testing of qualities relating to the affective domain, the area still remains largely neglected in the present system of evaluation. Therefore, it becomes necessary that evaluation in Civics is planned systematically to see how far the objectives set forth in the curriculum are achieved.

As a continuous process, evaluation should test interests, attitudes, civic competencies and values. Suitable tools and techniques of evaluation should be used at several points of time so that not only the content but the objectives and competencies developed are tested properly.

A serious defect in the school curriculum is the absence of provision for education in social and civic values. The syllabus should, therefore, contain at least one unit on project work with a detailed list of topics for practical activities. Ways and means should be found to make this unit effective in the sense that it should be obligatory for teachers and students to organize and undertake these activities. One of the ways is to make project work a part of evaluation. Some percentage of the total marks allotted to Civics should be assigned to the project work. Every student should take up at least two practical activities every year and prepare a short write-up or report on his project. The reports of the students should be evaluated by the Civics teachers.

The student who is a citizen in training, needs help in getting experiences and insight into the process of citizenship. Under this scheme, an opportunity should be provided to the student to develop abilities which are essential for any active citizen in India. It is suggested that 20 per cent of the total marks allotted to Civics should be assigned to the project work. Every student should take up at least two practical activities every year and prepare a short write-up or report on his project. The reports of the students should be evaluated.

(i) Sanitation problem of any particular locality.

(ii) Management and maintenance of civic amenities in a particular area and the related problems.

(iii) How police functions in an area.

(iv) Traffic problems in a locality.

(v) Celebrating festivals of different communities and national festivals.

(vi) Election process from nomination to declaration of results of elections of Students' Union, Village Panchayats, Municipal Committees.

(vii) Study of some major developments and events in the national life e.g. electrification, nationalization of banks, nuclear arms race, food, population, green revolution, study of local historical events connected with the Indian Independence Movement.

(viii) Functioning of the following in terms of their achievements and difficulties faced:

(a) Village Panchayat/Municipal Committee or Corporation

(b) Block Samiti

(c) Zila Parishad.

Syllabus

Class VI

Civic Life in the Community

Unit I: Development of the Community

1. Meaning of Civic life in relation to home.
2. Our village community: Its backwardness and its changing face.
3. Our economic life and cooperation: Role of cooperatives in the development of the community.
4. Programmes for social and economic development, with emphasis on human resource development, working of Community Development Block.

Unit II: Local Government: Rural

1. Need for local government, solution of local problems like health, sanitation, education and recreation. Special problems of rural areas.
2. Local government in rural areas: Gram Panchayat, Panchayat Samiti and Zila Parishad, their composition and functions, their strengths and weaknesses, democracy at the grass-root level.

(This unit may be studied with reference to the local government existing in a respective State.)

Unit III: Local Government: Urban

1. Local government in urban areas: Municipality, Corporation.
2. The structure and functions of urban local government, sources of income, elections, special problems of urban areas.
3. The duties of the people to help these institutions, wise choice of representatives, cooperation, paying taxes, taking and sharing responsibilities.

(This unit may be studied with reference to the local government existing in a respective urban area.)

Unit IV: District Administration

1. Law and order, land management and realization of land revenue, police, and administration of jails.
2. Maintenance of civic amenities, developmental functions.
3. Judicial administration.

Unit V: Preservation of Property of the Community

1. Public property in the locality
   (a) Panchayat Ghar, village ponds, trees, village well, school library, hospital, park, museum, post-office,

road, electric poles, railways, public transport, bus, telephone booth, etc.

(b) Historical monuments.

2. Their utility to the people, facilities, comfort, education.
3. Need for their preservation, public money spent, taxes imposed on all if misused, collective sharing of public property, nature and pattern of individual and collective suffering in the absence of public property.
4. Care of historical monuments, historical evidence, national wealth, special effort for their preservation.

Unit VI: Project Work

List of activities given in the introduction to this syllabus, two projects should be taken up by each student.

Class VII

Indian Constitution

Unit I: Features of our Constitution

1. Making of our Constitution, prepared by the people's representatives.
2. Some basic values enshrined in the Indian Constitution—Democracy, Equality, Religious freedom, etc. Constitution as an instrument of social change.
3. National government and State governments. Three Lists—Union, State and Concurrent.
4. Fundamental Rights and Fundamental Duties mentioned in the Constitution, Directive Principles of State Policy.
5. Indian Citizenship.
6. National Symbols.

Unit II: Law-making Process

1. Parliament: Lok Sabha and Rajya Sabha, their composition and functions.

2. State Legislature: Its composition and functions,
3. How laws are made—ordinance.

Unit III: Executing Laws

1. President, Prime Minister and the Council of Ministers, their functions and inter-relationship.
2. Governor, Chief Minister and the Council of Ministers, functions and interrelationship (with reference to a respective State).
3. Role of the civil service.

Unit IV: Interpreting Laws

1. Single judicial system of the country: Supreme Court, High Court and Subordinate Courts, their composition and jurisdiction.
2. How cases are decided, Lok Adalats.

Unit V: Project Work

Activities listed in the introduction to the syllabus. Two projects should be taken up by each student.

Class VIII

Independent India—Achievements and Challanges

Unit I: Our National Goals

Democracy, Socialism, Secularism, National Integration and International Undertaking.

Unit II: Strengthening Our Democracy

1. Qualities of citizenship in a democracy, wide information, freedom of the press and mass media, critical judgement, balanced opinion, wise use of the vote and discipline in public life, observance of legitimate means in public behaviour and abjuring violence.

2. Necessity of the social and economic reconstruction for the success of democracy.

Unit III: Our Social Problems

1. Indian Society: Rural and Urban
2. Social problems and their solution—government and voluntary efforts.
   (a) Illiteracy—education for all.
   (b) Special problems relating to the scheduled castes and tribal people.
   (c) Status of women.
   (d) Society and the child—rights of the child.
   (e) Anti-social practices.

Unit IV: Our Economic Problems

1. Impact of the British rule on economic conditions of the country. A brief review after independence.
2. Some major economic problems.
   (a) poverty and unemployment
   (b) Population growth
3. Production and productivity in agricultural, indus-trial and household sectors.
4. Planned economic development for self-reliance and social justice. Five Year Plans—achievements and failures.

Unit V: National Integration

1. (a) Indian population—a brief historical background.
   (b) Diversities—language, dress, culture, etc.
2. (a) Forces hampering the growth of national unity—communalism, linguism and casteism.
   (b) Forces promoting national unity, 'Indian Constitution and values enshrined in it, national festivals, cultural

unity, national symbols, economic development, regional interdependence, etc.

Unit VI: Defence of the Country

1. Our Armed Forces, their role in times of peace and war.
2. Second line of defence—Territorial Army, Border Security Force, NCC and ACC.
3. The citizen and defence.

Unit VII: India and the World

1. The world as a family of nations, interdependence of nations, need for cooperation and co-existence.
2. The United Nations: Organization and functions, its principal agencies: UNESCO, WHO, UNICEF, ILO, FAO.
3. India's Foreign Policy.
   (i) Policy of non-alignment, friendship with all
   (ii) India and her neighbouring countries.
   (iii) India as a member of the U.N.

Unit VIII: World Problems

Human Rights

1. Meaning of Human Rights.
2. The Universal Declaration of Human Rights and the Constitution of India.
3. (a) Apartheid
   (b) Problem of Human Rights.

Arms Race

1. The arms race, danger of nuclear war.
2. Interrelationship between arms race and human rights.
3. The arms race, danger of nuclear war.
4. Interrelationship between arms race and human rights.

Disparities between the Developing and Developed Countries

Existing disparities between the developing and the developed countries. Need for a new order.

Environmental Pollution

1. Human activities and environmental pollution
2. Types of environmental, pollution, pollution of air, water and land. Factors responsible for environmental pollution, impact of environmental problem on society and quality of life.
3. Ways and means to reduce environmental pollution at the local, national and international levels.

Unit X: Practical Work

Activities listed in the introduction to the syllabus. Two projects should be taken up by each student.

The Evaluation

The curriculum seems to be quite comprehensive. It provides for sufficient scope for the students to understand the main streams of the cultural heritage of India on the present context. Wherever possible application of knowledge has been stressed. With a view to broadening the outlook of the students, developments in other parts of the world too have been put in perspective. An understanding of the contemporary problems like environment protection has been duly highlighted.

Notwithstanding these merits, there are certain gaps. It has been taken for granted that the Aryans came from outside although this fact is still under dispute. Due emphasis is missing on the Gupta period. It has been clubbed with other kingdoms. No reference has been made to Rana Pratap while dealing with the Mughals. Similarly, Shivaji's name is missing. While mentioning social and religious reform movements and cultural awakening, Arya Samaj does not find mention. Reference to recent developments and contemporary problems should have been made. Social studies have been substituted by Social Science.

2

Motives and Goals

Below are some of the basic principles to be kept in view while stating instructional objectives after they have been derived:

1. The statement of an objective should include both (a) the kind of behavioural outcome expected and (b) the content. The former is sometimes called competence or modification part. The term modification implies that it is at the level of the individual's behaviour that the change occurs as a result of learning. Content on the other hand is the medium for the realisation of the desired behaviour. It does not acquire any direction unless it is harnessed to mental processes. It is the question of activising a product through the application of processes using various communication symbols. For example, "Summer monsoon" is just an item of knowledge but educationally it becomes meaningful only when we say: the pupil explains the causes of the reversal of wind movement during the monsoon season.
2. An objective should be conceived and stated in terms of pupil's behaviour.
3. Objectives should be worked out at the right level of generality (specificity) so as to be neither so vague nor

so specific or atomistic as to be non-functional. Complex or compound objectives need particular attention in this respect.

4. Objectives should be stated non-compositely, so as to avoid confusion, repetition and contradiction.
5. Objectives in a list should not overlap. It may be helpful to group together similar objectives.
6. Objectives should be so stated that there, is a clear indication and even distinction among learning situations required for realising different behaviour changes. For example, learning situations for memorizing certain facts would be basically different from the ones needed for developing critical thinking.
7. Objectives need to be conceived in terms of continuity of growth over a period. They should essentially be developmental in their purport representing roads to travel rather than the terminal points.
8. Worthwhileness of objectives should be carefully judged from various points of view, particularly their social acceptability.
9. Objectives should be realistic. They should be attainable through available or procurable resources and testable through available or manipulable tools.
10. The list of objectives as a whole should be comprehensive enough to cover different outcomes expected of an educational programme in the cognitive, affective and the psychon-motor domains.

Teaching Aims

The work of identifying well-defined behavioural changes requires that broader objectives should be broken down into more specific ones to a limit where they stand fully clarified and delimited. This step is often known as specifying objectives and its product comes to be known as "specifications." The specifications are thus the "behavioural outcomes" expected as a result of learning experience emanating from a learning situation. It is an exercise in meaningful analysis.

A practical way of getting at the specifications of an objective is first to state the objective, comprehend what we mean by it and then to seek answers to the question "what the students will be able to do to exhibit to us the achievement of the particular objective on their part" The answers will be specifications.

Objective

The pupil comprehends (understands) the information represented on a daily weather chart.

Particular Motives

To exhibit the achievement of the above objective. The pupil will be able to:

- identify and discriminate between the different types of information given on the weather chart.
- translate symbolic representations into verbal descriptions.
- see relationship between isobaric forms and wind speed and direction; wind direction and precipitation, etc.
- compare the information given on weather maps of different dates recognise the prevailing trend of weather.
- explain a particular information depicted on the weather chart in respect of its scope, as also antecedent, consequent relationship etc.
- summarise the information represented on the map in verbal form draw a simplified version of a given weather map, etc.

In order to clearly visualise, the relationship between objectives and pupils' activities, let us for a while study the following table giving the activities and the corresponding objective that each can help achieve and try to draw some conclusions from it:

Pupil activities	Objective
Practical work	Understanding, Skill
Organising an exhibition	Interest, Appreciation, Application, Skill
Excursion	Knowledge, Understanding
Discussion	Understanding, Critical thinking
Lecture	Knowledge, Understanding
Dramatisation	Comprehension, Interest

1. To acquire the knowledge (information) of facts, terms, concepts, conventions, trends, principles, generalizations, assumptions, hypotheses, processes etc. in Social Studies.
2. To develop an understanding of facts, terms, concepts, conventions, trends, principles and generalizations, assumptions, hypotheses, processes, etc. in Social Studies.
3. To apply the acquired knowledge of Social Studies and its understanding in unfamiliar situations.
4. To acquire practical skills essential for the study of Social Studies.
5. To develop interest in the subject and problems related to Social Studies and political life of the people of one's country and of those of the world.
6. To develop desirable positive attitudes necessary for developing a broader outlook.

Objective: To acquire the knowledge (information) of facts, terms, concepts, conventions, principles, generalizations, assumptions, hypotheses, problems, processes, etc. in Social Studies

Specification of the Objective

To demonstrate the achievement of the above objective, the pupil:

- recalls facts, terms, concepts, principles, trends, etc.
- recognises facts, terms, concepts, principles, trends etc.
- reads information from various forms of representation of data i.e. maps, charts, diagrams, graphs etc.

Objective: To develop an understanding of facts, terms, concepts, conventions, trends, principles, generalizations, assumptions, hypotheses, processes, etc. in Social Studies

Specification of the Objective

To demonstrate the achievement of the above objective, the pupil:

- discriminates.
- classifies.
- compares and contrasts.
- identifies relationships.
- detects the points of emphasis and the trends of arguments.
- cites illustrations.
- detects errors and fallacies and corrects them.
- explains (analyses or gives meaning or clarifies or elucidates).
- gives reasons or advances arguments. 2.10 interprets data presented in different forms.

Objective: To apply the acquired knowledge and its understanding to unfamiliar situations

Specifications of the Objective

To demonstrate the achievement of the above objective, the pupil:

– analyses the unfamiliar situations or problems and:
  (a) finds out what is given and what is required.
  (b) recalls knowledge relevant to the situation.
  (c) judges the sufficiency of insufficiency, adequacy or inadequacy of data or any other evidence for solving the problem.
– establishes relationships
– suggests alternative methods for solving a particular problem.
– selects the most appropriate method of attack.
– draws inferences and makes generalizations.
– makes predictions regarding the probable outcome of a given situation.

Objective: To acquire practical skills essential for the study of Social Studies

Specification of the Objective

To demonstrate the achievement of the above objective, the pupil:

– draws maps, charts, tables, diagrams, graphs etc. from the given data.
– translates data from one form of presentation to another.
– prepares models.

Objective: To develop interest in the subject and problems related to the civic and political life of the people of one's country and of those of the world.

Specifications of the Objective

To demonstrate the achievement of the above objective, the pupil:

- voluntarily studies literature related to Social Studies and tries to know about the inherent issues and problems.
- spends leisure in trying to know about civic problems and issues and exerts in finding solutions to them.
- closely observes civic and political processes and changes at local, national and international levels.
- discusses and is able to communicate various aspects of every day civic problems and their implications.
- enthusiastically participates in excursions, visits and field-trips to places of civic and political activities (e.g. Panchayats, Municipalities, Assemblies etc.)
- enjoys attending and participating in debates, symposium, discussions on civic and political problems.
- enjoys writing articles and preparing pamphlets, brochures, etc. on topics related to Social Studies.
- enjoys preparing display-materials related to civic and political life and events.
- enjoys collecting information about other political systems and facts about other location, regions and countries.

Objective: To develop desirable positive attitudes necessary for developing a broader outlook

Specifications of the Objective

To demonstrate the achievement of the above objective, the pupil:

- respects the views, opinions and problems of others and displays sympathy and fellow feeling towards them:
  - a) shows tolerance.
  - b) controls emotions and displays restraint.
  - c) develops social awareness.

- is able to examine the present situations in the light of a historical perspective.
- develops a sense of law-abidingness.
- assumes responsibility in cooperative and civic activities.
- judges issues objectively and on their merits.
- displays abhorrence towards socio-economic malpractices like hoarding, profiteering, black-marketing, smuggling, bribery for votes etc.
- shows sympathetic understanding of the problems of people belonging to different social, religious, linguistic and cultural groups.
- realises the importance of the contributions made by the leaders of the nation in different spheres.
- develops a sense of respect for the National Flag, the National Anthem, the National Emblem and the Constitution of one's country and those of other countries of the world.
- develops faith in democratic values.

Significance of the Motives

The aim and objectives of teaching social studies are necessary to point to the broad ideals and to enable us to selecting 'significant and meaningful content, teaching methods and techniques. They are the 'Crux' and 'Key' of the entire process of teaching and learning and therefore, they will have to be in consonance with the broader aims of education. John V. Michaels has aptly stated "The Social Studies are concerned with man and his interaction with his social and physical environment, they deal with human relationship – the central function of the social studies is identical with the central purpose of education – the development of democratic citizenship."

The Education Commission 1964-66, outlined the role of Social Studies as, "the aim of teaching social studies is to help the students to acquire a knowledge of their environment, an understanding of human relationships and certain attitudes and values which are vital for intelligent participation in the affairs of the community, the State, the nation and the world. An effective programme of social studies is essential in India for the development of good citizenship and emotional integration."

Acquaintance with the Environment. Social studies acquaints the child with his past and present social, cultural and geographical environment.

Interest in Socio-economic Institutions. Social studies in schools helps the students to take a keen interest in the ways people live through various socio-economic and political institutions.

Appreciation of Cultural Heritage. The teaching of social studies enables children to appreciate India's rich cultural heritage.

Sifting of Material. The teaching of social studies enables the students to recognize and get rid of what is undesirable and antiquated especially in the context of social change.

Development of Broad-mindedness. Social studies aims at ensuring that narrow, parochial, chauvinistic and obscurantist tendencies are not allowed to grow in our pupils and that they become tolerant and broad-minded.

Development of Social Commitment. Social studies endeavors to develop a will and ability in every pupil to participate in the most important task of the reconstruction of society and economy with a sense of social commitment.

Faith in the Destiny of Nation. Teaching of social studies aims at developing a faith in the minds of the students in the destiny of our nation in terms of promoting a spirit of tolerance and assimilation and peace and harmony among the people of the world.

Development of Insight into Human Relations. Social studies is intended to help pupils to develop an insight into human relationships, social values and attitudes.

Effective Participation in Social Affairs. Social studies enables the growing children to participate effectively in the affairs of the community, the state, the country and the world at large.

Promotion of Ideals Enshrined in the Constitution. Social studies promotes the values and ideals of humanism, secularism, socialism and democracy.

Maximization of Economic and Social Welfare. Social Studies inculcates attitudes and skills for maximization of economic and social welfare.

Promotion of Peace. Social studies inculcates attitudes and imparts the knowledge necessary for the achievement of the principal values of a just world order.

Profitable Use of Leisure Time. Social studies affords opportunities to the students to develop such interests that will enable them to use their leisure properly.

Foundation of Specialisation. Social studies provides a pattern and experience of study that will serve as a foundation for specialisation at a later stage of education of the students. At the early stages, students are made familiar with the elementary knowledge of various disciplines.

Multi-facet Development of the Personality. The primary objective of social studies is to develop an appreciation of 3 R's—Rights, Responsibilities and Relationships. Social Studies aims at developing qualities like clearness of thought, intellectual conscience, courage, love of truth, initiative, self-reliance, spontaneity, tolerance, unbiased attitude etc., which go a long way in the development of a well-balanced personality, physically strong, intellectually mature, emotionally stable and socially efficient.

Motives are Essential

The formulation of educational objectives is needed for a variety of reasons.

1. provide the desired direction to educational activities.
2. determine the nature of educational activities.
3. provide a basis for systematising or planning an educational programme.
4. decide the points of emphasis in an educational activity.

5. give unity and coherence to an educational programme.
6. provide the basis for the measurement of growth and thus guarantee valid evaluation.
7. help distinguish between various aspects of learning.
8. help focus attention on proper attributes of teaching and evaluation.
9. help grade learning experiences and also evaluation material.
10. help maintain a balance between different aspects of an educational programme.
11. help fix priorities in an educational programme.
12. guide educational decisions in curricular or co-curricular areas.
13. guide in the selecting of relevant content.
14. guide improvements in education.
15. give meaning to and clarify the structure and content of curriculum.
16. help make learning functional.
17. help articulate learning at various levels.
18. help discover or evolve proper learning situations.
19. help define educational processes.
20. help make the intangibles in education tangible.
21. help identify weaknesses and strengths of pupils in learning.
22. facilitate communication among educational workers.

Values and Mottos

Sometimes attempts are made to differentiate aims and values of teaching a subject. Aims are considered as conscious purposes and goals. Values on the other hand are the outcome or results achieved after teaching according to these aims. Aims are ideals which are not based on experiments. Values spring as a result of experimentation or after putting aims into practices. Values are based on reality and the aims on philosophical considerations.

Values of teaching Social Studies are: (1) Social learning (2) Training in social skills (3) Training in social standards (4) Training in understanding social problems (5) Training in understanding social changes (6) Training in bringing about desirable social changes (7) Training in developing social attitudes (8) Training in developing a sense of belonging.

In fact, it is very difficult to draw a line of distinction between one value and the other. All are complementary and supplementary.

The Outcome

The general objectives have been further broken down in probable results in more specific terms. The probable results are laid in terms of the following:

The subject of Social Studies is a content-subject and, as such, it abounds in facts. It is, therefore, very necessary to highlight or draw attention, to the more significant facts, generalizations and principles, commonly known as 'understandings'. For instance, 'A child that practices good manners and habits, is loved by all, both at home and school,' or 'Man has to depend upon communities far away for satisfying his daily needs,' are the understandings that one has to develop through the lessons on good manners, or national and international trade, respectively.

If our teaching is not to result in mere transmission of unrelated and isolated facts, it is an important task of the teacher to help the child to receive various facts in their proper perspective or in their relative importance. It should be the endeavour of the teacher to help the children in developing important concepts of understandings by providing them enough experiences in and outside the class. It has been a common experience that properly developed concepts and understandings are retained longer in our minds, than the host of unrelated and unorganised facts that are memorized for the purpose of examinations.

Understandings include the following:

(1) Making the child understand his environment so as to enable him to adjust better with his social and cultural environment.

(2) Enabling the child understand social concepts to family, community, state and nation.

(3) Enabling the child understand the world around him.

(4) Enabling the child develop an appreciation of social change.

(5) Enabling the child know the progress of society from primitive to the advanced stage.

(6) Acquainting the child about, man's ways of living, his significant achievements and the problems that he faces today.

(7) Acquainting the child with social institutions.

(8) Helping the child understand how far geographical conditions influence in moulding the growth of society in different parts of the world.

(9) Helping the child learn about vocational activities and opportunities.

Favourable Behaviour

An attitude is a feeling, developed towards an object, or person or group or anything, else. These attitudes last through a life time. The facts that a child learns in the class may be forgotten. But these attitudes linger, and mould his behavior-pattern for all that is to follow. The child may forget the facts, he learnt about the duties of a policeman or the postman. But the feeling of friendliness he gained, for these public officials will remain for life.

The development of these desirable attitudes and appreciation is an important aspect of any good education. The attitudes, appreciations and habits are an inseparable part of the personality of an individual. All agree that it is the attitudes that matter, more than anything else in the behavior of a person. The development of the attitudes is, however, not to be attempted as a separate item by lecturing or preaching. It should be the natural outcome of all the discussions and activities carried on by the class. They are developed unknowingly. It is often said that attitudes are caught and not taught. The teacher, should, therefore, be conscious of this aspect and reflect proper attitudes, through his disposition and behaviour, so that they are rightly adopted by the children under his charge.

Desirable attitudes imply:

(i) Developing attitudes to assume social and civic responsibility and thus making the child an active participant and an enlightened individual.

(ii) Developing attitudes to act in accordance with democratic principles and values.

(iii) Developing attitudes of personal responsibility, civic and world mindedness, emotional maturity, intellectual integrity, aesthetic appreciation and suspended judgement.

(iv) Developing attitudes of patriotism, cooperation and tolerance.

(v) Developing attitudes to appreciate the viewpoints of others and making one's own contribution.

Needed Skills

The development of essential skills, in every child, should be an equally important outcome of the teaching of Social Studies in schools. The skills may pertain to various subject areas. For instance, it may be map reading and map making, building a time-chart, of observing and handling apparatuses such as a thermometer or a rain gauge. Another category of skills refers to his ability to communicate with others. This may include asking questions, telling a story, addressing a meeting, presenting a report or dramatizing an event.

Then there are the intellectual skills. This may include an ability to distinguish between a fact and an opinion, sifting data to arrive at conclusions or judgements. Similarly, social skills may include ability to work with a group and to seek cooperation from other members. Development of basic skills includes as follows:

(a) Helping the child develop such skills as are necessary for effective participation in social life.

(b) Helping the child develop critical and scientific thinking and sense of time.

(c) Helping the child inculcate the social skills: (i) to interpret printed, pictured and chartered material; (ii) to place people, events and institutions a time, space and importance; (iii) to use words of social, cultural and economic significance correctly; (iv) to understand and interpret significant data and to compare, contrast, summarise, generalize and criticise them.

Learning Skills

Meaning of a Skill. James High of the University of California has stated, "A skill is the wherewithal to gain an end; in social studies this is to learn the facts, generalizations and formulation of social relations." The skill of citizenship is the ability to get along well and benefit from democratic social organisation. It is the responsibility of every social studies teacher to devote considerable time and effort to the matter of increasing his students use of skills and to introduce them to new ones.

Apart from the motor and social skills needed from achievement in social studies (eye movement in reading vocal organs in speech, getting alongwith others), there is another group of skills which is of primary importance in social studies.

Prof. Charles A. Beard has analysed these skills as under:

1. Skill in methods of obtaining access to information (a) use of libraries and institutions, (b) use of encyclopaedias, handbooks, documents, sources, authorities, statistical collections etc.
2. Skill in the sifting of the materials and the discovery and determination of authentic evidence in the use of primary sources.
3. Skill in the observation and description of contemporary occurrences in the school and community.
4. Skill in methods of handling information (a) in analysis-breaking down large themes or masses of data into manageable units and penetrating to irreducible ele-

ments, (b) in synthesis – combining elements, drawing inferences and conclusions, and comparing with previous conclusions and inference – logical and systematic organisation, (c) in map and chart making and graphic presentation.

5. Skill in memorising results of study with consciousness of application to new situations by exact reference and analogy.
6. Skill in scientific method-inquiring spirit, patience, weighing evidence, tentative and precise conclusions.

Significant Principles

Mccracken Carpenter and Alice W. Spieseke have suggested the following principles:

1. For the acquisition and improvement of skills, the learning activity must focus on skill development. Skill development will not take place by chance.
2. Experience designed to promote growth in skills must be meaningful to the learner. A certain skill must be accepted as important.
3. Experience used in skill development must be geared to the maturation level of the learner. Just as a five-year-old cannot usually master the flowing script with a fountain pen, neither can a junior high school student be expected to achieve the same degree of skill in synthetic thought as a college professor.
4. For the successful learning and retention of skills, repetitive practice is necessary. Reinforcement of learning is essential.
5. Skills should be developed in connection with on-going activities and not in isolation. Every social studies skill is in the end an integral part of the life equipment of the citizen.
6. Development of different skills should go on simultaneously. There is a gradual and steady growth of all of the parts in the process of education.

7. Evidence of skill development must be sought to changes in behaviour. The whole purpose of education is to induce an improved behaviour pattern.
8. Provision for the systematic development of skills must be made through the school programme. This is merely to re-emphasise the idea that skills begin with mastery of simple uncomplicated steps and proceed to more complex and various patterns of activity. This principle is a summary of all the other seven.

QUESTIONS

1. State the basic principles of stating instructional objectives.
2. Differentiate between general objectives and specific objectives of teaching Social Studies.
3. Specify instructional objectives of teaching Social Studies.
4. Why should we have aims for the teaching of Social Studies?
5. State the general objectives of teaching Social Studies.
6. Explain in brief the difference between objectives and values.
7. Describe the anticipated outcomes of Social Studies in terms of the following:
   (a) Understandings
   (b) Desirable Attitudes
   (c) Essential Skills.

3

Theory and Practice

Every individual is a part of the community and it is not merely a history or geography or a civics or an economics that matters, but rather the man himself who influences and is influenced by his history, his geography, his civics or economics and his community. The subject of Social Studies which deals directly with man and the society in which he lives, carries special responsibility of preparing young children to become well informed constructive participants in society and capable of developing healthy social relationships.

The dawn of independence in the year 1947, opened a new chapter in our history. By adopting a new constitution declaring us a sovereign, secular, socialist and democratic republic, we have entered a new era. We have decided to rebuild our society on a pattern that guarantees social justice to all members and groups. Likewise, we have also ventured to reconstruct our national economy on a sound foundation. In the international field, we have decided to develop friendship with all and to promote world peace.

An elementary course in social studies should help lay down, in every child, sound foundations of a good democratic citizenship which implies an all-round individual growth towards collective progress, in a welfare Stale.

This, then, demands a functional approach, which emphasises the development of certain basic understandings, certain essential skills, both intellectual and social, and certain desirable altitudes for unproved social living, in every child that studies the subject

Although the subject of social studies includes much of the subject-matter of history, geography, civics and economics, it does not limit itself to the fields formally covered by these formal disciplines nor does it attempt to give a regular- sequence of lessons in them.

The Definition

The term 'Social Studies' is of recent origin. Its widespread use was started in 1916 in the USA. Its origin in India can be traced back to the formulation of the Basic System of Education in 1937. The term Social Studies has been defined differently by different commissions, committees and writers. Some definitions are as follows:

1. The Curriculum for the Ten-Year School – A Framework published by NCERT in 1976 points out, "Environmental studies will include both natural and social environments in classes I and II. It would be more appropriate to use the term social studies rather than social science at the primary stage since it represents a broad and composite instructional area.
2. James Hamming in Teaching of Social Studies in Secondary Schools considers Social Studies "a study of relations and inter-relations – historical, geographical and social."
3. James High has observed in Teaching Secondary Social Studies "Most simply stated, the Social Studies are the school mirror of the scholarly findings of the Social Sciences. Such data as Social Scientist may gather is integrated and simplified to appropriate levels of expression for children in all the grades."
4. John V. Michealis states in Social Studies for Children in Democracy, "The Social Studies are concerned with man and his social and physical environment, they deal with human relationships."

5. Peter H. Martorella has observed in Social Studies: Strategies, Theory and Practice, "It is more accurate to think of social studies as an applied field which attempts to fuse scientific knowledge with ethical, philosophical, religious and social considerations which arise in the process of decision-making as practised by citizens."
6. In its publication 'Social Studies for Schools' the Social Studies Committee of Schools Board, Victoria (USA) has given me true concept of this subject in these words:

   "What we study in Social Studies, is the life of a man in some particular place, at some particular time. We, therefore, use every possible 'subject' to help us understand his problem and how he dealt or deals with them. The main aim is to give a better understanding of present problems. We try to give our future citizens some understanding of the development of man-kind. We attempt to trace with the children the fascinating of how man has developed through the ages, of how man has studied to use and control his environment and how his life has been influenced by this, how our institutions have grown out of the past and should, therefore, be respected and how they have undergone many changes to meet changing needs and must undergo many more from time to time. Man's struggle with his environment yesterday and today, man's use or misuse of his powers and resources, his development, the essential unity of civilization, these are the main themes of Social Studies. We are trying to break the habit of putting knowledge into watertight compartments, labelled History, Geography, Civics, Economics etc. We are also trying to train children in the habits of thinking clearly, to be able to use all the knowledge at their command to solve problems and to be able to find the necessary infor-mation."
7. In the words of J.F. Forester, "Social Studies, as the very name suggests, is the study of society and its chief aim is to help pupils to understand the world in which they have to live and how it came to be, so that they may become responsible citizens. It aims at promoting criti-

cal thinking and a readiness for social change, at creating a disposition for acting on behalf of the general welfare, at an appreciation of other cultures and a realization of the interdependence of man and man and of nation and nation."

8. The Secondary Education Commission of the National Education Association USA has defined Social Studies, in these words:—"Social Studies are understood to be those whose subject-matter relates directly to the organisation and development of human society and to man as a member of social group."
9. Mr. M.P. Muffatt is of opinion that a person may be learned in Chemistry or Mathematics, he may be a skilled technician, but if he is shortsighted in his attitude to his fellowmen, he is unsocial and perhaps ill-adjusted in many other ways. The way of living is a fine art to which Social Studies contributes understanding.
10. The framers of the Report of Secondary Education Commission in India, realising the novelty of the subject have clearly slated:—"Social Studies, as a term is comparatively new in Indian Education. It is meant to cover the ground, traditionally associated with History, Geography, Economics, Civics etc. This whole group for studies has therefore, to be viewed as a compact whole whose object is to adjust the students to their social environment which includes the family, community, state and nation — so that they may be able to understand how society has come to its present form."
11. An NCERT publication entitled 'National Curriculum for Elementary and Secondary Education' (1988) has used the term Social Studies. It has observed "Social Sciences is perhaps the singular curricular area which can prove to be the most effective tool for providing education in the context of all the core components indicating in the NPE (National Policy on Education) 1986." The common core envisaged by the NPE comprises (i) History of India's freedom movement, (ii) Constitutional obligations, (iii) Values such as India's com-

mon heritage, (iv) Egalitarianism, democracy, secularism, (iv) Equality of sexes, (v) Protection of environment, (vi) Small family norms etc.

The Effects

Social Studies deals with man, his relations with other men and his environment. It, therefore, draws its contents from several social sciences to help us understand the problems of man and how he dealt or deals with them. The main themes of Social Studies are – man's struggle with environment yesterday and today, man's use or misuse of his powers and resources, his development and the essential unity of civilization. The contents of Social Studies are drawn from several social sciences but are not determined by the discipline of any one of these. Social Studies is meant to cover the ground, traditionally associated with History, Geography, Economics, Civics etc. If the teaching of these subjects only imparts miscellaneous and unrelated information and does not throw any light on it or provide insight into social conditions and problems or create the desire to improve the existing state of things, their educative significance will be negligible. The whole group of studies has, therefore, to be viewed as a compact, whole whose object is to adjust the students to their social environment.

Social Studies includes the study of relationships and interrelationships – historical, geographical and social so as to provide to the young person with that basis of public knowledge and orientation of study, his personality denied the means of integration, his interests left unstirred and his energies untapped. It includes matter which reveals to the child where he is in time,, space and society.

Social Studies traces for the children the fascinating story of how man has developed through the ages; how his life has been influenced by the environment; how he himself has influenced the environment; how our institutions have grown out of the past; how man has struggled with his environment in the past; how he is struggling today; man's use or misuse of his powers and above all the essential unity of civilization.

Social Studies aims at breaking the habit of putting knowledge into water-tight compariments, History, Geography, Civics, Economics etc.

Social Studies includes that material which is conducive to the development of a well information, intelligent person who is capable of comprehending properly the current problems, is keen to accept responsibilities as a citizen for the all and has developed insights, skills and moral qualities which are so essential and desirable in a democratic society.

Area of Operation

The scope of Social Studies is very vast and wide and in fact, as wide as the world itself and as lengthy as the history of man on this earth. It includes the millions of years prior to recorded history and also the foreseeable future. In the words of John Michaels. "The breadth of Social Studies programme should provide for a variety of experiences so that the child's learning will be well-rounded and well-balanced. It should also be possible to draw upon other fields of learning so that significant problems can be considered in the light of their ramifications; a narrow compartmentalised programme limits social learning."

It draws material from all the social sciences relating to the study of human relations, human institutions and human behaviours. In doing so, undue emphasis is not laid on any one subject or part, at the cost of another.

It is true that the scope is very vast and wide but this does not mean that the course in Social Studies is limitless and fathomless ocean and that it knows no ends. Its frontiers have to be encompassed so as to provide an overall integrated outline of 'Minimum Essential Functional Knowledge' from various disciplines.

The Ingredients

1. A study of relationships, i.e., relationships between man and man, relationships between man and institutions, relationships between man and earth and relationships between man and goods.

2. A functional study of natural sciences and arts e.g., study of that part of chemistry which has helped a lot in the eradication of various diseases.
3. A study of current affairs which make us think about the social structure of the community or the society and the effects of social forces in their making.
4. A study of international affairs for promoting brotherhood of mankind.
5. A study of the actual working of social institutions like the Village Panchayat, State Legislature and Parliament etc.

The vastness of the scope of Social Studies may be explained with the help of a diagram as given below:

The Secondary Education Commission (1952-53) has observed, "It is not often realised that the complaint of overcrowding is largely due to the multiplicity of subjects, presented as separate entities, without bringing out their organic interrelationship. So, in framing the curriculum an attempt should be made to see whether certain subjects can be grouped in large, organically related units dealing with certain broad areas of human knowledge and interest. Thus, it is psychologically preferable to present subjects centering round the study of the social environment and human relations under the comprehensive heading of "Social Studies" than to teach a number of separate Subjects like History, Geography, Civics and Economics in watertight compartments.

"Social Studies" as a term is comparatively new in Indian education; it is meant to cover the ground traditionally associated with History, Geography, Economics, Civics etc. If the teachings of these separate subjects only imparts miscellaneous and unrelated information and does not throw any light on, or provide insight into social conditions and problems or create the desire to improve the existing stage of things, their educative significance will be negligible. This whole group of studies has, therefore, to be viewed as a compact whole whose object is to adjust the students to their social environment—which includes family, community. State and Nation—so that they may be able to understand how society has come to its present form and interpret intelligently the matrix of social forces and movements in the midst of which they are living. They help the student to discover and explain how this adjustment has taken place in the past and how it is taking place today. Through them, the students should be able to acquire not only the knowledge but the attitudes and values which are essential for successful group living and civic efficiency. They should endeavour to give the students not only a sense of national patriotism and an appreciation of national heritage, but also a keen and lively sense of obvious fact that these are but the formulation of the aims which have to be achieved; their translation into curricular terms will require careful thought and patient research."

Basic Ideas

An analysis of the foregoing paragraphs brings out the following characteristics of Social Studies:

1. Social Studies deals with the interrelations that develop between and among people and those that develop between people and their environment.
2. Social Studies is a broad and composite instructional area which draws its contents from different social sciences.
3. Social Studies is a compound rather than a mixture where the ingredients lose their identity and something tangible and worthwhile emerges out of the combination. If differs from the teaching of History, Geography, Civics, Economics etc. in the same sense in which the taste of ice-cream differs from that of its ingredients like sugar, cream, milk etc., lasted in isolation.
4. Social Studies aims at enabling the students to adjust to their social environment which includes the family, community, state and nation and in fact the entire humanity.
5. Social Studies deals with the way of living.
6. Social Studies deals with those areas of curriculum that enable the students to interpret intelligently the matrix of social forces and movements in the midst of which they are living.

7. Social Studies establishes relationships between present, past and future.
8. Social Studies integrates the knowledge of all social sciences and is, therefore, called 'Coordinated' and 'Coordinating.'
9. Social Studies is the applied branch of Social Sciences, introduced in the school curriculum with a view to developing proper attitudes, sensibilities and skills in future citizens.
10. The materials of Social Studies are useful for general education at school level, before collegiate education starts so that pupils can learn them with sufficient ease and interest.
11. The contents of Social Studies are continuously growing and changing with the changing social process. Hence, its contents will have to be revised periodically.
12. Social Studies covers the study of communities at all levels, local, regional, national and international with focus on man and his social environment.
13. Social Studies stresses contemporary human life and its problems rather than the past history of man.

Aims and Objectives

An NCERT publication Guidelines/or Upper Primary Stage (1988) points out these outcomes, "The child at this stage, could be initiated into the study of India's past in all its major aspects such as social, cultural and scientific development. He should also be helped to appreciate diversities in ways of living and interdependence of various regions of India and the world. He should also know the civic and political institutions and understand contemporary social and economic issues and problems. Social skills and civic competencies and a national perspective would, thus, equip him to participate in the task of social and economic reconstruction." The Social Studies Committee of Schools Board, Victoria (USA) has pointed out that through Social Studies, "We are trying to train children in the habit of thinking clearly, to be able to use all the knowledge at their command to solve problems and to be able to find the necessary information."

In the words of J.F. Forrester, the chief aim of Social Studies "is to help pupils to understand the world in which they have to live and how it came to be so that they become responsible citizens. It aims at promoting critical thinking and a readiness for social change, at creating a disposition for action on behalf of the general welfare, at an appreciation of other cultures and a realisation of the " interdependence of man and man and nation and nation."

M. P. Muffatt is of the opinion that a person may be learned in Chemistry or Mathematics, he may be a skilled technician, but if he is shortsighted in his attitude to his fellowman, he is unsocial and perhaps ill-adjusted in many other ways. The art of living is a fine art to which Social Studies contributes understanding.

The Secondary Education Commission, 1952-53, states that the object of Social Studies is "to adjust the students to their social environment which includes the family, community, state and nation so that they may be able to understand how society has come to its present form. They may be able to interpret intelligently the matrix of social forces and movements in the midst of which they are living." The Commission further adds that "This subject should help the students to discover and explain how this adjustment has taken place in the past and how it is taking place today. Through this subject, the students should be able to acquire not only the knowledge but attitudes and values which are essential for successful group living and civic efficiency. It should endeavour to give the students not only sense of national patriotism and an appreciation of national heritage, but also a keen and lively sense of world unity and world citizenship."

The role of Social Studies has been clearly outlined in 'The Curriculum for the Ten-Year School – A Framework' published by NCERT in 1976. It states as follows:

> "The instruction in Social Sciences should promote the values and ideals of humanism, secularism, socialism, and democracy. It should inculcate attitudes and impart the knowledge necessary for the achievement of the principal values of a world order, maximization of ecological stability."

Cyril Burt, in the Foreword to James Hemming's book entitled 'Teaching of Social Studies in Secondary Schools' has stressed the importance of social sciences as a core subject in these words, "the social, economic and political problem of the modern world are so intricate that few young people can be trusted to pick up the necessary information, or to teach themselves to think clearly and logically on the numerous problems that confront them... a well designed and well conducted course of social sciences can fulfil the main educational requirements of a field of study. It will satisfy the need of the child to understand his environment and his relations with it and it will go far to satisfy the need of society for well-adjusted citizens prepared to participate in solving ,the pressing problems of our times."

The Syllabus

The curriculum of a country, like its constitution, reflects the ethos of that country. As the Education Commission points out, there is a need to transform education so as to relate it to the life, needs and aspirations of the people and to make it an instrument of social change. For this purpose, the curriculum in social sciences and social studies is intended for the awakening of social consciousness, the development of democratic values and a feeling for social justice and national integration. Social Studies is a practical subject with a practical bias, it lays emphasis not only on practical knowledge but also on right doing.

Social Studies has been made an integral part of school curriculum as it aims at giving education for life. Social Studies through its functional approach, gives practical training to the pupils to live well. By providing an all-embracing comprehensive area, it enables the pupils to clear their relationships with their material, physical and social surroundings so that they 'are able to adjust themselves to the life of today. No wonder, therefore, social studies forms an integral part of school curriculum which has its concern as national integration, social justice, productivity, modernisation of the society and cultivation of moral and spiritual values.

Inclusion of Social Studies from Psychological Point of View. It is a well-known principle of teaching that children are interested in concrete things and social studies deals with the concrete things. There is nothing more concrete than life itself which is the central theme of social studies. Social studies is the subject which deals with the substance of life, for life and through life.

Besides, social studies provides knowledge in a correlated and integrated form a form needed by the child.

Inclusion of Social Studies from Sociological Point of View. With the changing pattern of life, the home fails to provide adequate opportunities to the young child for citizenship training. The disintegration of the joint family system and working of both the parents in offices or factories have deprived the child of developing interpersonal relationships. The failure of the home to provide the necessary social education to the child has placed an important obligation on the part of the school. Social studies provides opportunities for socialisation and for democratic living.

Inclusion of Social Studies from Pragmatic Point of View. Social, secular, economic and political problems of the modern life have become so intricate that left to themselves, only a few young men and women can adjust themselves amicably. It is, therefore, extremely important that appropriate experiences must be provi-ded to the student in the school to understand his nature, the nature of his physical and social environment so that he is helped to develop the attitudes and skills of social minuteness, cooperation and tolerance. A course in social studies offers such upper tunities. Social studies finds an important place in the school curriculum as:

1. It helps the child to acquaint with his past and present cultural, economic and social environment.
2. It helps the child to appreciate his rich cultural heritage.
3. It helps the child to get rid of what is undesirable and antiquated especially in the context of social change.
4. It helps the child to acquire right attitudes, knowledge, understanding and competence needed for adjustment with the environment.
5. It helps the child to gain insight into spiritual, economic and political values.

6. It helps the child to use his leisure properly.
7. It helps the child to solve social and individual problems.
8. It helps the child to develop democratic citizenship.
9. Ii helps the child to increase social competence.
10. It helps the child to foster national outlook.
11. It helps the child to foster international understanding.

Mutual Cooperation

David L. Sills in an article 'The International Encyclopedia of Higher Education' (1977) has observed, "Although knowledge is often broadly divided into the social and behavioral sciences, the humanities and the natural sciences, there is no full definition of the social sciences that is generally accepted. Nor is there any consensus concerning which individual disciplines are properly included under the heading. Accordingly, each generation of social scientists uses a different implicit definition of the field, sometimes resulting in controversies among colleagues and between countries. In general, however, the social and behavioral sciences include those disciplines that study social behavior and social institutions."

International Encyclopedia of the Social Sciences,-edited by David L. Sills includes the following disciplines under Social Sciences:

(1) Anthropology, (2) Behavioral Sciences, (3) Economics, (4) Geography, (5) History, (6) Law, (7) Political Science, (8) Psychiatry, (9) Psychology, (10) Sociology, (11) Statistics.

The New Encyclopedia Britannica gives the scope of social sciences as "The Social Sciences, which deal with human behavior in its social and cultural aspects, include the following disciplines: Economics, Political Science, Sociology, Social and Cultural Anthropology, Social Psychology, Social and Economic Geography; and those areas of Education that deal with the social context of learning and the relation of the school to the social order. History is regarded by many of its practitioners as a social science and certain areas of historical study today are almost indistinguishable from work done in the social sciences."

The Categorisation

Prof. M. Halayya has given the following classification:

1. Purely Social Sciences.
2. Semi-Social Sciences.
3. Sciences with Social Implications.

Purely Social Sciences. These may be said to constitute the purely social sciences: Politics, Economics, History, Jurisprudence, Anthropology, Penology and Sociology.

Semi-social Sciences. Among the semi-social sciences may be mentioned Ethics, Education, Philosophy and Psychology.

Sciences with Social Implications. These are Biology, Geography, Medicine, Linguistic and Art.

1. Social sciences are the advanced studies of human society which are taught at the high school stage, higher secondary stage and at college stage. Social studies are simplified portions of social sciences selected for instructional purposes at the primary and middle stages.
2. Social sciences represent an adult approach while the social studies represent a child-centrad approach.
3. Social sciences are the theory part of human affairs and social studies as the practical part of human affairs.
4. Social sciences lay more emphasis on knowledge and social studies on the functional part of knowledge.
5. Social sciences are concerned with the investigation of a diversity of human relations and pile up considerably more data than it is possible or desirable to include in social studies.
6. Social sciences aim at finding out how new truth about human relationships and social studies aim at guiding adolescents in their learning of selected portions of what has been discovered in social sciences.

Social sciences and social studies have many similarities. They are not only related generally but also share a common body of content. The centre of focus in social sciences and social studies is man's relationship to man and his environment and how he meets his needs. Human relationships are the common denominators. As a matter of fact there is no hard and fast line separating social sciences and social studies. The subject matter is generally known as social studies in the primary and middle classes where gradual unfolding of the total environment—physical, social and cultural—is needed. As the student gains more insight and becomes mature to interpret raw data at the secondary and higher secondary stages, he emerges from the social studies and enters into social sciences.

In a nutshell, social studies is the adaptation of the scholarly findings of the social sciences. It include those portions of social sciences which are pertinent to the immediate purpose of learning and can be adapted at the level of comprehension of the students.

According to 'The Curriculum for Ten-Year School' History, Civics, Geography and Economics are to be taught in social sciences at middle and secondary stage of education, i. e., for classes VI to X. In view of the limited time that will be available for each of the branches, it would be desirable to integrate their teaching in a way that pupils develop a proper understanding of the facts and problems in their right perspective without causing any damage to the totality of individual discipline.

History provides the youth an insight, appreciation and understanding of how our present life has come into being. Emphasis in History is to be shifted from dynastic history and political details to social and economic conditions and the growth of various aspects of culture.

Civics make an attempt at imparting training in civic life, development of civic competencies and civic abilities so that students eventually participate constructively in the life of the Community in the democratic way.

The NCERT in its documents on Curriculum 1986 and 1988 has used the term Social Sciences.

Economics makes the child familiar with the current multifarious activities and issues that affect the every day life of the common man and of the society to which he belongs. The course is intended to throw some light on the potential resources and the performance shown so far and the future economic prospects of the country.

In the earlier stages, it would be helpful if some rudimentary understanding of the economic forces that influence the citizen's daily life is given to the students. Some elementary knowledge of consumer economics, such as earning and spending, controls, price rise and the effects of increasing population should be given in a very simplified form.

Geography is intended to bring home to the pupils the interdependence of the various regions of the country and the world. Geography should enable them to appreciate that it is only through sharing with others that the peoples of the world can really enjoy the blessings of the mother earth.

The most important point to be kept in view in the teaching of social sciences is to encompass the vast frontiers of the subject matter in such a way as to deepen the understanding of the child on the social, physical and cultural world around him, develop an insight into human relationships, values and attitudes and appropriate skills.

Significant Elements

1. Social Sciences are those parts of cultural knowledge which have a direct bearing on man's activities in specific field.
2. Social Sciences are the advanced studies of human society which are meant for mature students.
3. Social Sciences aim at finding out new truths about human relationships so as to contribute to social utility.

Regarding the Study of Social Studies and Social Sciences the Education Commission observed, "At the higher secondary stage, there will be specialised studies in the social sciences. There is now an increasing trend to introduce in the curriculum of secondary education, at least in the seniormost classes, some elements of the social sciences and their methods. The new curriculum proposed in the higher secondary classes provides for the special study of history, geography, civics, economics and sociology. But something of the scientific spirit and methods of social sciences should permeate the teaching of social studies and of history, geography and civics even in the lower classes."

Ecological Awareness

Environmental studies is considered an approach based upon the child's investigation of his locality which leads to the progressive development of skills, concepts and attitudes required for the study of other environments in time and space. The communication media required for such studies also necessitate an ever increasing use of language and mathematics. It is not thought of as a subject with a body of factual information but rather as a way of learning through enquiry. Environment studies involves a child in activities which are based upon his observation and investigation of his surroundings. The approach has twofold aim of arousing and developing the child's desire to know more about his world and aiding him in the development of skills he needs to interpret it.

Environmental studies' approach is based upon the general view of learning and especially on the two stages which establish the development of children from a level of 'Concrete operation' to one defined as the level of 'Formal operations'. In more traditional terms it implies moving from concrete to abstract', from 'known to unknown' and from 'particular to general.

The basic concept is to train children to observe more closely and more accurately without at first making any attempt to differentiate historical, geographical and scientific investigation. Repeated opportunities for children to examine material which, by nature and variety is suitable for their age, will stress the development of a general scientific attitude. The pattern of observation, experimentation, recording and interpretation should become the recognised way for the children.

'The Curriculum for the Ten-Year School' has envisaged environmental studies to include both natural and social environments in class I and II. It has used the term social studies to that part of environmental studies that deals with the social environment at the primary stage (Class III to V) and general science to the part dealing with natural environment.

It may be pointed out that since the environment and the experiences outside the school vary from place to place, the activities provided in the school should also vary so that the edifice of knowledge is built not on abstract concepts alone but also on the solid foundations of experience drawn from the environment of the child.

Broader Perceptions

The Social Studies contains the following ideas:

Geography: To exist, man must utilise natural resources.

History: The life of man has been and is influenced by change.

Economics: Productive resources are scarce and human wants are limited.

Political Science: Man seeks to establish and maintain a public authority through which to govern and be governed.

Psychology: Man's behavior is purposive and goal-oriented.

Sociology: Man is a social being.

Anthropology: Man is man, yet everywhere he is unique.

Social Psychology: Man as a social being is both an individual and a member of group.

Summary: In a nutshell each letter of Social Studies stands for L

S	1.	Social relationship
	2.	Social efficiency
O	3.	Objective attitude
C	4.	Citizenship training
	5.	Constructive and critical thinking
I	6.	Integrated knowledge
	7.	Intelligent understanding
A	8.	Adaptability
	9.	Appreciation of other's viewpoint
L	10.	Learning.

S 11. Sensitiveness to social issues

T 12. Tolerance

U 13. Unbiased attitude

D 14. Devotion to ideas

I 15. Inter-relationships

E 16. Emotional balance

S 17. Self-discipline

18. Social attitude

QUESTIONS

1. Define Social Studies. Which definition you consider the most appropriate?
2. Bring out clearly the scope of Social Studies.
3. Distinguish between 'Social Sciences' and 'Social Studies'. What is the scope of both?
4. State any three chief features of Social Studies.
5. Explain the true concept of Social Sciences.
6. Why should Social Studies be included in the school curriculum?
7. What are the main themes of Social Sciences?
8. What are the values of studying Social Sciences?

4

Art of Teaching

Teacher's Role

The teacher of social studies has to relate to with attitudes, ideals and appreciations to a large extent than is the case in other branches of study. The subject of social studies more than any other subject demands well-prepared conscientious men and women of sound knowledge and training, whose personalities rank high among men. The study of mathematics, the appreciation of a poem, the knowledge of the natural world, important as they may be, cannot be compared with the teacher of social studies who deals with the teaching of pupils to live together in a democracy and raising the tone of democracy by developing thoughtful, appreciative and an intelligent electorate.

Teaching of social studies has suffered very much from poor teaching especially at the elementary stage. It is in general held that anyone could teach social studies. All that was essential was a textbook and the ability to read it. The teacher's task was merely to see that the pupils knew the facts presented in the book. This attitude towards the teaching of social studies still exists. A social studies class is frequently given to a physical education teacher or a drawing or music teacher in order that he may complete the schedule. When one considers the aims and objectives of education and the role that the social studies is destined to play in accomplishing these aims, one venders why the teaching of social studies has been neglected and deals with very indifferently in so many of our schools.

If the social studies are to assist pupils to understand this complex world in which we live in order that this may better adapt themselves to it and prepare themselves for an intelligent and constructive citizenship we must provide well-trained teachers of social studies at all stages of education.

Qualities of a Teacher

These may be categorised as:

I. Scholarship.

II. Professional Training.

III. Personality.

IV. Teaching Skills.

V. Human Relations.

Scholarship. This includes:

1. Acquaintance with problems of present day life.
2. Background of a liberal education.
3. Reader of magazines and newspapers.
4. Reader of books on the subject taught.
5. Sound knowledge of the subject taught.

Professional Training. This incorporates:

6. Desire for improvement.
7. Professional attitude.
8. Reader of professional books.
9. Reader of educational magazines.
10. Sound professional training.

Personality. It has three aspects:

(a) Physical aspects.

(b) Passive virtues.

(c) Executive abilities.

Physical aspects. These include:

11. Personal appearance including dress, carriage, social expression, mannerism and personal cleanliness.
12. Etiquette including good manners, observance of social forms, cour-tesy and refinement.
13. Voice, rich and mellow.
14. Good language command including pronunciation, enunciation and grammar.
15. Health.

Intrinsic qualities. These include:

16. Enthusiasm.
17. Fairness.
18. Friendliness.
19. Optimism.
20. Patience.
21. Self-control.
22. Sincerity.
23. Sympathy.
24. Tact.
25. Understanding.

Executive abilities. These include:

26. Adaptability.
27. Directive ability.
28. Industry.
29. Initiative.
30. Organising ability.
31. Resourcefulness.
32. Self-confidence.
33. Self-reliance.

Teaching Skills. The Core Training Programme Package (CTPP) of the NCERT (1979) aiming at enabling the teachers to acquire mastery of manipulative skills for making their teaching effective includes the following skills:

(a) Skills of class management.

(b) Skills of communication (Teacher's Acts).

(c) Skills of interaction (Teacher-Pupil Acts).

(d) Skills of the use of Teaching Aids.

(e) Skills of Attitude and Behaviour.

Skills of Class Management. These include as below:

(1) Control and modification of facial expression. The teacher should enter the class as a balanced person. It is necessary to emphasise the need for neatness and simplicity in his dress and appearance. Gaudy dress and shabby appearances have to be avoided. The teacher must maintain his calm and confidence in the face of gesticulation and mimicking of the group.

(2) Greetings and taking up proper positions in the class. The teacher is expected to offer the greetings while entering the class and then take the central place facing the class. He is also required to keep moving to the central place when students are offering greetings orally or by standing up in their seats and then face the class and respond to the greetings.

(3) Movements (locomotion in the class-room). Appropriateness of movements lies in providing a balanced supervision to the class and in being available at the right time to the student who needs help.

(4) Use of appropriate gestures in various situations and various stages. Expressions of gestures of approval, appreciation and disapproval also have a great bearing on learning. The tendency of offering undue smile or encouragement or displeasure would form the negative points. Praise like gold and silver owes its utility to scarcity.

Skills of Communication (Teacher's Acts). This comprises five skills : narration, recitation, dramatisation, explanation and demonstration. These skills are teacher-dominated.

Narration. It involves the art of articulated speech making, it is of the following:

(i) Event centred read out from a written text.

(ii) Event centred delivered with the help of notes.

(iii) Event centred spoken extempore.

(iv) Theme centred read out from a written text.

(v) Theme centred delivered with the help of notes.

(vi) Theme centred spoken extempore.

Recitation. This includes:

(a) Reciting poems with a written script.

(b) Reciting poems without a written script

(c) Reciting songs and rhymes with a written script.

(d) Reciting songs and rhymes without a written script.

Dramatisation. Dramatisation involves creation of both visual and audio environment appropriate to the event. Facial expressions appropriate to the occasion, modulation of voice, movements, pauses, creation of appropriate environment and proper sequence of presentation are very important. Dramatisation may be done in the following cases:

(i) Short events with the help of a written script.

(ii) Short events without the help of a written script.

(iii) Full story with the help of a written script.

(iv) Full story without the help of a written script.

Explanation. This involves:

(a) Paraphrasing and correlating a given passage.

(b) Elaborating and correlating a given passage.

Demonstration. Following are the main steps:

(i) Preparing for a demonstration.

(ii) Explaining and demonstrating each step while performing.

(iii) Winding up a demonstration.

Skills of Interaction (Teacher-pupil Acts). This includes:

Questions and Feedback

(a) Framing various types of question.

(b) Framing questions pertaining to hierachical objectives.

(c) Presentation and distribution of question to the whole class and feedback by verbal and non-verbal cues.

Discussion. This relates to:

(i) Selecting a suitable topic for discussion.

(ii) Collecting and systematising information.

(iii) Initiating, sustaining and guiding a discussion.

(iv) Concluding a discussion.

Problem Solving. This pertains to:

(i) Presentation of a problem.

(ii) Analysis of the problem.

(iii) Initiating and sustaining the process of problem solving.

(iv) Guiding problem solving activities.

Skills in the Use of Teaching Aids. This consists of:

(a) Selection of teaching aids as per needs.

(b) Preparation of charts, models, maps and diagrams.

(c) Operation of mechanical aids.

(d) Positioning while writing on and explaining from the blackboard.

(e) Writing on the blackboard with reference to size, shape, boldness and colour of letters.

(f) Drawing, sketching, preparing tables and graphs on the blackboard.

Skills of Attitude and Behaviour. This comprises:

(a) Patient Listening.

(b) Suggesting.

(c) Guiding.

(d) Counselling.

Correlationship

This comprises:

1. Relations with students.
2. Relations with colleagues.
3. Relations with parents.
4. Relations with school personnel.
5. Relations with administrators, inspectors, supervisors etc.
6. Relations with the community.
7. Relations with publishers, stationers, sports dealers etc.
8. Relations with professional organisations and workers.

Particular Capabilities

A Specialist in Human Relations. Social Studies have always been the 'proper study of mankind' meaning, the study of human relationships. Such studies have a special broad emphasis because they are clustered problems of social behaviour involving much diverse information drawn from many standard disciplines of knowledge. A social studies teacher, therefore, has to be very much concerned with this aspect. I.B. Berkson has observed, "As a specialist in human relations he is called upon more often than many of his colleagues for public appearances and as a moderator of discussion of current and public interest."

Objectivity. Another responsibility of the social studies teacher lies in recognition and acceptance of objectivity as a continual criterion. The teacher's job is not to indoctrinate but to equip students to make decisions based on sound and objective knowledge. The teacher's objective duty is not to select for the student but to point out to him the choices which he may make himself and a method by which such choices may be made. The social studies teacher is perhaps always the focus of public eye more than others because of the very nature of his subject-matter, dealing as it does with people and with the contemporary scene. He must discuss issues that are considered controversial and, therefore, he must be doubly careful to pursue his investigations and teaching with objectivity.

Deep Knowledge of the Subject. The primary task of any teacher is through knowledge of the subject-matter which the teacher will attempt to get his students to learn. It is very necessary to bear in mind that 'lack of subject preparation stands near the top of virtually every list of causes of teacher failure'. This certainly does not mean that every school teacher must be a specialist scholar in some branch of study. This is the function of doctors of philosophy in Colleges and Universities. The teacher, however, must know, broadly and deeply, the field in which he teaches.

Trained in Field Study Theory. Teachers of social studies should early get into the habit of "field study" i.e. an application of a field theory to the process of learning, both for themselves and for their students. Each problem that comes up for investigation and learning is a field of inquiry which can be examined from many different points of view and by drawing upon the knowledge of many different disciplines.

Well-informed. The contents of social studies change as rapidly as the world changes. The children of today grow up in a rapidly changing, moving and accelerated universe. They want latest and upto-date knowledge. It is, therefore, very imperative that the teacher of social studies should be keenly interested in latest developments in economics, social, political and cultural life not only of their own country but also of the world at large. The teacher of social studies should also acquire a broad understanding of the family, community, state, nation and the world.

A Widely Travelled Person. First hand information of the important and significant cultural, geographical and historical buildings and places, art galleries, museums, dams, factories and projects etc. will greatly help the social studies. Travels will also enable him to develop breadth of outlook and width of understanding which will assist him to interpret the culture of different parts of the country and the world to his pupils and thus promote emotional, national and international understanding.

A Good Communicator. Only a good communicator can guide discussion, stimulate interest and create in the classroom an environment which is rich in materials and where pupils are challenged to work and learn together. He should be a good story teller and man of imagination.

Skilled in the Use of Technological Aids. A social studies teacher is expected to possess adequate skill in the use of various aids which enables him to bring vividness and attractiveness in the lesson. Skill in map drawing is also very essential.

An Interpreter of Experiences. M.L. Jacks, while discussing the functions of a social studies teacher, has observed, "Above all he is an interpreter – interpreting not the experiences of his pupils but also the community to which they belong, its past no less than its present, its purposes and efforts to achieve those purposes, its cultural and technical achievements, its opportunities and possibilities, the invitation for service which it extends and the rewards, glittering or dimly discovered which it offers." A social studies teacher is in a very advantageous position to bring together the past and the present, the new and the old, the alien and the native, the near and the distant.

QUESTIONS

1. State the role of the Social Studies teacher in enabling the students to understand the contemporary problems.
2. What are the specific teaching skills needed in a social studies teacher?
3. Elucidate the qualities of a social studies teacher.
4. 'A social studies teacher should be well-versed in current affairs'. Explain this statement.

5

Methods of Teaching

The effect of recent developments in educational philosophy and educational psychology upon the methods of teaching has been revolutionary. The central place in the school, in theory at least, has been given to the student. Any process that is not based upon the 'student-activity' is not in accord with recent educational theories. The present century has been termed as 'The Century of the Child'. Rousseau considers that 'child' is a 'hero' in "The drama of education' and as such he must play the dominant role.

The origin of modern methodology may be traced to 'Great Didactic' of Johann Amos Comenius who lived in the seventeenth century. Comenius believed that all instruction should be carefully graded and arranged in a natural order. He advocated, that the teacher, in his methods, should appeal through sense perception to the understanding of the child. He set forth his principles in his 'Great Didactic'. The work of Comenius, however, like that of other educators of his time was buried beneath the sea of religious controversy and bigotry of his age.

'Emile' of Rousseau in the second half of the eighteenth century laid the foundations of the methodology and became the inspiration of forward looking and progressive educators. Comenius provided some ideas, Rousseau improved and enlarged and others worked them and put them into practice. In his chief educational work 'Emile', Rousseau begins with his principle "Everything is good as it comes from the hands of the Author of Nature; but everything degenerates in the hands of man." He points out that there are three great teachers, "nature, man and things."

Johann Heinrich Pestalozzi attempted to "psychologise instruction". He declared that the basis of all education was a drawing out process and not a pouring in process that the basis of all education lay in the nature of the child and that methods of instruction must be sought and constructed to that end.

Wilhelm August Froebel and Johann Friedrich Herbart, disciples and followers of Pestalozzi developed elaborate systems of education. The work of Froebel dealt largely with the Kindergarten stage. Herbart gave his famous 'Herbartian Steps' which cast a flood of light on existing methods. Herbartian steps became the stimulators of various other movements in the field of education. Herbart condemned the rote method and stressed comprehension and association. The concept that the outcome of education was not the strengthening of the mental faculties but rather the building up of an "apperceptive mass" of ideas was very revolutionary. Herbartian theory and practice became popular in Germany between 1865 and 1885. Teachers and students from many lands studied at Jena, a centre of Herbartian teaching. By 1890, these ideas were brought to America where they received an almost universal acceptance.

The period of Herbartian influence, one the whole, was a transitional one. It prepared the way for newer and better concepts of education. By 1910, Herbartian as a system of education was quite generally criticised. Herbartianism stressed the teacher and the formal procedure of teachings; the new theories of educational philosophy emphasised the pupils. Emphasis during recent years has been on individual instruction in the classroom but the socialisation of the individual is not to be neglected. Almost all modern methods and procedures can be used to promote both. It is believed that socialisation can be used in connection with individual development. In the social studies, even more than any other subject in the school, socialization is necessary. Through his own activities intermingled with the activities of the group, the pupil can learn and develop. Education must begin with the child and must be adapted to the needs and requirements of the child as he grows. Only in this manner, according to this philosophy, can the individual be made socially efficient.

The Secondary Education Commission has emphasised the need for right methods of teaching in these words, "Every teacher and educationist of experience knows that even the best curriculum and the most perfect syllabus remain dead unless quickened into life by the right methods of teaching and the right kind of teachers. Sometimes even an unsatisfactory and unimaginative syllabus can be made interesting and significant by the gifted teacher who does not focus his mind on the subject-matter to be taught or the information to be imparted but on his students—their interests and aptitudes, their reactions and response. He judges the success of his lesson not by the amount of matter covered but by the understanding, the appreciation and the efficiency achieved by the students."

In the world of Herbart Ward and Frank Roscoe, "While it is true that good method is not merely a collection of artifices or mechanical devices and that every teacher must devise his own method, it is important to remember that good method can result only from the constant observation of certain broad principles. These include orderly procedure in teaching, an arrangement of the subject-matter which will avoid waste of time and of energy and a distribution of emphasis which will secure the greatest co-operation from the pupils and maintain their active interest."

A method is not merely a device adopted for communicating certain items of information to students and exclusively the concern of the teacher who is supposed to be at the "giving end." To quote the Secondary Education Commission, "Any method, good or bad, links up the teacher and his pupils into an organic relationship with constant mutual interaction; it reacts not only on the mind of the students but on their entire personality; their standards of work and judgment, their intellectual and emotional equipment, their attitudes and values. Good methods which are psychologically and socially sound may raise the whole quality of their life; bad methods debase it. So, in the choice and assessment of methods, teachers must always take into consideration their end products, namely, the attitudes and values inculcated in them consciously or unconsciously."

Practical Learning

Children have been endowed by nature with tremendous vitality. They have within them the springs of youth, joy and vigour. They possess curiosity and wish to know things for themselves. In the words of T.S. Avinashilingam, "The Great Ganga of life flows majestically on. But if anyone tries to retain and dam it, the dam will break unless attempts are simultaneously made to divert it into other channels. These waters can only be diverted, but cannot be dammed indefinitely. If anyone tried to do the impossible, it would be at his peril, for the dam will break, sooner or later. So is the nature of children. The great vitality of our children cannot be permanently restrained without providing a positive purpose. In ordinary bookish classroom education, the teacher teaches, students are but passive listeners. Their energy has not to be restrained by fear, inducement or punishment. This is against their nature and that is why we see much outbursts of so-called indiscipline. But, on the other hand, if we provide such activities in which the children themselves can take part we will find that discipline becomes natural. Thus, providing for various types of activities which will interest the children and give them opportunities for observation and the use of their hands is to offer them the fulfilment and satisfaction, which nothing else confers."

The principle of 'Learning by Doing' has been accepted by all the progressive educators and in all the progressive countries. All educationists recognise that activity is an important instrument of education.

Comenius's View. According to him "impression must be ensured by expression and what has to be done must be learnt by doing."

Rousseau's Views. Rousseau protested against the traditional methods of teaching very vehemently and he declared, "Children are first restless and then curious. Instead of making the child stick to his books, I keep him busy in workshop, his hands will work to the profit of his mind."

Prestalozzi's views. He called the traditional system as 'the wordy system of teaching'. According to him, "Our unpsychological schools are essentially only artificial stifling machines for destroying all the results of the power and experience, the nature herself brings to life in them. After they enjoyed sensuous life for five years, we make all nature round them vanish before their eyes: tyranically to the delightful course of their unrestricted freedom; peg them up like sheep; pitilessly chain them for hours, days, weeks, months, years to the contemplation of unnatural and unattractive letters."

Teaching Sports Way

Froebel's Views. "Play is the chief activity of childhood" which Froebel considers as "the highest phase of child development....for it is self-active representation of the stage.... It gives, therefore, joy, freedom, contentment, inner and outer rest, peace with the world. It holds the source of all that is good." But, "without rational conscious guidance," says Froebel, "childish activity degenerates into aimless play instead of preparing for those tasks of life for which it is designed."

Gradual Learning

Dewey's Views. Dewey endeavoured to substitute bookish learning by experience. He strongly recommended investigation and experimentation. According to him the school is a 'special environment' where a certain quality of life and certain types of activities and occupations are provided with the object of securing children's development along desirable lines. "The teacher", according to him, "is a guide and director, he steers the boat but the energy that propels it must come from those who are learning."

Educating Oneself

Madam Montessori's Views. She shifted the emphasis from "teaching to learning'. She believed that self-education is the best method by which the child learns in his own way and at his own rate. She used the word 'Directress'.

James Welton's Views. "The teacher is like a guide and the pupil like a traveller in an unknown country. The traveller knows where he wants to go, but knows neither the way nor the exact character of the place he wishes to go.... But unless the traveller that is the pupil takes the journey himself, nothing is accomplished. Many a lesson is too much like a guide describing the journey to the would-be traveller who sits and listens but does not leave his chair to undertake it. In ether lessons, the guide himself laboriously takes the journeys again and again, but the traveller that should be, remains inert. In short, no matter how admirably a lesson is planned, there is no really methodical teaching unless the pupils by their own efforts pass along the road traced for them; for as has been said, "true teaching is nothing but arousing and directing learning activity of another."

Gandhiji's Views. "Let us now cry a halt and concentrate on education of the child properly through manual work, not as a side activity but as a prime means of intellectual training."

Thus we find that a long line of distinguished experts in education have advocated that knowledge can best be given through constructive activities suitable to the child. These new ideas on education have brought a new and hopeful message to our children.

Activity does not mean mere physical activity. Of course, it comes first. But it means, as Rybum puts, "Activity of the intelligence and also of the emotions, and of the will. If a pupil is to develop all sides of his personality, then it is necessary for him to be active in all ways, to exercise all the different powers he has." Doing is necessary in learning. It is not a mere device but a part and parcel of the learning process without which learning is not complete. Doing must be with a purpose.

Instinctive Tendencies. Children are active by nature. Construction is a powerful drive roused in childhood. The hands of the child are ever ready to make new things. If he does not find material to construct, he begins to destroy. In fact, construction and destruction are the aspects of the same activity. The teacher should utilise this instinct by encouraging children to construct and create things.

Children Possess Curiosity. They want to understand the environment and put hundreds of question to teachers, parents and friends. This urge must be exploited. Children are fond of collecting things. They should be encouraged to collect useful things for their museum.

Self-motivation. Motivation facilitates the process of learning by doing. It arouses the interest of the child and once interest is aroused, the child becomes active, attentive and learns by doing.

Purposeful Activities. Abstract things cannot be followed and understood by children. Mental activities should be followed by concrete activities and this gives them the idea what they are doing and that with some purpose and aim.

Utilisation of All Senses. The children are required to utilize all of their senses in learning by doing. They have to be attentive in learning, seeing, feeling, smelling and sometimes testing even. This makes learning fruitful.

Close Relation of Mind and Body. Mental activities fail to develop harmoniously the mind and body which are closely related. In learning by doing the hand and the head work in close cooperation and the learning becomes successful.

The Principle of Linking with Life. Learning is linked with the life and the environment of the child and thus it becomes pan and parcel of our nature. In a lesson on gardening, if we take the students to a garden and explain to them the relevant topic, it creates more impression and the students learn it easily.

Lessening of Fatigue. Undoubtedly mental work is more fatigue-giving than the manual one and if children are kept busy in purely mental activities, they feel mental fatigue. But when we coordinate both mental and manual work, fatigue is lessened to a great extent.

Social Development. Social development is as important as individual development. Children want to work in groups. In learning by doing they learn from each other and thus develop qualities like co-operation. Sometimes learning by doing takes the form of productive activities as is the case in basic education. The students then produce things for society. Thus they develop feelings of being a part of the community and try to be useful for it.

Inferiority Complex Resolved. Learning by doing affords opportunities to backward children in studies to show their talents in various kinds of productive and constructive activities and in physical activities. This helps them in gaining confidence which further assists them in resolving their inferiority complex and they succeed in mental activities also.

Use of Almost all the Theories of Learning. Various theories of learning have been put forward. 'Learning by trial and error,' 'learning by imitating' and 'learning by insight'—all are employed in learning by doing. Thus, learning becomes quicker, easier and more effective.

Various Levels of Progress

Primary Classes. This method can be employed at all stages of education. In the primary classes some manual work or craft work is at the centre. This may take the form of building a room, or making post office or making envelopes. It may take the form of action songs, games, clay modelling, paper-cutting etc. The use of apparatus as devised in Kindergarten and Montessori systems also implies learning by doing. The Project Method is also an activity method which provides life situations and presents purposeful activities.

Middle and Higher Secondary Classes. The principle of learning by doing takes various forms in the higher secondary classes. Dalton Plan is an activity method which provides many opportunities to do work independently, to find out answers to a large number of question by studying many books. It also provides for conferences and discussion work. The Heuristic Method places the children in the position of discoverers, inventors and experimenters.

Principle of Learning by Doing and Out-of-class Activities. The scope of this principle is not related only to the learning of various subjects but also to the out-of-class activities. Students should be engaged in debating, editing, scouting, dramatising, etc. Games and sports are other fields. Students should be provided opportunities to render social service to community. Social education centres, social service clubs etc., should be started. N.C.C., B.S.S., all provide useful channels to harness the energies of the youth and thereby sublimate the instincts of the students.

Learning by Doing in Social Studies. The principle can be employed in all the school subjects.

History. Children should be taken to places, of historical interest, i.e. ancient monuments, caves, forts, ruins, edicts, museums etc. Charts and models of the various battles should be prepared. Maps of various dynasties and the extent of empire should be prepared.

Historical Plays may be Dramatised. The students may be encouraged to read historical novels.

Geography. Excursions to the places of geographical interest should be arranged. The students should be asked to prepare geographical maps, models and charts to show geographical facts in colours and lines on paper as well as on earth.

Civics. Visits to the meetings and sessions of village panchayat. District Boards, State Assemblies, etc., may be arranged.

Types of Methods

Inspirational Methods. These methods are primarily based on high activity on the part of the instructor-teacher. Giving a sermon to the students or to any group of learners is a good example of this methodology.

Expository Methods. In these methods cognitive emphasis is very high, while student activity and emphasis on experience is low. One good example of expository method is the lecture method in which the main emphasis is on imparting cognitive information to the learners.

Natural Learning Methods. The main rationale of these methods is that learning takes place in a natural way and planning for learning is not necessary. Learners are left on their own, with free and unplanned activity. Thus, the emphasis on learning activity is high, whereas it is low on planned experience and on cognitive inputs.

Individualized Methods. These methods are quite well known mainly through the popularity of programmed instruction. The main characteristic of these methods is the guided search encouraged by the instructor or the teacher. In addition to programmed instruction, self-study, computer-oriented instruction, case method, and prescribed experiments in science are other examples of individualized learning in which the main emphasis is for each learner to learn at his own pace.

Encounter Methods. Carl Rogers had popularized the term 'encounter', although several other terms are used like T-Group, sensitivity training, interpersonal confrontation and so on. In these methods the main emphasis is on experience and learner activity. Since the emphasis is on providing experience through confrontation or through encounter, and not through cognitive understanding, these methods are affective for changing basic behavioural patterns and developing new ways of looking at things. Role play also involves some amount of encounter.

Discovery Methods. These methods are high on all the three dimensions: learner activity, experience and experimentation by the learner, and cognitive understanding. Simulations primarily come under the category as also self-generated experiments in science. The main emphasis of methods in this category is on problem-solving and providing necessary framework to the learner, so that while solving the problem the learner is also able to learn the rationale and logic of what he has done.

Group Methods. Methods like Project method come under this category.

Identifying Methods

We can charaterise the good methods of teaching as below:

1. They should aim at inculcating love of work.
2. They should aim at developing the desire to do work with the highest measure of efficiency of which one is capable. The motto of every school and his pupils should

be 'Everything that is worth doing at all is worth doing well'. Whether it be making a speech, writing a composition, drawing a map, cleaning the class-room, making a book rack or forming a queue.

3. They should provide numerous opportunities of participation in freely accepted projects and activities in which discipline and co-operation are constantly in demand.
4. They should aim at developing the capacity for 'clear thinking' which distinguishes every truly educated person, "whether a student is asked to make a speech in a debating society or to write an essay or to answer a question in history, geography, or science or to experiment, the accent should always be on clear thinking and on lucid expression which is a mirror of clear thought."
5. The methods of teaching should expand the range of students' interest. "We would urge all schools to provide in the time-table, at least one free period every day in which students may pursue their favourite hobbies and creative activities individually or in groups, preferably under the guidance of some interested teacher", recommended the Secondary Education Commission.
6. They should aim at providing opportunities to pupils to apply practically the knowledge that has been acquired by them. They should aim at transforming present bookish schools into "work schools" or "activity schools."
7. They should aim at the quickening of interest and training in efficient techniques of learning and study.
8. They should train the students in the art of study. They should train the students in the use of reference material such as the list of contents and index in books, the dictionary, the atlas, and reference books like the encyclopaedia.
9. They should be adapted to suit different levels of intelligence.

10. They should be such as they balance the claim of individual work with co-operative or group effort. The training of emotions, attitudes and social capacities take place best in the context of projects and units of work undertaken co-operatively. The Secondary Education Commission has recommended that the teachers should be so trained that they are able to visualise and organise at least a part of the curriculum in the form of projects and activity-units which groups of students may take up and carry to completion."

Various Methods

1. Assignment Method.
2. Dalton Plan.
3. Discussion Method.
4. Laboratory Method.
5. Lecture Method.
6. Observation Method.
7. Questioning.
8. Problem Method.
9. Project Method.
10. Review Method.
11. Socialised Classroom Recitation Method.
12. Source Method.
13. Story Telling Method.
14. Supervised Study Method.
15. Text Book Method.

Assignment Method

Significance of Assignment. N.L. Bossing has observed, "The central position of the assignment in the techniques of teaching has remained unquestioned." G.H. Belts asserts, "Upon the proper assignment of the lesson depends much of the success of the recitation, and also much of the pupil's progress in learning how to study." W.N. Drum suggests, "Teachers generally do not appreciate the importance of the assignment, and the work of the pupils probably suffers as much from hasty or careless assignment as from any other single cause." H.R. Douglass and others are of the view, "The assignment represents one of the most important phases of teaching." Essentials of an assignment.

1. The assignment should be clear and definite.
2. The assignment should be concise but sufficiently detailed to enable each student to understand the task assigned.
3. The assignment should anticipate special difficulties and suggest ways to remove them.
4. The assignment should relate the new unit to past experience.
5. Students should understand the importance of the assignment.
6. The assignment should arouse an interest in advance work.
7. The assignment should provide for differences in the ability and interest of students.
8. The assignment should be motivated chiefly by the hope of worth while achievements, rather than scholastic reward or the fear of punishment.
9. The assignment should stimulate thought.
10. The assignment should provide necessary and specific directions for the study of the lesson.
11. The assignment should be adjusted to the time and opportunity of the class.
12. Materials of the assignment should be varied and adaptable to the needs and interests of the students.

Types of Assignment. N.L. Bossing has listed the following:

Page or Paragraph Assignment. Often thought of as the textbook assignment. Unfortunately, this method is still widely used as recent studies have revealed.

Chapter Assignment. Another form of the textbook assignment though vastly different from the page or paragraph form. Chapters usually are of a unitary nature and involve some elements of completeness within themselves.

Topical Assignment. This type may or may not centre around a single chapter in a textbook. It has a wealth of possibility in the social sciences particularly.

Problem Assignment. Where an arbitrary distinction is set up between a problem and a project the type becomes very valuable form of assignment.

Project Assignment. Adapted especially to the workshop, natural sciences, and some measure to the social sciences. Its special appeal is through the natural motor activity required.

Experience Assignment. Most frequently used in mathematics. It represents the old traditional approach to teaching although if used in combination with other types, this form can be used very effectively.

Individual or Group Report Assignment. Used extensively as a device to supplement other types and to provide for individual differences in interests and capacities within the class; very effective.

Unit Assignment. It may apply to any extensive segment of classroom activity that presents factors of cohesion and a relatively complete additional element around which the unit may resolve itself as a core. A rather pretentious problem may serve as this unitary core.

Experimental Assignment. This is a form of the problem and project types characteristic of the science laboratory. Too often in practice, it does not represent either an experiment or a problem in the true sense. It can be made a vital instrument of educational training if properly used.

Practice Assignment. This type represents an assignment of repetitions of activities designed to produce mental or motor skills. Mastery of the simple combinations in arithmetic, memorization of a poem, or practice in speed on the typewriter are examples of this type of assignment.

Difficulties in the Preparation of a Good Assignment. Fleming and Woodring have listed the following difficulties:

1. Insufficient thought and preparation in planning the assignment.
2. Inability to obtain an acceptance by the pupil of a worthy purpose for performance of the task.
3. Simulation in the preparation of the assignments by appealing the interests of adolescents and by providing 'for real needs growing out of pupil experience.
4. Prevention of loss of interest due to too long phase of time between the assignment and preparation.
5. Avoidance of assignments so long that successful accomplishment is impossible in the time available for preparation, with consequent loss of interest.
6. Guarding against too many and too varied activities, resulting in dividing interests with consequent bad habits of work, and unsatisfactory accomplishments.
7. Difficulty in presenting work to be done so that it is clearly understood by the pupils; also, the difficulty of ascertaining whether every pupil understands.
8. Gauging the difficulty of work so that success is possible for each pupil.
9. Determining essential requirements, and differentiation of assignments to suit the various levels and types of ability existing in the class.
10. Inclusion of challenges to mental exploration by the pupil, thereby stimulating real thinking.
11. Provision for continuity of work by presenting new problems as a continuation of previous experience and anticipation of future problems.
12. Correlating with other subjects and outside activities.
13. Focusing attention on important elements in the new problem of task, and directing the attack in such a way as to increase interest rather than lessen it, to stimulate

effort, and to overcome seeming obstacles to accomplishment.

14. Providing the necessary tools for preparation by training in study procedures and techniques, and in selection, organization, and use of materials, thereby developing effective habits of independent work.
15. Giving to pupils devices for checking the mastery and performance of work undertaken.
16. Evaluating the effectiveness of an assignment by the quality of response during the presentation of the assignment, and by the adequacy of pupil preparation.
17. Providing sufficient time for adequate consideration of the assignment and determining the psychological moment for its presentation.

Suggested Assignment Procedure. The procedure suggested for the preparation of a good assignment is as follows:

1. Analyse the nature of the learning process required in the advance unit. This is without exception the first step in a good assignment procedure. Much of what follows in any good assignment-depends upon this analysis.
2. Study the various types of assignments available and select the one, or modified form of it, that appears to fit best the learning situation. Some assignment types are admirably adapted to one form of learning for teaching but not to others.
3. Provide the essential background for the advance work where uncertainty exists that such background obtains. At this point too many teachers are likely to assume the adequacy of this background when in fact it may not exist. Scarcely can one emphasize too strongly the apperceptive preparation for the new.
4. Whether this is the next step in the assignment procedure or not, it is obvious that very early in the assignment phase the teacher must throw out a challenge to the student that will enlist his interest and maximum effort in the new unit.

5. Outline in sufficient detail the advance unit to be studied.
6. Suggest some plan of attack upon the new unit. It is well to remember one caution—do not do the student that which he may be led to do for himself. This suggests the desirability of leading the class in a cooperative discovery of desirable leads for the general attack upon the new.
7. Where reference to source material other than the textbooks is necessary, this should be made specific. The most satisfactory plan in the large unit assignment is to provide the select list of available sources in mimeographed or hectographed form with chapter or inclusive page references given.

Home Assignments

Whether or not homework should be given to the students is a controversial point. Extreme views have been expressed regarding the usefulness of home work. The assignment of home task has been emphatically denounced by Bray. He writes, "Under normal conditions a reasonable day's work for a child has been done at the close of the afternoon and homework as it is generally organised does more harm than good as a rule in this country except perhaps from the point of view of examination success." On the other hand, P.C. Wren commends the assigning of homework. An average guardian also feels that some work should be given to the student which he should do at home.

Purpose of Home Task in Social Studies. Following purposes can be stated.

1. To provide opportunities to students to work independently and thereby to develop in them self-reliance and initiative.
2. To develop habits of reading regularly among the students.
3. To provide opportunities to the students to utilise their leisure time profitably. It is generally seen that our school

children waste their precious time in loitering about or making mischief when no such work is given to them.

4. To give them an opportunity to do practice what is done in the school.
5. To finish the prescribed courses in time. The syllabi is too heavy to be finished in the classroom work.
6. To serve as a link in the parent-teacher co-operation. It enables the parents to know that regular work is being done in the school.
7. To develop permanent interests and to train the students in the profitable use of leisure.
8. To enable the child to revise his previous lesson and prepare the next one.
9. To provide remedial measure for backward children.
10. To give chance to every child to progress at his own speed.

Type of Homework Given. Following are the types of homework.

1. Writing of essay type answers to questions arising out of the subject-matter already done in the class.
2. Verbal memorising work pertaining to curricular and co-curricular activities. It may take the form of cramming facts, principles, poems, spelling etc. of memorising work in respect of dramatics and debates etc.
3. Practical work, e.g., preparation of charts, maps, knitting, sewing and drawing, etc.
4. Transcription, calligraphy etc.
5. Advance preparation for the coming lesson.

Disadvantages and Objections. These are as follows:

1. It deprives the children of participating in recreational activities when it imposes heavy demands upon them.
2. It is a great hindrance in the way of the students of enjoying family and social life.

3. It deprives children of the opportunity to help their parents in supplementing their income.
4. It imposes a great physical strain to small children and thus endangers their health.
5. It becomes a constant source of fear and worry to the students and therefore it endangers their emotional stability.
6. Children are tempted to copy whenever they find that the home task is difficult to do.
7. Sometimes children are tempted to tell a lie that due to certain reasons they have failed to do home task.
8. Unhealthy home conditions make study more harmful than profitable. There is a lack of adequate light and quietness in a large number of Indian homes and the atmosphere is not congenial for study.
9. Too much of homework develops an attitude of indifference on the pan of the pupils and they become careless.
10. Lack of proper correction by the teacher, sometimes, gives rise to carelessness on the pan of the pupils. It also develops wrong habits of work if the work is not properly checked.
11. Too much work is set by some over-enthusiastic specialist teachers in their subjects completely disregarding what other teachers of the same class might have set for the same day.
12. The task is generally too academic in nature and ignores those activities which are needed most for an all-round development of the personality of the child.
13. It is not properly adjusted to pupils' needs and capacities.

Principles of Assigning Homework. Following are the principles of assigning homework.

1. The nature of the homework should be such as it does not require any kind of assistance from a private tutor or guardian.
2. It should not be purely mechanical, i.e., requiring no general knowledge on the part of the child.
3. Homework should aim at developing the taste of the individual child. This purpose can be very conveniently realised if homework is in the nature of hobbies.
4. Homework should be very definite.
5. It should be supplementary rather preparatory as far as possible.
6. A single assignment for the whole class may not be considered as appropriate. It should vary according to the mental and physical makeup of the students.
7. Homework in different subjects should be co-ordinated. Homework time table should be framed so as to avoid confusion.
8. While assigning homework "Principle of sliding scales" should be adapted. The primary classes might be given home task to keep them busy for about half hour or so; in the middle, secondary and Senior secondary classes time involved in doing home task should not exceed one hour, Normally it should be given on alternate days.
9. Home task should not be set as a punishment
10. Home task should be properly checked.
11. Library books should be given for reading at home as a home task.
12. Copies of the homework time tables may be sent to the parents to seek their cooperation which is very important.
13. While assigning homework the teachers should take into consideration the home conditions of the child such as domestic employment, working condition in the home, etc.

14. 15% marks should be reserved for the evaluation of the student's work based on the assignments done through the year.

Corrective Methods

The following methods of correction may be adopted:

1. Correction by the teacher.
2. Correction with the help of the bright students in the class.
3. Correction with the help of the blackboard.
4. Correction by interchanging the exercise books among the students.
5. Glance checking and signing by teachers.

At the primary stage, teachers should correct all the assignments without any help from the children. At this stage it is not possible for the children to do any self-correction.

Note: For Dalton Plan, see the next chapter.

Teaching by Discussion

Meaning and Significance of Discussion Method. This method has been used in the teaching-learning process since times immemorial. It was widely used at the famous Nalanda University. The Greek scholars in their walk used to discuss various problems and issues with their disciples. Discussion has been described as a thoughtful consideration of the relationships involved in a topic or problem under study. It is concerned with the analysis, comparison, evaluation and conclusions of these relationships. It aims at uniting and integrating the work of the class. It is carried out by organising, outlining and relating, the facts studied. It encourages the students to direct their thinking process towards the solution of a problem and to use their experiences for a further clarification and consolidation of learning material.

Discussion is to be distinguished from debate in which the participants seek to prove a point rather than to discover a truth.

Debate may also be marked by uncontrolled exchange of verbalism.

Discussion is very important in stimulating mental activity, developing fluency and ease in expression, clarity of ideas in thinking and training in the presentation of one's ideas and facts. An exchange of ideas and opinions, offers valuable training to students in reflective thinking.

Essential Parts or Constituents of Discussion. These are as under:

1. The leader – the teacher
2. The group – the students
3. The problem or the topic
4. The content – body of knowledge.
5. Evaluation – change in ideas, attitudes etc.

Organisation of Discussion. Following are the main techniques of organising discussion.

1. Introducing a topic or a problem by the teacher by giving points or explanations to serve as the basis of discussion.
2. Calling upon a pupil by the teacher to give facts, describe a scene or situation, explain an incident, event or happening for getting the discussion started.
3. Preparing an outline of points cooperatively by the teacher and a few students which may become the starting point for discussion.
4. Asking the students to describe their own experiences connected with the subject, topic or problem and making them points for discussion.
5. Presenting detailed papers by the teacher and discussions thereon.
6. Presenting detailed papers by the students and discussing them in the class.
7. Showing special works and projects to the class and discussing them.

8. Showing some pictures, charts, diagrams or any audio-visual material and discussion about them.

Merits of Discussion. Following are the merits of discussion:

1. It helps in clarifying issues.
2. It helps children in crystallising their thinking.
3. It helps students in discovering what they do not know and what they have overlooked.
4. It engenders more reflection. It is farther from rote learning.
5. It represents a type of pooled knowledge, ideas and feelings of several persons.
6. It develops team spirit.
7. It engenders toleration of views which are at variance.
8. It affords opportunities to the students to learn together, make suggestions, share responsibility, comprehend the topic, evaluate the findings and to summarise results.
9. It provides opportunities to the students to speak distinctly, stand and sit correctly, respect the ideas of others, share interests, ask pertinent questions and comprehend the problem before the group.
10. It helps the teacher in discovering talented students who have potential for becoming good leaders.

Limitations of Discussion. Limitations of discussion are:

1. It is not suitable in all topics.
2. It is likely to be dominated by a few students.
3. It is likely to go off the track.
4. It may lead to unpleasant feelings.
5. It may create emotional tensions.
6. It may involve unnecessary arguments.

Directing Group Discussion. The teacher has to show immense patience and skill to ensure that discussion takes place on right lines and in the appropriate environment. Following points may be considered in this respect:

1. Students should be well acquainted with the significance of the topic, its nature and scope and causes why the class should discuss it.
2. Discussion should be confined to important aspects.
3. Students should be encouraged to participate in the discussion.
4. Ideas may be invited without pressure or embarrassment.
5. Explanations, where needed, should be provided.
6. Personality cult should be avoided.
7. Cooperation rather than competition should be encouraged.
8. Efforts should be made to develop team spirit.
9. Doubts, mistakes and wrong interpretation should be made clear by the teacher.
10. Facts and points should be evaluated.
11. Facts and points should be summarised.
12. Students should be guided to appreciate difference of opinion and views.
13. Goals of discussion should be kept in view.
14. Only a few students should not be allowed to dominate classroom discussion.
15. Shy students may be given training in discussion in small groups so that their hesitation is removed while participating in bigger groups.

Teaching in Laboratory

H.C. Hill presents a picture of the Laboratory Method as used in the University of Chicago High School in a class in civics. He says, "The greater part of the students will be studying and writing at their work tables. Two or three may be having a quiet conference on some moot point. Others may be comparing notes or outlines of some phase of the work. One student may be busy at the dictionary, hunting for the explanation of some phrase or term;

another may be consulting an atlas; a third may be sharpening a pencil or filling his fountain pen; a fourth may be making a map or preparing a graph; a fifth may be conferring with the teacher about some difficulty or asking for a criticism on his notes or outlines. Usually one or two students will be browsing among the volumes in the bookcases or going through tables of contents or indexes to find a clue to some obscure item. Now and then an idler or a dawdler will be observed. In general, however, the room is a place of quite, disorderly order, in which students are busily engaged in profitable activities of one kind or another."

Bining and Bining sum up the situation, "Conviction on troublesome issues and questions must come as a result of analysis, judgement and experience. Teachers must be loyal to the ideals of tolerance, truth, justice, and honesty. They should emphasize, in their teaching, attitudes, ideals, intellectual habits, and other qualities that will bring about an educated citizency in a great democracy. A few educators have suggested that the teaching of ideals—even those ideals upon which there is general agreement—is a form of indoctrination. From this viewpoint, we are being indoctrinated. If it means going to the extremes of Fascist Italy and Nazi Germany or present-day Soviet Russia, it is to be condemned. On the other hand, a social and civic training that is in accord with democratic ideals— call it what we may—is not only desirable but essential if our schools are to have any part in training citizens who will build a nobler society, freer from faults and defects than the present one."

Teaching by Lecture

Significance of Lecture Method. It is the oldest teaching method given by philosophy of idealism. As used in education, the lecture method refers to the teaching procedure involved in the clarification or explanation to the student of some major idea. This method lays emphasis on the presentation of the content. Teacher is more active and students are passive but he uses question answer to keep them attentive in the class. It is used to clarify matters, to expand content and motivate the students. By changing his voice, by impersonating characters, by shifting his position and by using simple devices, a teacher can deliver his lesson effectively. While delivering his lecture, a teacher can indicate by his facial expression, gestures and tones the exact shade of meaning that he wishes to convey.

Merits of the Lecture Method. Following are the merits of the lecture method.

1. It is economical as it needs no apparatus and no laboratory. A large number of students can be taught at a time.
2. It saves time and covers syllabus in a limited time.
3. It is very effective in giving factual information and in relating some of the thrilling anecdotes with historical lessons. The life stories of great adventurers, experimenters, investigators and thinkers can become very interesting and valuable talks by a teacher.
4. Lecturing makes the work of the teacher very simple. He need not make elaborate arrangements.
5. A good lecture not only stimulates the students but also lingers long in their imagination. It motivates students to become good orators.
6. It provides better scope for clarification and for laying stress on significant ideas.
7. It brings a personal contact and touch to impress or influence the pupils.
8. It provides flexibility. As the teacher is in close and intimate contact with his pupils, he can adjust his technique in accordance with their abilities, aptitudes and interests.
9. It gives the students training in listening.
10. It gives the students training in taking notes rapidly.
11. It develops good audience habits.
12. It provides opportunities of correlating events and subjects.
13. It enables the linkage of previous knowledge with the new one.

Limitations. The limitations of this method are as follows:

1. There is very little scope for pupil activity.
2. It does not take into consideration individual differences.
3. Lecturing is against the principle of 'Learning by Doing'.
4. It spoonfeeds the students without developing their power of reasoning.
5. Speed of the lecture may be too fast for the learner to grasp the line of thought.
6. An average student may not be able to fix up his attention to a lecture of forty to forty-five minutes.
7. A lecturer is likely to cover more content without realising that little learning takes place.
8. A lecture may become monotonous to the students after a while. Very few teachers can keep the interest of the students upto the end.

Guidelines for the effective use of the lecture method, the following points should be kept in view in using this device of teaching.

1. Matter should be arranged in such a way as to leave a single clear impression on the minds of the students.
2. The teacher should have pauses in between the lesson so that the students may learn the new knowledge bit by bit.
3. The rate of exposition should be slow when the class is backward. The teacher should utilise different ways of presenting the same information.
4. There should be abundant repetition but it should be in a new way so that the class may not feel dullness.
5. Children's way of looking at things should be considered in exposition. Language used should be familiar and suitable.
6. The lesson should be divided into sections which have a logical sequence. This will enable the students to understand easily and will also train them in systematic

thinking besides assisting them to put their own thought logically.

7. The rate of exposition and the size of the subject-matter are determined by the individual capacity of children and teacher's natural rate of speech.
8. Proper use of the blackboard should be made.
9. Actual objects, models, diagrams, sketches etc., should be used.
10. The students should be encouraged to ask question. This will enable them to get their doubts removed.
11. Verbal illustrations such as examples, comparisons, etc., should be used to enable the students to grasp the exposition.
12. Pictorial illustrations such as pictures, maps and charts should be freely used as these help in motivating the students.
13. The aim of the lesson should be kept in view and the students fully made conversant with the aim.

Teaching by Observation

It is rightly believed that observation under the careful guidance of a social studies teacher proves very effective in the process of learning, and facts, skills and behaviour learnt are retained for a longer period. Observation or direct experience or visits to actual places, say, a monument, a fort, a field, a river, a temple, an institution etc. provide ample opportunities to students, for 'seeing', 'hearing', 'examining', 'gathering data' and 'asking' questions. Visits to hospitals, telephone exchanges, telegraph offices, study trips to airports, etc. show how people and goods are trans-ported from one place to another. Pupils understand better the working of markets, cooperative stores and factories when they see their working and thus acquaint themselves with the processes of production, distribution, exchange and consumption. Such experiences are most conducive to learning. Concrete data on cultural, industrial, political and geographical facts and relation-ship being more 'tangible', 'visible' and 'describable' serve as a great motivating force for further enquiry in social sciences. Observation lends vitality to the subject-matter of social studies.

Techniques of observation method. Following techniques are adopted in the observation method:

1. Field Trips or Educational Excursions
2. Community Surveys.
3. Community Service Projects.

Teaching by Review

Meaning and Significance of 'Review'. N.L. Bossing states, "The term review connotes not a mere repetition of facts to fix them more firmly in mind, but rather a new view of these facts in a different setting that results in-new understandings, changed attitudes or different behaviour patterns." H.N. Rivilin regards review as, "deepening the students insight into the problem......... increasing his appreciation of its ramifications." Review must recall essential facts and appraisals of segments of experience in a final summary that actually involves a new view and a new understanding and provides a basis for changed behaviour.

Purposes of Review. Following are the purposes of review:

1. Fixing in mind activities or materials learned.
2. Organising the materials and experiences into larger units for understanding.
3. Enabling the students to gain perspective.
4. Providing for desirable expansion and supplementation of materials and experience.
5. Providing an apperceptive basis for future study.
6. Diagnosing student weakness in preparation and understanding.
7. Diagnosing teacher weakness.
8. Creating new interest in old materials.

Teaching by Source

Meaning of Source Method of Teaching Social Studies. Source method implies the use of original material and original sources in the teaching of social studies. A source method provides first hand experiences and leads to better understanding of the subject. Sources may be divided into two categories:

(a) Primary Sources.

(b) Secondary Sources.

Primary Sources. These include as given below:

(i) Physical remains or relics or unconscious testimony in far off his-torical sites, roads, pyramids, human remains, clothing, food, fortification, utensils, pottery, building, implements, machinery, furniture, weapons, fine arts and museum pieces of many kinds, inscriptions, chiselled stories, monuments, tombs, coins, stamps, tapestrips, scenery and portraits, sculptures, historical paintings etc.

(ii) Consciously transmitted information in the form of oral or written testimony. Written sources include constitutions, charters, court decisions, official minutes or records, autobiographies, letters, diaries, geneologies, contracts, deeds, wills, permits, licences, affidavits, depositions, declarations, proclamations, certificates, bills, receipts, magazines and newspapers, accounts, advertisements, maps, diagrams, books, pamphlets, films, catalogues, paintings, inscriptions, recordings, transcriptions and research reports. Oral tradition includes ballads, anecdotes, tales and saga.

Secondary Sources. These are those sources which are written by those who are not on the scene of the event. They simply describe the reports of those persons who either participate in an event or were eye-witnesses of the events. Generally, they are several times removed from the original first hand account of events and as such they are usually of limited worth.

An act passed by the Parliament is a primary data whereas its extracts published in newspapers are covered by the secondary data. The report of the University Education Commission is primary data but contents published in textbooks form the secondary data. Many history textbooks and encyclopaedias are examples of secondary sources.

Use of Source Method. It can be used at the following stages of the lesson:

Pre-lesson Use of Resources. Visits to actual sites of monuments, forts or museums may be arranged. The teacher can ask the students to read selected passages connected with the lesson before hand.

Mid-lesson Use of Resources. Extracts from original or secondary sources can be read during the course of the lesson. They create real situations, impart reality and vividness to the lesson and reinforce the impact of teaching.

Post-lesson Use of Resources. Pre-lesson use of resources can also become the post-lesson use of resources and vice-versa. Students may be given assignments which need the use of resources and vice-versa. Students may be given assignments which need the use of resources. They may be encouraged to pursue their interest in a particular topic, do some critical thinking and analysis and prepare their own account.

Merits of Sources Method. Following are the merits of sources method:

1. It develops a sense of reality and vividness.
2. It develops a sense of objectivity.
3. It provides a congenial and motivating environment.
4. It arouses curiosity among the students.
5. It develops elementary skills of collecting data, sifting the relevant and organising the same.
6. It provides opportunities for useful mental exercises—right thinking and imagining, comparing and analysing, drawing inferences etc.
7. It promotes interest in the study of the subject.
8. It initiates the students in social studies research.

9. It provides functional knowledge. Even the slow and backward children feel interested when they see original sources. Their learning becomes functional because it is gained in the real context.
10. It supplements class-room lesson.

Limitations of the Source Method. Limitations are given below:

1. It is very difficult for the school teachers to have an easy access to original sources.
2. Utilisation of original sources is a very difficult task for the school students as they lack the requisite training.
3. The method is very complex and technical.
4. There is the difficulty of languages. Almost all the original sources are in Sanskrit, Pali, Arabic or Persian and a few in English.
5. Contemporary authors and writers have given their own prejudices, preferences and limitations with the result that it becomes very difficult to sift fact from fiction. The students are, thus, lost in the maze of conflicting views about the same event or movement.
6. Source method of teaching social studies is very expensive.
7. Source method of teaching social studies is time consuming. How to make source method effective. The students should be encouraged to study the resource books in the library. Educational tours to places of importance may be arranged. The students may be asked to write their own impressions and inferences about the places they visit. Copies of important extracts from the relevant records may be pasted on the blackboard for the use of students.

Dr. Keatings thinks that original sources can be used for creating suitable environment in the lower form. Well planned, purposive and well directed efforts have to be made by the teacher in the use of this method. By suggesting the use of resource method in social studies, we do not aim at making our students research scholars. Use of the method in selected topics is likely to make the study of social studies more meaningful and real.

Teaching by Story Telling

Story Telling as an Art. Story telling is one of the most important methods of teaching social studies. It is an art which enables the teacher to come very close to the heart of the students and thereby he attracts their attention. Some teachers are born story tellers and they are very fortunate in this respect. This art of story telling aims at presenting to the pupils, through the medium of speech, clear, vivid, interesting, ordered sequences of events, in such a way that their minds reconstruct these happenings and they live in imagination through the experiences recounted either as spectators or possibly as participators. Story telling enables the teacher to make lessons lively and interesting to the pupils. Stories of great personalities, reformers, writers, saints, discoverers and scientists etc. must be told to the students. Story telling helps in enhancing the interests of the students in the subject. It goes a long way in firing the imagination of the students. Story telling can be relied upon by the teacher as the best companion for helping in developing in his pupils traits of character such as charity, piety, truthfulness and valour etc. The art of story telling can be cultivated by:

1. Observing skilful narrators.
2. Studying the work of successful story writers.
3. Practising story telling.
4. Critically evaluating one's own performance and bringing about necessary changes.

In telling a story the teacher should be guided by the following points:

1. Suitable stories for the age of the students should be selected. A story that appeals and interests the seven-year child will not suit the child for four years of age. Small children of 4 or 5 years are interested in stories of boys and girls. The child of 7 or 8 years takes interest in

hearing to stories of magic and wonder, stories of giants, adventure and romance.

2. The stories should be short and the plot easy.
3. The teachers must know the story well that he wants to narrate. If he stops in the middle, it will detract charm from the story.
4. Language employed in telling a story should be very simple and easy.
5. A story should be told and not read. The story loses a great deal of its interest for the children if it is read.
6. The teacher himself should like the story and take interest in story-telling.
7. There should be plenty of action in the stories. Key sentences and phrases should be repeated as the children enjoy this repetition. The stories should be loaded with activities and experiences familiar to the children. R. Strang has observed, "Stories for young children, therefore, should be told in terms of action and sense impressions. Upto the age of six years, a child is most alive to moving things—engines, boats, horses and wagons, animals, boys and girls in action. Children lose interest when the action is interrupted by a long descriptive passage. In telling a story one can notice the drop in interest during descriptive and explanatory portions, and the flare-up of interest again when the action is resumed. Since the young child's own activities and experiences are the ones most interesting to him, the first stories should be about experiences familiar to children."
8. Conversation, if any, in the story should be given in direct speech and not indirect.
9. The method of introducing and developing the story should be thought out before-hand.
10. The story should be told in a natural way and very vividly.
11. Humour makes the story more interesting and should not be neglected.

12. To make the story more realistic, the teacher may use pictures and draw diagrams on the blackboard.
13. The story should suggest and inspire the students to action.
14. Rybum suggests that well-known and familiar stories can be made fresh if they are told as though one of the characters in the story were telling it. He writes, "The story of Asoka and the Kalinga war could be told as if Asoka, himself, were telling it."
15. The story must have some aim besides mere enjoyment. The teacher must keep in mind the aim while narrating a story. It is all the more better if the students too know the aim.

Method of Supervised Study

Meaning of Supervised Study. Arthur C. Bining and David H. Bining describe the meaning of supervised study as, "By supervised study, we mean the supervision by the teacher of a group or class of pupils as they work at their desk or around their tables. In this procedure, we find pupils busy at work that has been assigned to them by the teacher. When they meet a difficulty that they cannot overcome, they ask the teacher for direction and assistance. The teacher, when not called upon, walks up quietly up and down the classroom or remains at his desk watching the pupils do their work continually alert for any wrong procedures that the pupils may follow. He is always ready to direct and aid them."

Individual Attention. Supervised study is an aid in helping to solve the problem of individual differences. Supervised study aids in preventing failures. The pupil works along his own mental level and at his own capacity. Assignments can be given to meet all levels of ability.

Better Pupil Teacher Relations. Another good feature of supervised study is seen in the better pupil teacher relations that it promotes. In the usual class teaching procedure, the teacher is frequently considered a hard task master and the procedure often produces a "class versus teacher" attitude. Under the supervised study programme, he appears in the role of a helper and guide. There is greater opportunity for the display of sympathy and understanding. The teacher is able to understand the pupil and his difficulties better and in a position to spurt him on to a greater effort.

Development of Skills. There are certain skills which can best be developed under this procedure. A thorough use of the supervised method would reveal weaknesses in the learner. Following skills can be developed easily.

(a) Skills as to how to read social studies material.

(b) Skills as to how to use encyclopedias.

(c) Skills as to how to use dictionaries.

(d) Skills as to how to use maps, atlases, indexes and almanacs.

(e) Skills as to how to read graphs.

Objections to Supervised Study. There are some objections such as:

1. Some investigations have concluded that the bright pupil is not helped under this method and in some cases in even hindered by the method.
2. Supervised study requires the lengthened school day and which is not possible due to various pressures of co-curricular activities.
3. Supervised study is a costly method. It would necessitate an increase in the teaching force that would mean an increased cost of education.
4. Supervised study depends too much on the initiative and enthusiasm of the students which they seldom display.
5. Supervised study destroys the supremacy of the teacher as he plays a secondary role in the teaching learning process.

Supervised Study and Socialised Recitation. Bining and Bining have explained the difference, "The socialised recitation has been used successfully with a supervised study procedure. In a class period of sixty minutes, however, it would be better to use a simplified form of socialised recitation. The first part of the period can be devoted to the socialised study. For example, the procedure could be as follows. During the socialised recitation, the direction of the class is under a pupil Chairman and a discussion leader. The Chairman first calls upon a pupil, previously chosen by the Chairman, teacher or class, for review of the work of the preceding day. Corrections and additions are then voluntarily made. The Chairman next calls for the topic or problem of the day, in order to be sure that subject is clearly in the minds of the members of the group. The discussion leader now takes charge. Each phase of the topic or problem is then discussed by the group, under the direction of the leader. After the discussion the teacher examines or comments on any points that have not been clearly brought out."

Dramatic Manner

Meaning: Dramatisation has been described as 'a synthetic art', involving the purposive coordination and control of the delicate organs of speech and muscles of the body combined with a sense of rhythm, with a view to free and intelligent expression of emotions and ideas.

Dramatic art affords innumerable opportunities for the correlation of a large number of subjects. In the preparation of their roles, the students indirectly and unconsciously improve their speech habits and language. A systematic study of historical events has to be made when pageants of the life of great persons are prepared i.e. pageant on the life of Buddha, Chandragupta, Vikramaditya, Gandhiji, etc. Children prepare costumes suiting different ages and thus come to know about the dresses of the people during different periods of history. Dramatics also add to the geographical knowledge of the students. Carpentry and other mechanical arts facilitate the work of construction of the stage. Dance and music add to the beauty of a drama.

Drama has its great social value. It is a cooperative enterprise and develops qualities of cooperation and social understanding. It helps in fostering *esprit de corps* among the students. In various school functions dramas form the chief items of the programme. For the honour of the school, every student works to the best of his capacity.

Dramatics afford the students many opportunities for training in team work. They are very helpful in providing the students with opportunities for the release of the inhibitions to which they are subjected by the conventions of society.

There are many activities in a drama and as such students of diverse aptitudes get chances to choose items for which they are best suited and satisfy their urges, e.g., self-expression through the various activities of a drama.

Conditions for Success. A number of rehearsals bring grace and success to the play when it is staged. Pupils should prepare as much stage material as they can.

Children should be encouraged to write their own plays. The usual participants in this activity should be given opportunities to play different roles. The same pupils as far as possible should, however, not be allowed to play the role of a villain.

Selection of Play

1. Plays chosen should depict the evils of the social customs.
2. A play should have a literary value also.
3. The students should be able to understand and appreciate the play.
4. It should also have entertainment value.
5. It should be free from objectional subject-matter.
6. There should be no vulgarity in the play.

By Way of Dictation

V.D. Ghate has observed, "There is too much dictating of notes in our schools and the history teacher seems to be by far the worst culprit." Dictating notes, by and large, has become a coaching and not a teaching device. It has, of course, a great significance in teaching of social studies. It is used due to the following reasons:

1. Lack of suitable history textbooks.
2. Pressure of work with the teacher and less time for preparing the lesson.
3. Short cut to finish the over-crowded subject-matter.
4. Short cut to pass the examination.
5. Lack of adequate power of expression of the teacher.

Methods of Dictating Notes

1. Detailed notes on important topics after discussing the topic in the class.
2. Notes in the question-answer form primarily from examination point of view—guess questions and their answers.
3. Explanatory notes and summaries on the blackboards.

Defects in the Method of Note Dictation

1. It does not provide training in the developing critical approach.
2. Note dictation makes history teaching synonymous with memorisation of facts communicated by the teacher.
3. Note dictation fails to develop proper insight into the subject.
4. Note dictation proves to be a great hindrance in developing the habit of consulting reference books and textbooks also.

Instead of dictating notes to the students, they should be encouraged to prepare their own notes.

Teaching Techniques

NCERT has laid great stress in adopting appropriate strategies in teaching-learning. The question of adopting appropriate strate-gies for providing learning experiences and organising teacher-pupil activities is crucial for effective use of curricular content and achievement of curricular objectives, While dealing with curri-culum organisation, the curriculum designer should teaching-learning strategies as an essential component of curricular cycle, and, while transacting the curriculum, the curriculum practitioner should be consistently conscious about careful selection of appropriate strategies. It would be imperative that, in spite of the mastery over the content on the part of the teacher, he/she should be appropriately oriented with regard to the importance and various types of instructional strategies and the principles that should govern their selection and administration.

A teacher, in relation to pupils, has to act essentially as a friend, philosopher and guide. His/her role should generally be to suggest and present rather than to command. He/she must show the pupil how to learn the subject and how to devise his/her own methods of learning and organising the knowledge which he/she gathers or discovers. The child-centred and activity-based approach should be the main strategy for curriculum transaction. This implies many things which a teacher should be consistently aware of. The curricular content, books, instructional materials, classroom and teachers should serve as means to the pupil's development and not as ends in themselves dominating over him/her. There should essentially be a warm, welcoming and encouraging approach that takes fully into consideration the needs and motives and the interests of the pupil. The involvement of the pupil in the learning process should go beyond the process of listening passively to that of thinking, reasoning, feeling and doing. In a nutshell, whole of the pupil's personality should be involved in the process of learning. Doing and discovering has been the natural and normal course through which the mankind has been able to gather, gradually, to this day, the vast fund of knowledge about, and control over, various facts and events. By following the same process as a teaching-learning strategy it would be possible to make learning more absorbing, meaningful, satisfying and stable.

While evolving an appropriate approach and method, -a teacher has to take into consideration certain basic tenets that guide the direction in which he/she should proceed, viz., from simple to complex, easy to difficult, known to unknown, concrete to abstract, particular to general, and whole to parts.

Motivation is basic to learning, and teacher should judiciously adopt appropriate strategies accordingly. Application of positive reinforcements like, praise, recognition and other rewards promote better learning than the negative incentives like punishment, rebuke and embarrassment. The positive approach to motivation has an important implication for evaluation system as an integral part of teaching-learning process: that success is in itself a strong source of motivation for further success, and, hence, repeated failure is most damaging to the learning process.

Teaching-learning strategies may assume a variety of modes and may involve a variety of activities on the part of learners and teachers, viz., observation, collection of materials and information, demonstration and experimentation project assignments, play-way activities/educational games, educational excursions, role playing and dramatisation, group discussions and group activities, explaining/describing conversations and discussions, inductive-deductive teaching, problem solving/discovery learning, creative writing, supplementary reading, story-telling, etc.

A number of factors on which the selection/choice of a particular strategy depends should be taken into consideration while adopting appropriate approach to teaching-learning: learner's capabilities, availability of resources, entry behaviour, type of organisational climate available, quality of teacher preparation, objectives to be achieved and nature of curricular content.

Use of physical, economic and socio-cultural environment, found around the school, for making learning more concrete and meaningful, should be regarded as one of the important approaches to teaching-learning. The teacher should identify the elements in the environment having a natural correlation with the curricular content. For example, the kind of vegetation and soils and natural resources found in the environment around the school could help in making many lessons in general sciences more lively and relevant. The religious and cultural celebrations observed by the community may be of help in adding meaning and reality to many content points in social studies and languages. Similarly, visits to various local industries and artisans, social institutions, government and administrative bodies, farming houses, poultries, etc. could be of great help in providing concrete learning experien-ces to children in the context of various subject areas.

Receiving regular feedback for the improvement of both teaching and learning should form an in-built component of teaching-learning strategy. A system of continuous evaluation plays an important role in providing regular feedback indicating strengths and weaknesses of the process. A vigilant teacher should always be on a look-out for behaviour indicators through various interactions with pupils inside and outside the classroom that would provide feedback to him/her.

Paying individual attention to each learner, and allowing him/her to proceed at a pace suiting to his/her abilities and aptitudes, is one of the fundamentals of pedagogical approach. Pupils with special talents or aptitudes should be provide with opportunities to proceed at a faster pace and good quality education should be provided to them. Similarly, there should be provision for remedial instruction for those who are slow learners.

Need for adopting appropriate strategies directed at the development of non-scholastic dimensions of child's personality has generally not been fully appreciated and efforts on that count are seriously lacking. The so-called co-curricular activities should rather be treated as an integral part of school curriculum and should receive as careful attention of the curriculum practitioner as the scholastic activities. A long list of such activities could be prepared under various categories, viz., school assembly programmes, cultural and recreational activities, school beautification activities, activities in community living, creative activities, auxiliary activities celebrations of special days/weeks, and celebration of days of national importance. Even bookish content in various areas provides enough scope for carefully gearing it, through scholastic activities, to the non-cognitive development of the learner.

QUESTIONS

1. Discuss the need for dynamic methods of teaching Social Studies.
2. Explain the use of group discussion in the teaching of Social Studies. What measures would you adopt to make it effective?
3. What place would you give to the following in the teaching of Social Studies?

   (i) Source Method (ii) Note Dictation (iii) Lecturing (iv) Story Telling (v) Assignment Method (vi) Socialised Recitation (vii) Laboratory Method.
4. Elucidate the role of instructional strategies in the teaching of Social Studies.
5. How will you adopt the approach 'Learning by Doing' in Social Studies?

6

Problem Method

Problem solving may be defined as a planned attack upon a difficulty or perplexity for the purpose of finding a solution. It is a method in which a person uses his ability to solve problems which confront him. It enables a person to exercise control over his activities and environment. It is an instructional device whereby the teacher and the pupils attempt in a conscious, planned, purposeful effort to arrive at explanation or solution to some educationally significant difficulty. Yoakam and Simpson define it as "a problem occurs in a situation in which a felt difficulty that is clearly present and recognised by the thinker. It may be a purely mental difficulty or it may be physical and involve the manipulation of data. The distinguishing thing about a problem, however, is that an individual who meets it as needing a solution. He recognises it as a challenge." It is a method in which some difficulty to act in an educational setting is felt and an attempt is made in a conscious, planned and purposeful way to find its solution.

Dewey observes, "Whenever-no-matter how slight and common place in character-perplexes and challenges the mind so that it makes belief at all uncertain there is a genuine problem." He further explains problem solving in these words, "The problem fixes the end of thought and the end controls the process of thinking."

Gates has defined the problem thus, "A problem exists for an individual when he has a definite goal he cannot reach by the behaviour pattern which he already has available."

Problem solving is not merely a method of teaching. It is, in fact a method of organisation of a subject matter. It is an approach to deal with subject matter. The researches of Quitten and Hanna reveal that as compared to the chronological and topical treatment, problem approach in social sciences is much more useful.

Why Problem-solving? Life is full of problems and the successful man in life is he, who is fully equipped with adequate knowledge and reasoning power to tackle these problems successfully. There are problems and puzzling situations which are a normal feature of a child's everyday life. These problems grow in complexity as he grows older and older. The solution of these problems enables him to have a mastery of the environment. Therefore, if the function of education is to enable the child to prepare him for life, problem solving must be encouraged in school life.

Children are curious by nature. They want to find out answers of many questions which sometimes are puzzling even to the adults; nevertheless they must be helped to satisfy their curiosity, whenever possible, by solving various problems. We must teach the pupils, how to think so that they are able to transfer these techniques to a vast number of varied problem situations.

Examples of Wide Range of Problems. We may note the following:

(a) For younger children. To build a house of toy bricks, to make a toy stage. These are practical problems and can be solved by trial and error methods.

(b) For children of ten to twelve years of age. To find out whether a given plant or a variety of cultivated vegetables will flourish under given conditions of soil, water, etc., to reason out what results are likely to accrue under certain conditions in History, Geography, Civics, Science, etc.

(c) For older children. To decide whether India could grow its own food essentials; to reason out why did Akbar succeed and Aurangzeb failed? Why is sky blue? Why is coal black and paper white?

Steps in Problem-solving. The steps of problem solving are as given below.

(1) Formation and appreciation of the problem. The nature of the problem should be made very clear to the students. They must also feel the necessity of finding out a solution for the problem.

(2) Collection of relevant data and information. The students should be stimulated to collect data in a systematic manner. Full cooperation of the students should be secured. They may be invited to make suggestions as to how they could collect the relevant data. The teacher may suggest many points to them. He may ask them to read extra books. He may also ask them to organise a few educational trips to gather the relevant information.

(3) Organisation of data. The students should be asked to sift the relevant material from the superficial one and put it in a scientific way.

(4) Drawing of conclusions. Discussions should be arranged collectively and individually with each pupil. Panton suggests that the teacher's aim should be to secure that, as far as possible, the essential thinking is done by the pupils themselves and that their educative process produces the particular solution, formulation of generalizations at stake. "Care should be taken that judgement is made only when sufficient data is collected."

(5) Testing conclusions. No conclusion should be accepted without being properly verified. The correctness of the conclusion must be proved. The students must be taught

to be critical, to examine the "truths" which they "discover" to see "whether they fit all the known data." We should have our minds free from every bias in the process of problem-solving.

Role of the Teacher

Valentine Davis quotes Prof. Pasher who suggests the following points in problem-solving:

1. Get them (the students) to define the problem clearly.
2. Aid them to keep the problem in mind.
3. Get them to make many suggestions by encouraging them: (a) to analyse the situation in parts, (b) to recall previously known similar cases and general rules that apply, (c) to guess courageously and formulate guesses clearly.
4. Get them time to evaluate each suggestion carefully by encouraging them: (a) to maintain a slate of doubt or suspended conclusion, (b) to criticise the suggestion by appeal to know facts, minister experiments, and scientific treatises.
5. Get them to organise the material by proceeding: (a) to build an outline on the board, (b) to use diagrams and graphs, (c) to formulate concise statement of the net outcome of the discussion.

It has been stated that for the success of the problem-solving teaching technique we need "a teacher who has the ability to see problems clearly, the power of analyse with a keen discernment and the faculty to synthesize and draw conclusions with an uncanny accuracy."

Procedures in Problem-solving. There are two procedures in problem-solving and they are (i) the Inductive, and (ii) the Deductive.

Essential Features of a Problem. Following are the essential features of the problem:

1. The problem should be meaningful, interesting and worthwhile for children.
2. It should have some correlation with life.
3. It should have some correlation with other subjects.
4. It should arise out of the real needs of the students.
5. The children must possess some background of the problem which they are going to discuss.
6. The problem should be clearly defined.
7. The solution of the problem should be found out by the students themselves working under the guidance and supervision of the teacher.
8. The problem must have some educational value.

Merits of Problem-solving. Following are the merits of problem-solving:

1. It helps in stimulating thinking.
2. It develops reasoning power.
3. It helps to improve knowledge.
4. It helps in developing good study habits.
5. It affords opportunities for participation in social activities. Problems are solved with the joint efforts of many students. The students learn to appreciate the different points of view and thus become tolerant.
6. The students learn to be self-dependent.
7. Discussions help to develop the power of expression of the students.
8. The method provides opportunities to the teachers to know in detail their pupils. They learn which students are shy in nature and which are very active and accordingly they assist the students.
9. Students learn facts which are meaningful and which have been discovered by their own efforts.

10. It helps in the maintenance of discipline. The students remain busy in finding out the answers to their own problem.
11. Knowledge is easily assimilated as it is the result of a purposeful activity.
12. Learning becomes more interesting in place of a dread.
13. It gives the power of critical judgement.
14. It helps to verify an opinion.
15. It satisfies curiosity.
16. It helps to learn how to act in a new situation.

Demerits of Problem-solving. The demerits are given below:

1. Generally speaking problem-solving involves mental activity only. There is less of bodily activity.

The logical method of presentation gives life to two distinct types of lessons of the informative type when the knowledge is acquired.

2. Small children do not possess sufficient background information and therefore they fail to participate in discussions.
3. There is a lack of suitable reference and source books for children.
4. It involves a lot of time and the teachers find it difficult to cover the prescribed syllabus.

Deductive and Inductive Method

Broadly speaking, there are two general approaches or procedures in problem-solving – the Inductive and the Deductive. The whole method of teaching and learning is based on induction and deduction.

Inductive Method

The inductive method is a method of development. In the inductive method, the child is led to discover truth for himself.

The various processes in the inductive method are: (i) observation of the given material: (ii) Discrimination and analysis noting differences and similarities, (iii) Classification, (iv) Abstraction and generalization, and (v) Application or verification.

In the inductive method, the pupils are led from particular instances to general conclusion. Concrete examples are given and with their help students are helped to arrive at certain conclusions or principles. In the teaching of science including geography, mathematics and languages, this method is very helpful. The students by examining a number of examples in science, conclude that heat expands and cold contracts.

In a geometry lesson the students by measuring the angles of a triangle come to the conclusion that their sum is equal to two right angles.

In a geography lesson the students by examining the heights of the places located at high places conclude that temperature decreases as height increases. The students may examine the heights and temperatures of places like Simla, Nainital, Dalhousie, Darjeeling, etc.

In a lesson in economics the students by examining a number of cases, may conclude that agriculturists in India are in debt. The process runs like this. Ram is in debt. Sham is in debt Krishna is in debt and so on. Ram is an agriculturist. Sham is an agriculturist. Krishna is an agriculturist and so on. From this, it will be concluded that all these persons are agriculturists and are in debt. In a language lesson, the teacher while teaching proposition may give examples, like 'Ram is in the room.' 'The cat is undy the table'. 'The book is on the table' and may lead the students to find out the definition of 'preposition'. We find that a crow is black; we find another crow also black; still another crow black and so on and say that all crows are black. This method is more useful in lessons where rules, definitions, generalisations, laws and casual connections between facts are to be established.

The Merits. Following are the merits of the Inductive Method:

1. Knowledge is self-acquired and is soon transformed into 'wisdom.' 'General truths in order to be learned must

be earned' is a famous saying and the inductive method is true to it.

2. It promotes mental activity on the part of the pupils and makes them active participants in the learning teaching process.
3. It makes the lesson interesting by providing challenging situations to the students.
4. The method affords opportunities to the students to be self-dependent and develops self-confidence.
5. The student's curiosity is well-kept up till the end when generalisations are arrived at.
6. This method is very natural because the knowledge in possession of man has been acquired in this way from the practical side of experience.
7. The child learns how to tackle problems. He not only acquires more facts but also learns the way of acquiring facts which proves him useful for practical life.
8. The method is based on sound psychological principles. Learning by doing is the basis of this method.

The Demerits. Following are the demerits of Inductive Method:

1. There is every possibility that the students may draw conclusions very hastily and these may be based on insufficient data and, therefore, may be wrong.
2. The method is very slow and lengthy.
3. It is not very helpful in the case of small children.
4. It is not suitable in the teaching of subjects in which there is more stress on the teaching of facts. It is not possible for us to experience facts in history and in so many other subjects.
5. The inductive method is not a complete method in itself. It has been said, "Induction does not prove but only provides the material to prove, it only discovers." When

we have discovered a principle, we have to apply it again on some concrete instances for its verification. Therefore, we need deductive method to ensure the value of inductive process.

Deductive Method

This method is the other way round. In the deductive method rules, generalisations and principles are provided to the students and then they are asked to verify them with the help of particular examples. The students are told that places situated at this altitudes are cold and then particular examples are taken to prove it. Such examples can be multiplied.

Merits of the Deductive Method. The merits of the Deductive Method are as below:

1. The teacher's work is simplified. He gives general principles and the students verify them.
2. This method is very economical. It saves time and energy both of the students and the teachers. Many principles for the discovery of which mankind has taken a lot of pains can be told to the students easily.
3. It is very suitable for small children who cannot discover truths for themselves. They get ready-made material.

Demerits and Limitations of the Deductive Method. These are as follows:

1. Knowledge is not self-acquired and, therefore, not assimilated properly.
2. The child is deprived of the pleasure of self-activity and self-effort as ready-made formulae, principles and rules are given to him.
3. It encourages memorisation of facts which are soon forgotten and, therefore, knowledge is rendered useless.
4. This method is unnatural and unpsychological for the students who do not possess ability to appreciate abstract ideas in the absence of concrete examples.

5. It fails to develop motivation and interest in the learning as the truths are not of much value to the students.
6. It fails to develop self-confidence and initiative in the students.

Combination of Deductive and Inductive Method. According to I.E. Miller, induction is the making of the tools of thought and deduction is the using of tools. Both supplement each other and are not opposite things. Both are wanted for the discovery of truth as both legs are wanted for walking.

The only method for the teacher is the method by which minds add to its knowledge.

Induction should be followed by deduction and deduction by induction. Our approach should be inductive-cum-deductive.

Many a Problem

1. What does a citizenship mean?
2. What does the government do to protect our life and property?
3. How can we attain a well-rounded life?
4. What does the community do in helping character formation?
5. What is meant by public opinion?
6. How are our governments financed?
7. In what ways has man conquered time and space?
8. How are human needs satisfied?
9. How is man today extremely dependent upon his fellow-men for his existence?
10. How do we pay for goods and services?
11. How are products and goods distributed?
12. What are the various means of making a living?
13. What was the impact of Industrial Revolution in England?

Deductive and Inductive Method Compared

Deductive	*Inductive*
1. General laws are first stated and particular cases are taken as examples to prove them.	1. First particular cases are dealt with and then laws are derived from them.
2. It does not lead to new knowledge.	2. It leads to new knowledge.
3. It is a methodof verification and explanation and, therefore, it is a method	3. It is a method of discovery and, therefore, it is a method of education.
4. This method is very quick. The child gets readymade knowledge and he makes use of knowledge acquired by	4. This method is very slow. The child acquires first-hand information by actual observation of alot of material.
5. This method encourages dependence upon others as it is based on borrowing from others.	5. This method gives training to the child to depend upon himself and develops self-confidence and initiative.
6. It is a downward movement of thought and leads to a more perfect comprehension of	6. It is an upward movement of thought and leads to rules, definitions or principles.

14. How did America gain independence?
15. What are the effects of French Revolution?
16. What were the outcomes of the Russian Revolution?
17. What is the contribution of UNO to world peace?

QUESTIONS

1. What is a problem method? How would you make use of it in the teaching of Social Studies?
2. Explain the merits and demerits of deductive and inductive approach in the teaching of Social Studies.
3. Select any problem and prepare a lesson plan accordingly.
4. Elucidate the role of the teacher in problem solving method. Is it possible to use it in the teaching of every topic? State reasons.

7

Project Method

Project method is the outcome of the pragmatic educational philosophy of Dewey, the well-known American philosopher-cum-educationist. It was developed and perfected by Dr. William Head Kilpatric of the University of Columbia. It is a revolt against the traditional environment of the school which is usually marked by listlessness and passivity and which lacks keenness and real life. Much of the subject-matter taught and many habits formed in school do not conform to desirable social life in the outside world. The project method is the expression of the widespread dissatisfaction against the bookish, encyclopaedic passive method, whereby children as obedient masses are carefully drilled and spoon-fed with fact and information. The modern educators speak in no uncertain terms about disconnected facts, disconnected subjects, water-tight compartments and pigeon-hole time tables. "Ignore these." they say, "Give the class a real life project to bite at and watch the result."

The Meaning

Project Method has been defined by various educationists as:

Ballard. A project is a bit of real life that has been imported into the school.

Burton. The problem is a project which results in doing. The motor element is not what makes the activity a project, but the problem-solving of a practical nature accompanying the activity.

J.A. Stevenson. A project is a problematic act carried to completion in its natural setting.

Snedden. Project is a unit of educative work in which the most prominent feature is some form of positive and concrete achievement.

W.W. Charters. In the topical organisation principles are learned first while in the projects the problems are proposed which demand in the solution the development of principles by the learner as needed.

The following points have been stressed in the above-mentioned definitions of the project:

1. A Project is a Problematic Act.
2. A Project is a Purposeful Activity.
3. A Project is a Whole-hearted Activity.
4. A Project is an Activity in a Natural Setting.
5. A Project is an Activity in a Social Setting.
6. A Project is a Bit of Real Life introduced in School.
7. A project is a Problem-solving of a Practical Nature.
8. A Project is a Positive and Concrete Achievement.
9. A Project is an Activity through which Solution of various problems are found out.

Basic Rules

The Principle of Purpose. Knowledge of purpose is a great stimulus which motivates the child to realize his goal. The child must have an ideal. 'Why is he doing certain things?' Purpose motivates learning. Interest cannot be aroused by aimless and meaningless activities.

The Principle of Activity. Children are active by nature. They love activity. The instincts of curiosity, construction, pugnacity and herd make them active by nature. Therefore, such opportunities should be provided to them that make them active and learn things by doing. Physical as well as mental activities are to be provided to them. They are to be allowed to 'do' and to 'live through doing'.

The Principle of Experience. Experience is the best teacher. What is real must be experienced. The children learn new facts and information through experience.

The Principle of Social Experience. The child is a social being and we have to prepare him for social life. Training for a corporate life must be given to him in his childhood. In the project method, the child works in groups.

The Principle of Reality. Life is real and education to be meaningful must be real. The child who is to live in a life of reality must be trained as such through his education. The project method is a method of educating the child and, therefore, it must also be real. Real life situations should be presented in the life of the school.

The Principle of Freedom. The desire for an activity must be spontaneous and not forced by the teacher. The child should be free from imposition, restrictions or obstructions so that he may express himself fully and freely. He must be given the freedom to choose an activity, to do an activity according to his interests, needs and capacities.

The Principle of Utility. Knowledge will be worthwhile only when it is useful and practical. The traditional system of instruction simply stressed formal and vital information for its own sake and was of little utility. The project method develops various attitudes and values which are of great significance from the practical point of view.

Different Types of Projects. W.H. Kilpatrick mentions four types of projects:

1. 'The Producer Type', in which the emphasis is directed towards the actual construction of a material object or article.

2. 'The Consumer Type'. Where the objective is to obtain either direct or vicarious experience, such as reading

and learning to stories, listening to a musical delectation etc.

3. 'The Problem Type,' in which the chief purpose is to solve a problem involving the intellectual processes, such as determining the density of a certain liquid.
4. 'The Drill Type,' where the objective is to attain a certain degree of skill in a reaction—as learning a vocabulary.

Various Steps in a Project. These steps are given below:

Providing a Situation. It is not right to force a project on the unwilling students. The students themselves should define, state and choose their problems. Of course, the teacher's function would be to provide real and worthwhile situations. He would discover the tastes, temperaments and needs of the students and would provide situations wherein the students feel a spontaneous urge to carry out projects according to their felt needs. Stevenson taught the uses of the electric bell to his high school students by the Project Method. The necessity of completely overhauling the bell system in the school building arose and this occasion was utilised in providing a situation.

Choosing and Purposing. Purposing is very important. It is the centre round which a project moves. The project selected must be such as to satisfy a definite need or purpose. This purpose, as far as possible, must be acceptable to all the students of a class. Dr. Kilpatrick remarks, "The part of the pupil and the part of the teacher in most of the school work depend largely on who does the purposing. It is practically the whole thing." The students themselves should choose the project. The teacher should not be in a hurry to choose the project. Better results and better satisfaction can be had only through self-choice. Many situations should be provided to children. These situations should be discussed and the teacher should give useful suggestions. Decision should always be democratic. The teacher should merely guide and not thrust his opinion. The children must feel that the project is of their own choice.

Planning. When the decision of a project has been arrived at, the next problem is of planning. The teacher should draw the attention of the students to the need of planning before undertaking any activity. The task of planning is quite difficult. Good planning leads to better results. Each child should be encouraged to give his suggestions. The teacher should point out to the students to take into consideration their resources. Different proposals should be discussed and alternatives considered. The best plan is agreed upon after a good deal of discussion, suggestions and counter suggestions, rejections, and then students should be asked to write down the plan in their project book.

It must be stressed that the teacher must be ready with some proposals regarding the plan beforehand so that it may be possible for him to help the students in the best possible manner.

Executing the Plan. This step is the longest of all and requires a lot of work. The whole project is to be executed through the co-operative efforts of all students. The various activities of the project should be divided according to the individual interests and abilities of the different children in the class.

The teacher should give sufficient guidance to the students. He should not dictate them.

This is the state at which the students perform many activities and learn various useful experiences. The children keep themselves busy in collecting information, reading and writing in various languages, keeping accounts, calculating prices, looking up maps, collecting specimens of different things, measuring length and area, visiting markets, museums and zoos, visiting fields and crops, seeking help from others and the like.

Judging. The work is to be reviewed when it is completed. Lessons must be learnt from the mistakes that have been made in the various steps of a project. The students must learn to criticise constructively their own work. Self-criticism is valuable form of training. The students should find out what things they have learnt from the project.

Recording. A complete record of all activities connected with the project must be maintained. The project book should be well maintained. All the details in the various steps should be noted down. The project book should give a comprehensive picture of the project as a whole. It should give the procedure of providing a situation and of choosing the project, duties assigned, difficulties felt and experience gained etc.

Essentials of Good Project. These factors are given below:

Timely. Project should be related directly to the lesson and vocational interest. Projects should suit the particular mental and chronological ages of the students.

Environmental and seasonal factors should also be taken into consideration. It is a well-known fact that are there definite relationships between the seasons of the year and current community interests and those of pupils. Projects should be timely.

Usefulness. Practical aim of the project should not be lost sight of. It must fulfil a long-standing need. The learning experiences in a project must be capable of being applied in life.

Interesting. Projects should be interesting to students. They must make an appeal to the emotional hungers or drives of the students.

Challenging. Projects should neither be too simple and easy nor too long and difficult They should be challenging. It is an admitted fact that the youth wants to do tasks which are challenging in nature.

Economical. The projects should be economical. They should not unnecessarily tax the energy and pocket of the students. There should be the least wastage of time also.

Rich in Experiences. Many experiences of the sociable nature should be provided in a project. The project selected should be capable of correlating different subjects and practical activities of life.

Co-operativeness. The students should be allowed to think and plan independently as well as cooperatively. The projects should be executed in such a way as the students are kept active both physically as well as mentally.

Merit of the Project Method. These merits are given below:

Based on the Laws of Learning. It is in accordance with the psychological laws of learning. It is based upon:

The Law of Readiness. According to this law, we learn most when our minds are ready to receive. The project method prepares the mind of the students by providing them with suitable situation.

The Law of question. Learning to be effective must be practised. The project method affords many opportunities to the students to learn by doing.

The Law of Effect. This law states that if learning is to be effective and fruitful, it must be accompanied by satisfaction and happiness. The students derive immense pleasure when they manipulate their own activities.

Related with Life. Learning becomes practical and intimately related with life when meaningful and purposeful activities are provided to the students. The children get opportunities to acquaint themselves with the real problems of life. The students learn the practical usefulness of different subjects of the curriculum.

Correlates all the Subjects. The project method gives unity to the curriculum. The water-tight treatment of the various subjects which is commonly found in our schools gives way to an integrated programme. Subjects do not remain isolated. Learning comes as a by product of purposeful activity.

Trains for a Democratic Way of Life. The method provides sufficient opportunities to the students to work co-operatively for a common purpose. Decisions are arrived at democratically. The students have a say in the activities they choose, plan and execute.

Gives Training in Citizenship. This method imparts training to the students to inculcate in them primary virtues like tolerance, independence, open-mindedness, resourcefulness, etc.

Upholds the Dignity of Labour. Dignity of labour is engendered through the project method. The students have to perform their activities with their own hands and thus they develop a taste for all kinds of work. They learn that there is nobleness in working and doing things with their own hands.

Stresses Problem-solving. It discourages cramming and memory work. It stresses problem-solving. It develops the thinking and reasoning powers of the students.

Provides a Source of Happiness for the Backward. The project method provides a great relief to the backward children by providing them opportunities of participation in practical situation. Such children as are incapable of thinking abstract things keep themselves busy in concrete and practical situations.

Provides Freedom. The students work with great enthusiasm for the completion of their self-chosen project They do not feel tired as there is a good deal of variety in their work and atomosphere is full of freedom.

Solves the Problem of Indiscipline. As the children remain busy with their self-chosen work they do not get opportunities to think of anti-social ways. Demerits, limitations and difficulties. These are given below:

Neglecting Intellectual Work. There is a widespread misconception that the project method glorifies hand work at the cost of intellectual work. The critics argue that the children are kept busy in model-making and the like.

Haphazard and Unconnected Teaching. Projects many a time do not keep the examination and curriculum in view.

It is not possible to deal with all the subjects in a single project. There are many topics which cannot be taught through this method.

This difficulty can be met with by setting aside some periods in which the gaps may be covered up.

Upsetting of the Time-table. In a project method it is not possible to follow a rigid time-table. It upsets the routine work of the school.

Neglect of Drill Work. This method neglects practice and the development of skill in various subjects. The students do not get adequate drill in arithmetic, reading, spelling, drawing etc.

Difficulty in Getting Suitable Text-books. Preparation of books suitable for the project method is by no means an easy task. Moreover, material required for the implementation of a project is very costly. The method is not suitable for ordinary schools.

Artificial Correlation. Sometimes teachers show over-enthusiasm in stretching the projects upon which the class is working beyond its natural limits and try to connect those topics which have remote connections with the project in hand.

Unsuitable for the Shirkers and Shy. Some students/who are not inclined to take responsibility may remain in the background and do very little work.

Too Much Reliance on Young Children. It is not wise to depend too much on the choice of the children.

Lack of Competent Teachers. For the successful working of this method, very learned, efficient and resourceful teachers are needed. The method imposes heavy burden and responsibility upon the teachers.

Unsuitable for Transfers. A child reading in an ordinary school finds it very difficult to adapt himself to a school that follows project method and vice versa.

Conclusion. A review of the above brings us to the conclusion that most of the limitations are unreal and without much significance. Whenever a new method is suggested, criticisms are unnecessarily levelled.

Traditional methods have been tried and found unsuitable to the changing needs of the time. New methods must be tried and if found suitable should be accepted even if they are a bit expensive.

Teaching in Classroom

The project to be successful must be based on a definite procedure. The first and the main responsibility of the teacher is to provide those situations to the students wherein they should feel a spontaneous urge to solve some of their practical problems. The teacher must be on the lockout of discovering their interests, tastes, aptitudes and needs. There are different methods of providing situations. As far as possible, problems or situations which are provided to the students should be social ones. These provide better social training and give more satisfaction.

The teacher may converse with the class on different topics of interest to them. Pictures of different scenes may be shown to them. Surveys of the surrounding conditions may be undertaken.

The projects for study and work may arise out of the festivals like Diwali or Dussehra. The teacher is to tap all resources to provide worthwhile situations.

Most of the educators are of the view that the projects should be selected by the students themselves. They think that this will stimulate pupil purposing and that they will be more interested in their work if they have a share in determining what they are to make.

Others who think that the teachers should select the projects argue that this method will ensure that the students undertake only those projects which are within their reach. Students are immature and they require adequate guidance to select their projects.

However, the safer course would be to arrive at a compromise. According to this, the 'planning' and 'doing' should be under the guidance of the teachers. There should be no hard and fast rules in the selection of the project.

The relation of the teacher with his students is closer in the Project Method than in the ordinary class teaching. The teacher is like a friend, an elder brother who works together with the students and helps them to gain rich experiences. He must stimulate the shy students to put in their best. He must help the students to help themselves. He must see that the project is carried on in a democratic way. He must read intensively as well as extensively. He should have adequate patience, skill, knowledge, tect and sincerity.

History. History of the village, if any, relics and monuments, dwellings of primitive man—caves, huts etc., houses through different ages and at different places.

Geography. Source of water supply, climate, crops, fruits, vegetables and other products.

Economics. Occupation of the people, agricultural yield per acre, village handicrafts, rural indebtedness, co-operative societies.

Civics. Working of the Village Panchayat, co-operative store, educational facilities.

General Science. Health and sanitation of the village, water facilities, causes of diseases, village dispensary, ventilation etc.

Arithmetic. Estimate of the cost of the village draninage system, calculation of the per capita income of the villager, measurement of land holding, calculation of different items in the family budgets, total area of the village land, are a sown and cultivated, calculating agricultural produce per acre.

Language. Description of the various details of the survey.

Art Work. Preparation of charts depicting conditions of an ideal village.

Project: the Pageant on the Life of Buddha

History. The social, religious and political conditions of India at that time, sources of information regarding the life of Buddha.

Geography. Different places connected with the life of Buddha, preparation of maps showing these places.

Language. Study of books which throw light on the life of Buddha, writing of the various details of project.

Religion. Evils of untouchability, love for all, truth and non-violence, teachings of Buddha.

Civics. Co-operative spirit to make the project a success.

Drawing. Preparation of stage, making lighting arrangement.

Art. Beautification work in the project.

QUESTIONS

1. What is a project method? How would you make use of it to make your teaching effective?
2. Select any Project and prepare a lesson plan accordingly.
3. State the role of the teacher in the project method.
4. What are the limitations of the project method? How can it be used effectively in our schools?

8

Teaching Programme

The essential idea of programmed learning is that the most efficient, pleasant and permanent learning takes place when the student proceeds through a course by a large number of small, easy-to-take steps.

The History

It may be noted that the origins of programmed learning are not essentially new. Socrates may be regarded as one of the earliest programmers who developed a programme in Geometry. This was recorded by Plato in the dialogue, MENO. Socrates used to guide his followers to knowledge by conducting them conversationally along a path from fact to fact and insight to insight.

Some educators hold the 'Gita' as the first programmed text in the world. They maintain that it has all the ingredients of programming; initial behaviour, small steps, active participation, terminal behaviour, immediate knowledge and self-evaluation by the learner.

New Trends

The method of programmed learning or programmed instruction as it is often called today emerged from the efforts of American psychologists during the second decade of the 20th century. E.L. Thomdike (1874-1949) was the first psychologist whose findings bear direct relevance to programming. Programmed learning is related with the 'Law of Effect' as explained by Thomdike. Sidney L. Pressey, a psychologist of Ohio State University, is credited for developing in the middle 1920's practical machines which could teach as well as test. The teaching machines as developed by Pressey present a series of question to a student and inform him immediately whether his response is right or wrong.

In 1943, Skinner and his two other colleagues started programming by teaching a pigeon to roll a small bowling ball by operant conditioning. By 1954, Skinner and James G. Holland devised the auto-instructional methods which have served the present generation as the basis for present work in programmed instruction. In Skinnerian programmed instruction whether mechanised or otherwise the learner is initially asked questions which he can easily answer correctly without any previous study of the particular lesson. The learner is taught by the sequence of question. He is asked more and more as the lesson proceeds in very small steps.

In 1955, Norman A. Crowder developed what he calls "automatic tutoring by intrinsic programming" as against "extrinsic programming" developed by Skinner.

Robert Mager (1958) gave a new concept known as "Learner Controlled Instruction" which is a kind of Socratic dialogue in reverse, in which the learner led the instructor. The instructor remained silent until the learner himself stimulated the instructor with questions that suggested the needed illustrations, demonstrations, practice or some other help.

Stoluron at Illinois has been developing a process which should provide for greater individualization by measuring needs and developing programmes that require a computer to assist instruction.

In 1962, T.F. Gilbert gave formalized expression of his technology of education called Mathetics. Pennington and Slack expressed in 1962 further detailed methods of preparing lessons from mathetic principles.

Rothkopf in 1965 suggested a term "mathemagenics". Mathemagenic behaviour involves three characteristic activities: (1) The transformation of a nominal stimulus into an effective stimulus (which is to take place within the organism); (2) Some form of elaboration (which, for instance, may take the form of echoic responses); and (3) Process exemplified by problem solving and inductive reasoning. These activities must take place before any learning can occur. Rothkopf points out that as the learner reads a text, he experiments with and internalizes various kinds of mathemagenic behaviours. The test questions that learner encounters sort out and extinguish those behaviours which were not effective.

Significant Elements

1. Programmed instruction is a process of constructing sequences of instructional material in a way that the rate and depth of learning are maximised, understanding is fostered and the motivation of the student is enhanced.
2. Assumptions about the learner are clearly stated and put in definite terms in a programmed learning type of situation. These assumptions may relate to the particular level of reading competence of the learner, his command of vocabulary and his background in the subject-matter.
3. The objectives underlying the programme are defined in explicit and operational terms. This makes the terminal behaviour desired to be built up through the programme measurable and observable.
4. The subject-matter of the programme is presented by breaking into small steps in a logical sequence. The small steps stress the gradual nature of the increase in complexity and the smoothness of the transition from one item to the next. Information grows in depth. Changes occur in quality and quantity.
5. Programmed learner emphasises the interaction between learner and the programme.

6. The learner is made to respond actively by asking to fill in the blank, count the number of coins in a row or complete a series of numbers. For doing it correctly the student receives enforcement and establishes a pattern of stimulus-response interaction.
7. A programmed instructional sequence takes into consideration the initial behaviour of the learner with which it starts and the terminal subject-matter competence which the learner is to achieve.
8. A programmed test provides for immediate feedback information. This is based on the theory of reinforcement which emphasises that the learner learns from the sequence of responding and not from the making of response itself.
9. In a programmed learning situation, the learner progresses at his own pace.
10. Programmed instruction takes care of the fact that there are even differences in the rate at which an individual learner learns various kinds of subject-matter.
11. Programmed learning enhances the capacity of the learner to discriminate or to generalise by frequent application and thus offers the learner an interesting and challenging prospect.
12. Programmed learning provides for constant evaluation through the record of learner's responses. The quality of the programme can be improved through checking the number of errors at each step and the learner's progress can be a evaluated by looking into various types of responses produced by the learner.
13. Programmed learning is based strictly on the behaviouristic principles of psychology. A fair amount of stress is given to the explanation and development of understanding through the handling of various cues in the learning process.
14. In programme learning a learner moves in a very specific way as opposed to traditional procedures of teaching where the learner moves in a very general way.

Programmed Instruction and Traditional Method

Programmed Instruction	*Traditional Method*
1. It is based on the teaching principles that have been known for years.	1. It becomes difficultto apply teaching principles in crowded classrooms.
2. It is a group technique.	2. It is a group technique.
3. It presents the matter as a whole.	3. It presents the matter as a whole.
4. The learner does not get immediate feedback.	4. The learner does not get immediate feedback.
5. Objectives are not well-defined and are usually vague.	5. Objectives are not well-defined and are usually vague.
6. Little preparation is made.	6. Little preparation is made.
7. The student usually remains a passive listener and the teacher himself does the summarising and reviewing.	7. The student usually remains a passive listener and the teacher himself does the summarising and reviewing.
8. The unit is a lengthy one. There is no provision for response from the students in the form of answers to questions.	8. The unit is a lengthy one. There is no provision for response from the students in the form of answers to questions.
9. It is usually found to be very difficult to modify traditional instruction on the basis of student reaction.	9. It is usually found to be very difficult to modify traditional instruction on the basis of student reaction.

The Advantages

It has been universally envisaged that programmed instruction as a method of teaching-learning has many advantages and it has potentialities to revolutionise the theory and practice of teaching. Programmed instruction is considered to be a more efficient method of teaching-learning for the accomplishment of the objectives of education. Its superiority has been established in comparison with the traditional methods of teaching in the advanced countries of the world. Following are the major advantages of programmed instruction:

1. Good teachers are freed from the boredom of routine classroom teaching and they are in a position to devote their time to more creative activities.
2. The programmed instruction has been used more successfully in leaching the discernment of the logic of various disciplines and inspiring students to creative thinking and judgement.
3. Certain motor skills and intellectual abilities normally taught by frequent drills and rote can be very efficiently taught by self-instructional devices.
4. Self-instructional materials have been found to be very useful in the West in revolutionising the social setting of the classroom. Problems of discipline have been solved and a new hope for eliminating emotional and social problems has been generated.
5. Programmed instruction enables the teacher to diagnose the problems of the individual learner.
6. The teacher can give explanation in the classroom if the error is common or he may arrange individual conferences on specific points.
7. A well-programmed instruction is a great thrust in the direction of individualised instruction as it is tailored to cater to the needs of the individual students of the class.
8. Learning material in a programmed instruction is presented in such a way that learning becomes an interest-

ing game and the learner is motivated to meet the challenges set by his own capabilities.

9. Programmes are developed by experts. They are empirically tested and modified till they are standardised. A number of students can use a single good programme and thus save on texts.
10. Since a programme requires continuous response from the learner it overcomes the passivity and inertia on the part of the learner.
11. In programmed instruction the learner is immediately reinforced to correct his response and this reinforcement sustains the motivation of the learner.
12. It permits individual student to progress at his own speed. An intelligent student needs no longer be bored or allowed to lose interest due to slow progress of the other students of the class. He may progress as rapidly as he is able.
13. The self-instructional techniques present a material in which the complexity of the material is simplified through the analysis of the subject-matter into small and more easily assimilated segments of information.
14. A well-programmed instructional material gives the teacher the method and the individual learner adequate time to comprehend more complex of the concepts.
15. The introduction of programmed instruction is very helpful in certain situations where human instructors are not available, e.g., small isolated schools in the hilly areas.
16. The introduction of programmed instruction is of great significance for developing countries which are set on the path of educating millions of masses and are short of teachers.

Basic Principles

Klaus has summed up in 12 rules of programming and building instructional frames:

Active Responding. Learner learns from making a response and not from hearing or seeing it.

Proper Cuing. This is the main difference between a test question and an auto-instructional frame.

Appropriate Context. This is the kind of stimuli that will be capable of evoking the desired response at some time in future.

Small Steps. It is very desirable that there should be more small steps.

Careful Sequencing of Topics. The topics of the subject-matter should be carefully sequenced so as to provide for proper motivation.

Frequent Repetition. Cues associated should be changed and frequent repetition provided in frames.

Knowledge of Subject-matter and Technical Accuracy. Without these, it is very difficult to prepare a suitable and effective programme.

Lecturing to be Avoided. The learner should be helped to learn and this is possible when we provide facts to the learner.

Evoking a Relevant Response. Right kind of illustration should be used.

Providing Cues in Adequate Number. Excess of cues will prevent the learner from making his own generalisation and discovering principles.

Not Assuming too much Knowledge. The programmer should not assume too much knowledge on the part of the learner.

Presenting of Facts in Frames. No two new facts should be presented in one frame.

The Hindrances

Progrmmed materials have been severely criticised as a threat to replacing the teacher.

It is also argued that there is too much emphasis in learning facts and very little emphasis on the mastery of principles and concepts.

Some critics of programmed instruction maintain that the user of a programme does not know where he is headed.

They also point out that the learners are not aware of the organisation and programmed instruction is unrelated to other aspects of instruction.

It is also argued that the programmed instruction material is very costly and only rich nations can afford it.

It is also stated that the development and use of programmed instructional material require expert knowledge and training. An average teacher finds it very difficult to make use of this device.

The Effects

1. Tutorial experiences are provided for individual learners on a large scale whereby the learner may proceed at his own rate.
2. Programmed instruction can exercise control on homework and individual study.
3. Programmed instruction can enable the learner to catch up the loss of absence from school.
4. Programmed instruction provides a technological solution to the problem of individual difference. Programmed instructional materials enable the teacher to gear up his presentation to what he senses is the average, too show for the bright student and too fast for the slow one.
5. The availability of instructional material of a programme and its powerful tools make the teacher much more a professional man than he now is.
6. By interpreting the feedback obtained through oral questions and discussions in the class, the teacher can intelligently vary the flow of information or further instruction.
7. A basic feature of teaching machines is 'immediate knowledge of results' followed by immediate correction of errors and rewards for correct answers. It has been

established by research that more frequent the rewards, the better the learner assimilates the material.

8. It eliminates cheating because the learner has to gain nothing by it.
9. The students like the use of machines than studying a textbook.
10. It eliminates the influence of teacher variable in research.
11. Immediate scoring promotes the learning process. The techniques is valuable in giving tests which can automatically be scored.

Most materials of instruction can be used or abused. They will be used when employed creatively and abused when employed mechanically.

Programme No. 1
CLASS X – CIVICS
Topic – Constitution of India

1. The Constituent Assembly of India was set up under the provisions of the Cabinet Mission Plan to frame the Constitution of India which was formally adopted on 26th November 1949 and came into force on 26th January 1950. It took nearly three years to complete the work.
   (i) What was the work assigned to the Constituent Assembly?
   (ii) Under whose provision was it formed?
   (iii) When did our Constitution come into force?
   (iv) When was it adopted?
   (v) How much time did Constituent Asembly take to complete its work?
2. The Preamble of the Constitution has a great significance but is not a part of the Constitution. The Constitution was framed by the people of India through their representatives. It stresses the fact that the reign of the land lies with the people of India.

(a) Is the Preamble a part of the Constitution?

(b) By whom was the Constitution framed?

(c) In whose hands does the reign of law of India lie?

3. The Preamble of our Constitution is as under:

We the people of India having solemnly resolved to constitute India into a Sovereign Socialist Secular Democratic Republic and to secure to all its citizens:

Justice, social, economic and political;

Liberty of thought, expression, belief, faith and worship;

Equality of status and of opportunity; and to promote them all;

Fraternity assuring the dignity of the individual and the unity and integrity of the Nation.

In our Constituent Assembly this twenty-sixth day of November 1949, do hereby adopt, enact and give to ourselves this Constitution.

Note—Three new terms—Socialist, Secular and Integrity were added to the original text of the Preamble when it was amended in 1976 with the 42nd Amendment.

The Preamble stresses the democratic basis of the Constitution by stating that the People of India gave to themselves this Constitution. It also states the objectives like justice, liberty, equality and fraternity.

(i) Who has given the Constitution of India?

(ii) What kind of justice has been ensured by the Preamble?

(iii) What type of Republic is to be constituted?

(iv) What kind of equality has been given to its citizen?

(v) How many types of liberties can a citizen enjoy?

4. Another important feature of the Preamble is that the people themselves adopted and enacted the Constitution. Thus, the representatives of the people frame the laws of the country and they have the power to change or amend the Constitution.

(a) Who frames the laws of the country?

(b) Who has the power to amend the Constitution?

5. The Constitution of India has many unique features which distinguish it from other Constitutions. The framers of the Constitution freely borrowed ideas but took care to adopt these to the needs of the country.

The Constitution makes India a Sovereign, Socialist, Secular, Democratic Republic. The word Sovereign means that India is completely free from external control. No outside power has the right to interfere either in her internal administration or direct her in the conduct of her foreign policy.

This was emphasised to ensure that India was no longer 'dependent' on the British Empire as she had been before Indian Independence Act 1947 or 'dominion' as she had been from 15th August 1947 to 26th January 1950.

(a) What kind of status did India enjoy during 15th August 1947 to 26th January 1950?

(b) Was India sovereign between 15th August 1947 to 26th January 1950?

(c) What is the meaning of the word 'sovereign'?

(d) Does the Constitution of India has unique features?

(e) Did the framers of the Constitution borrow ideas?

Answers

1. (i) To frame the Constitution of India.

(ii) Provisions of the Cabinet Mission Plan.

(iii) 26th January 1950.

(iv) 26th November 1949.

(v) Nearly 3 years.

2. (a) No.

(b) People of India through their representatives.

(c) People of India.

3. (i) People of India.
   (ii) Social, economic and political.
   (iii) Sovereign, Socialist, Secular, Democratic.
   (iv) Equality of status.
   (v) Five.
4. (a) Representatives of the people.
   (b) Representatives of the people.
5. (a) Dominion.
   (b) No.
   (c) India is completely free from external control.
   (d) Yes.
   (e) Yes.

Programme No. 2
CLASS X—HISTORY
Hinduism

1. It was revealed thousands of years ago in India. It is considered to be the oldest religions of the world. It made significant progress during the Golden Age of the Imperial Guptas.
   (i) During which age did Hinduism make a great progress?
   (ii) Which is considered to be the oldest religions of the world.

   Ans. (i) Golden Age of the Guptas.
   (ii) Hinduism.
2. Following are its main tenets.
   (a) Belief in an Omnipotent God.
   (b) This belief does not debar them from worshipping several gods signifying the different forms of the same divine.

(c) Worship of several gods gave birth to numerous religious sects of which two are more important having their respective God as head

Religious Sects	God Head
Vaishnavism	Lord Vishnu
Shaivism	Lord Shiva

(i) What is the belief of Hinduism?

(ii) Name important religious sects in Hinduism.

(iii) Name the God heads of these sects.

Ans. (i) Belief in an Omnipotent God.

(ii) Vaishnavism and Shaivism.

(iii) Vishnu and Shiva.

3. The principal Hindu Scriptures are the Vedas, the Upanishads, the Darshanas, the Gita, the Mahabharata and the Ramayana etc. Name 5 principal Hindu Scriptures.

Ans. (i) The Vedas.

(ii) The Upanishads.

(iii) The Darshanas.

(iv) The Gita.

(v) The Ramayana.

4. The Hindus believe in the Salvation or 'Moksha' as the aim of man's life. This can be had by exercising full control over one's own senses.

There are believed to be three courses to achieve ultimate salvation—the 'Karma Marga' or the way of Good Deeds, the 'Gyana Marga' or the way of true knowledge and 'Bhakti Marga' or the way of Divine Devotion.

(i) What is the aim of man's life in Hinduism?

(ii) What is the meaning of the word 'Karma Marga'?

(iii) How many courses have been described in Hinduism for Salvation? Name them.

(iv) What is the other term used for the word salvation?

Ans. (i) Salvation.

(ii) Way of good deeds.

(iii) Three Karma Marga, Gyana Marga and Bhakti Marga.

(iv) Moksha.

5. The Hindus firmly believe in the theory of 'Karma' which means that the actions in one's present life bear their fruit in the next life.

The soul itself is immortal but is involved in an unending cycle of births and rebirths as a result of its deeds in this world.

(i) Does the soul die?

(ii) Do the Hindus believe in rebirth?

(iii) What is the theory of 'Karma'?

Ans. (i) No.

(ii) Yes.

(iii) Actions in one's life bear their fruit in the next life.

QUESTIONS

1. Explain the concept of Programmed Learning. To what extent is it possible to use in Social Studies in our schools?
2. Prepare Programme on any topic of Social Studies.

9

Teaching Devices

Utility of Laboratory

A modern teacher of social studies has come a long way from those old days when 'chalk' and 'talk' were the only aids of teaching. Modern technology has placed different types of instructional aids at his disposal. Apart from text books, there are different types of reference books, pamphlets, magazines, maps, globes, charts, projects, etc. which must be used to make the teaching-learning process effective.

A social studies room or what a few subject specialists would like to term as social studies laboratory, fully equipped with modern aids, will provide a pleasant social and cooperative environment where the teachers and the learners feel homely. It is a must for every school. It has been observed by M.P. Moffatt, "Class-room furnishings and their arrangements have directed bearing upon the quality of results obtained. Satisfactory outcomes can be expected from any class-room situation only when adequate facilities are provided. It should be furnished to provide a suitable environment for acquiring and practising social studies skills."

It has been recognised that like sciences, social studies also require a specially equipped room or laboratory. This alone can facilitate the use of modern methods and techniques like Play-way Method, Problem Method, Project Method and the Socialized Recitation Method, etc. Special setting and equipment are needed for utilising these methods.

A social studies laboratory should serve the purpose of a classroom, a library, workshop, an amateur theatre, a students' club, a stock room, all combined into one. It may grow steadily and constantly as regards equipment. It should become the exciting 'hub' of activity for the students and teachers of social studies. It should be so planned and arranged that it provides an inviting and stimulating environment. It should be a place of 'doing' rather than of 'talking'. Social studies library is an integral part of social studies programme and it helps in making it as living and vital discipline. Social studies library is the treasure vault of the store house of ideas. In fact, it is the flowing stream of living thought. Social studies library provides suitable opportunities to the student to use facts in a creative and productive way to arrive at their own independent conclusions and enable them to grow in enriched knowledge, abilities, skills and interests.

Following are some of the considerations which necessitate the provision of a special room or laboratory for social studies.

1. Providing 'home of their own' to social studies teachers for developing enthusiasm for the subject and faith in themselves and the students.
2. Creating and maintaining an effective teaching-learning environment.
3. Providing a quick and ready functional environment by making available work room for the students.
4. Introducing variety in teaching methods and facilitating the use of teaching aids readily and conveniently.
5. Saving energy and time in carrying round equipment like charts, maps, models, pictures and projectors etc.

The Tools

The room should be well-equipped with adequate teaching equipment so that functional environment is created and the teacher and the students are motivated to work. It should have the following equipment:

1. Audio-visual material which includes epidiascope, film-strip, magic lantern, projector, tape-recorder etc.
2. Bulletin Boards.
3. Charts and Graphs.
4. Hags.
5. Globes.
6. Maps and Atlases.
7. Models.
8. Meteorological Instruments—Barometer.
9. Rain Gauge, Thermometers of different kinds, Wind Vane.
10. Rocks-stones and Minerals.
11. Slide Album containing slides showing architecture, dancing, music, painting, sculpture etc.
12. Stamps of different kinds.
13. Survey Instruments—Box Compass, Compass, Chain and Arrows, Divider, Foot Rule or Scale, Hags, Plane Table, Prismatic Compass, Protector, Spirit Level, Survey Field Book, Tape, Tripod.
14. Time Charts and Graphs.
15. Text Books.
16. Reference Books.
17. Unit booklets dealing with a variety of topics, ranging from family life and neighbourhood to people of other lands and places.

18. Literary materials which include tales of adventure, easy biographies, historical series, travel stories, animal stories, historical novels etc.
19. Periodicals and magazines dealing with current events and various aspects of life showing art, literature, music, dance etc.
20. Pamphlets published by various agencies including Central and State Governments and specialised agencies and also by international agencies like the UNO and UNESCO etc.
21. Newspapers.

Utility of Museum

The museum as an instrument of popular education is a twentieth century phenomenon. Until very recently museums were private clubs for the intellectually privileged and exhibits were arranged in such a way as to be almost meaningless to the scientifically or artistically uninformed visitor. All this has changed, at least in theory, in the modern concept of the museums as a cultural centre of the community greater efforts are being made to make museums informative.

The Secondary Education Commission, on the role of school museums observed, "Museums play a great part in the education of school children as they bring home to them much more vividly than any prosaic lectures, the discoveries of the past and the various developments that have taken place in many fields of science and technology." Again the Commission observes, "We believe it is necessary from the educational point of view to establish such museums in important centres at least wherein both ancient and modern collections will be exhibited and in some cases even demonstrations given of the actual process of development of various scientific discoveries. Nothing can impress students in the formative age so much as the actual visualising of these experiments in a graphic manner."

These museums are made up of materials used in classroom teaching which, in many cases, are collected, classified and exhibited by students, with or without the help of a teacher. The museum activities may be an extracurricular function of the class or the school or they may be incorporated into a scientific-experimental method of teaching. The objectives of this type of museum are:

(a) to form within the school or the classroom an embryonic community dedicated to the usual occupations reflected in the school life of adults;

(b) to permit visual instruction and experimentation with actual museum specimens;

(c) to stimulate enthusiasm for study and research among both teachers and students;

(d) to stimulate interest, co-operation and participation in the cultural activities and scientific research conducted by the larger museums;

(e) to instruct students in proper scientific methods of laboratory research and museum conservation and exhibition techniques;

(f) to form, in the absence of larger museums in the community, a nucleus from which the classroom museum can grow beyond the limits of the school to serve ultimately the community and the region as a whole.

The Exhibition

What then are some of the ways in which museums as cultural and educational centres of the community can communicate successfully with their transitory visitors of heterogeneous composition? Based on various audience-testing experiments the following media can be used to heighten the effectiveness of visual communication.

Dramatic Labels. Usually they are far too short in the art museums or far too long. They actually frighten away rather than entice the average museum visitor. Experiments suggest that large letters placed at the focal point of the case or exhibit area will successfully headline the exhibit and catch the visitor's attention. Like a newspaper headline, the main label tends to direct the eye to smaller, less conspicuous letters that outline the most important points of the exhibit.

Dramatic Lighting. Light is a means of visual communication as well as an attention getter. Coloured lights that change, fade or highlight an exhibit can be used with great dramatic effect. Light can also be used to tell a story and to convey a sense of passing time. Light is particularly important in art museums.

Dramatic Utilization. Again experiments suggest that museum visitors should be given a chance to touch exhibits as well as to see them. Of course, much depends on the nature and expendability of the object involved but certain types of material—objects of wood, stone and metal and special "touch me" samples of animal skins and fabrics—can be used with great success to satisfy the visitor's urge to touch while permitting a minimum of danger.

Dramatic Sound Effects. Sound, like light, can be used to heighten the dramatic effect of visual communication. For example, an Amazon rain forest exhibition can be made vastly more effective by adding the sound of tropical rain, the croaking of frogs, the chattering of monkeys, and the beat of drums. An exhibit of medieval art can be made more meaningful if it is accompanied by music of the same period.

Effective Use of Space. Special concepts are also important in planning visitor traffic patterns within the exhibit areas.

Importance of Dalton Plan

The plan is named not after its originator Miss Helen Parkhurst but after the name of the town in which it was first adopted in a High School.

Laboratory Plan. Miss Parkhurst attaches importance to the use of the word 'Laboratory'. She writes, "I cling to it in the hope that it may gradually shift the educational point of view away from the atmosphere of prejudice which the word 'school' calls up in our minds. Let us think of school rather as a sociological laboratory where the pupils themselves are the experimenters, not the victims of an intricate and crystallised system in the evolution of which they have neither part nor lot. Let us think of it as a place where community conditions prevail as they prevail in life itself." Her aim was to create 'a new type of educational society' by putting boys and girls under entirely different conditions of living from those provided in the ordinary class-room and to re-organise the community life of the school.

Plan at Work

Assignment or Contracts. The teachers outline the work of the year to be done in their respective subjects to enable the students to know about the scope and the nature of the work they are required to complete in each subject. The work is further subdivided into suitable monthly units by the subject teachers. While preparing the assignment the teachers bear in mind factors like holidays, time available, revision at various stages, co-curricular activities and the demands of other subjects.

Each unit of work is accepted by the pupil as a 'contract' and he promises to complete the work and to satisfy the teacher before going to the next unit.

Each subject has its separate assignment. The child will be given the new assignment only when he has completed his assignments in all the subjects. A pupil is not allowed to do more than the month's work in a single subject unless he finishes the month's contract in every other subject. The child is free to undertake an assignment of a month in any manner he likes, i.e., he may devote one week completely to complete his assignment in one subject and may ignore assignments, in other subjects during that particular week and take up assignments in other subjects in the second, third or the fourth week. He may spend his whole day in one assignment of a subject and so on. The only limitation is that he must finish the whole contract, i.e., monthly assignments in each subject for a particular month, before the second contract is entered upon.

Subject Teachers. The Dalton Plan does away with class teachers and accepts specialist teachers. Each specialist teacher supervises each child in his subject and guides his work. He renders all possible help to the child to complete his assignment in time.

Subject Rooms. The plan scraps classrooms and gives their place to subject-rooms which are called subject-laboratories. Each specialist is the incharge of his room. Each subject-room is adequately equipped with the material required in that subject. It contains books and magazines, charts, maps, models, apparatus and appliances etc., concerning that subject.

There is no fixed time-table and no fixed period. Each student is free to devote more times to the subject in which he is weak and less in which he is up to the mark.

Records. Graphs are kept to show the work done by each child and in each subject so that the pupil himself and the teachers may know how he is progressing. Two records are maintained by the pupil himself; one showing his progress in each subject and the other in all subjects. The third record is kept by the subject-teacher himself and is hung in the subject-room.

These records serve as a mirror to indicate the work of the pupils and are kept up-to-date. These serve as a link also between the teacher and the pupil and bring them in close co-operation for the effective learning. The graph, in fact, is a constant reminder of the 'contract' or 'promise' and helps to make one conscious of the extent to which progress is made and is to be made.

Conferences. Usually the morning time uptil recess is devoted to individual work by each child or may be devoted for voluntary group work. The afternoon time may be used by the teacher for oral lessons in his subject. Group discussions under the guidance of the teacher may be held. These oral lessons or group discussions are called 'conferences'. These conferences may be devoted to remove common difficulties or to explain certain items of common interest and importance.

Teacher's Responsibilities

The duties of a teacher in the Dalton Plan may be summed up as under:

(i) Preparation of assignments and giving them to the pupils as and when required.

(ii) Keeping an atmosphere of study in the room.

(iii) Giving explanation of any details of the assignment and removing the difficulties of the pupils.

(iv) Giving information with regard to the use of relevant equipment and material.

(v) Ensuring that each assignment is finished properly before the new assignment is given to the pupil.

(vi) Keeping full records of the progress made by pupil in different classes.

(vii) Keeping the subject-library and other equipment up-to-date and in proper order.

The teacher, in the Dalton Plan, is 'a helper, not a driver; the pursued, not the pursuer.'

Major Principles

The Principle of Individual Work. John Adams says, "It is the most dramatic and systematic break away from the class-teaching unit". It is now generally accepted that the students differ in various respects and it is folly to tag them together for keeping pace in studies. The plan aims at providing equal opportunities to all pupils to work at their own rate and speed. The time taken is not necessarily equal but a minimum uniform achievement is required. In the words of Miss Parkhurst, "It is a piece of machinery for putting into operation the principle of individual work."

The Principle of Freedom. Children work well when they are allowed freedom to do so. There are no arbitrary fixed periods. There are no class-room restrictions or rigidity of discipline. In the Dalton Plan, children are free to move about, to consult one another and to work in any particular subject. In the words of an educationist, "It aims to giving to the older child that freedom for self-development which has proved so valuable in the school life of the "infant" while at the same time ensuring that he shall master thoroughly the academic work required by the curriculum of the school."

The Principle of Self-effort. Learning to be effective must be the product of one's own self-effort. In the Dalton Plan, the child learns through his own efforts.

The Principle of Co-operation. In a subject laboratory pupils of different age groups not only assist each other when occasions demand but are very much helped in turn, without being distracted, in the task of a companion being similar if not identical. According to Miss Parkhurst, the school can only reflect the social experience of the community when all its parts or groups develop the same intimate relations with one another as is found in society as a whole. The schools should be organised in such a way as the pupils and teachers come in close interaction with one another. Miss Parkhurst has used the term 'interaction of group life'. The students live and work together with the same teachers, in the same shared common workshops or laboratories.

The Principle of Setting Goals. The child is enabled to survey the whole field, to see the goal at which he is aiming at and thus a stimulus is provided to him and he takes up the work bit by bit thereby increasing and ensuring better learning.

Merits of the Plan. Dalton Plan is a continuation of Montessori Method and is especially applicable to secondary school work. The plan has the following advantages:

Individual Teaching. Each pupil is permitted to work at his own rate. The plan approaches teaching and instruction from the point of view of the pupil. The weak are not hurried along at the speed of other pupils and the bright are not kept back because of their slow class-fellows. The teacher pays individual attention to each child.

Continuity of Work. There is no waste of time as is usually the case in the conduct of various examinations for promotion or other purposes. There are no failures and the promotions from one grade to another may take place at any time.

Absence from school of a child due to ill-health or otherwise does not stand in his way of working smoothly. He can start the work just from where he had stopped and can make up his deficiency in his own speed. There is no danger that some courses have been covered in his absence and he has missed them.

Development of Qualities like Self-effort and Self-confidence. There is absolutely no spoonfeeding in the Dalton Plan. Ready-made knowledge is not given to the child. He has to depend upon himself in the solution of his problems. He has to consult suitable books and other reference material. He, himself has, to experience difficulties and to solve his problems. All this makes him self-confident.

Purposeful Learning. Student's 'contract' or 'assignment' is like a project in front of him and for its completion he tries his best and devotes his heart and soul into the work. Thus learning becomes motivated and purposeful.

Development of Desirable Study Habits. The students have to make use of a variety of material to complete their assignments. They have to study reference books, source books, etc., and all this helps to develop desirable study habits in them.

Development of Sense of Responsibility. The 'contract' is a constant reminder to the children to complete their work in time.

They feel that they must fulfil their responsibility that they have accepted in entering upon the 'assignment'.

Solving the Problem of Home Task. There is no need for giving home task. The child in order to complete his assignment may of his own accord devote extra time in the subject-laboratory. Thus compulsory homework loses its terror in the school.

Solving the Problem of Discipline. No restrictions are put on children. They work in an atmosphere of freedom. They accept their own responsibility and work for its fulfilment. There is no rigid time-table and the students are not forced to attend to studies according to a set time-table. Problem of truancy, mischief and delinquency are rare.

Simplification of the Problem of Evaluation. The graph system is a valuable check on the progress of each child. The records show the progress of each pupil and enable him to know where he stands. In a way records can help to give incentives to him. There is no necessity of frequent tests and awarding of marks.

Better Pupil-teacher Relationships. The plan enables the teacher to know the child individually. Every child is free to seek the teacher's guidance at any point when a difficulty occurs. The teacher is essentially a guide and a helper.

Problems and Hindrances

Limitations and difficulties of this plan are given below:

Not Suitable for the Average Child and a Shirker. The clever and the bright students can derive a lot of benefit from this scheme. It is not possible for the average child to learn new principles without a formal lesson. The shirkers also find opportunities to develop the attitude of 'postponement'.

Development of Individualistic Tendencies. As a child has his own assignment to do, he may not like to help his other friends if he is required to do so on the plea that he is absorbed in his own work. Pinkevitch observers, "We cannot but express the fear that it will be instrumental in developing individualistic tendencies in children."

A Purely Intellectual Plan. The plan fails to provide for liberal group activities. There is little scope for social service activities. Dr. Cox states, "The Dalton Plan is highly inadequate for social education."

Unsuitable for Lessons that Require Inspirational Treatment. There are certain subjects which require collective lessons for appreciation purposes. Physical training, music and drill in languages need group teaching. Therefore, the plan is unsuitable for these subjects.

Lack of Suitable Teachers. For the successful working of the plan, competent, liberal and progressive teachers are required. The plan puts heavy demands upon the teachers who are expected to prepare good assignment and be able to guide and help the pupils if and when such guidance or help is needed. Teachers must be in a position to inspire students to work hard independently. It is very difficult to get such teachers.

Lack of Well-equipped Libraries. Most of the libraries of our school are not adequately equipped and are without any trained librarians. But under the Dalton Plan, we require a wide variety of suitable text-books, source books and other relevant material so that the children may prepare their assignments.

Unsuitable for Junior Classes. The plan is more suitable for children above nine years of age.

Very Costly. The plan is very expensive. It requires many more teachers and well-equipped libraries and other equipment.

No Provision for Individual Differences. It is very difficult to change the attitude of the teachers who are accustomed to old methods of class teaching. They do not like sweeping changes. Moreover, they do not like to give freedom to pupil.

A review of the limitations and difficulties of the Dalton Plan shows that it is not possible to introduce this plan in its entirety in our schools. However, there is much that can be introduced in ordinary teaching. We should try to evolve some system in which class teaching may be done in the morning and individual teaching in the afternoon. More individual attention should be given to the students. They should be encouraged to read extra books and a record of that should be kept. Some son of day-to-day assessment should be made of the work done by each child and the results communicated to them so that they may be motivated to work hard.

QUESTIONS

1. Why do we need a Social Studies Room? How can we equip it?
2. How can a Social Studies room serve as a laboratory?
3. Write notes on:
   (a) Social Studies Museum
   (b) Social Studies Library.
4. Explain the merits and limitations of the use of Dalton Plan in Indian context.
5. State the role of the teacher in Dalton Plan.
6. Can we combine class teaching method with Dalton Plan? Give arguments in support of your answer.

10

Micro-teaching

Micro-teaching is a training procedure aiming at simplifying the complexities of the regular teaching process. In a micro-teaching procedure, the trainee is engaged in a scaled down teaching situation. It is scaled down in terms of class size, since the trainee is teaching a small group of four to six pupils. The lesson is scaled down in length of class time and is reduced on five or ten minutes. It is also scaled down in terms of teaching tasks.

These tasks may include: the practising and mastering of a specific teaching skill such as lecturing, questioning or leading a discussion Mastering of specific teaching strategies; flexibility; instructional decision-making; alternative uses of specific curricula, instructional materials and classroom management.

The short lesson is recorded on an audio or video-tape recorder and the trainee gets to hear and see himself immediately after the lesson. The pupils who attend the lesson are asked to fill in rating questionnaires evaluating specific aspects of the lesson. The trainee's own analysis of the lesson based on the authentic feedback from the tape together with the pupil's reaction and a supervisor's analysis and suggestions, assists the trainee in restructuring the lesson, which he then immediately reteaches to a new group of pupils. Further assessment by the 'learners' and the supervisor lead to further improvements when he teaches again, either immediately after or several days later. This micro-teaching sequence is practised usually in a micro-teaching laboratory in a teacher-training institution, or an in-service training programme in regular schools.

Main Propositions of Micro-teaching. Alien and Ryan in their book on the subject give the following main propositions of micro-teaching:

(1) Micro-teaching is real teaching, although a teaching situation is constructed in which the student-teacher and pupils work together in a practice situation. Bonafide teaching does take place.

(2) Micro-teaching lessens the complexities of normal classroom teaching. Class size, scope of content and time are all reduced.

(3) Micro-teaching focuses on training for the accomplishment of specific tasks. These tasks may be the practice of instructional skills, the practice of techniques of teaching, the mastery of certain curricular materials, or the demonstration of teaching methods.

(4) Micro-teaching allows for the increased control of practice. In a micro-teaching setting, the time, number of pupils, methods of feedback and supervision, etc., may be manipulated.

(5) Micro-teaching greatly expands the normal knowledge of results or feedback dimensions in teaching. Immediately after teaching a brief micro-lesson, the trainee is engaged in a critique of his performance. All this feedback can be immediately translated into practice when the trainee re-teachers shortly after the critique conference.

Two related areas can be pointed out where there are clear advantages:

(i) training in teaching skill

(ii) research in teacher-training.

Significant Elements

The Micro-element. The micro-element, which systematically attempts to simplify the complexities of the teaching process is the cardinal feature of micro-teaching. Underlying this is the basic supposition that before one attempts to understand, learn and perform effectively the complicated task of teaching, one should first master the components of that task. By focussing the training on a specific task, and by reducing the complexities of the teaching situation by diminishing the number of students, the duration of the lesson and subject-matter to be covered, it is possible to concentrate the training process and assure greater effectiveness.

Technical Skills of Teaching and Teaching Strategies. A repertoire of teaching skills such as lecturing, questioning, or leading a discussion and mastery of teaching strategies is the second important feature of micro-teaching. The concept of teaching skills is not new, and many text books on teaching methods refer to specific skills or teaching strategies. But never before has there been such a systematic approach to analysing classroom interaction for the purpose of research and training. For example, teaching skills can be classified under five general headings of response, questioning, increasing student participation, creating student involvement, and presentation, with three or four skills further delineated within each category. Detailed manuals and series of model films explaining and illustrating these skills have been prepared for training purposes.

The Feedback Element. The feedback element is the third important feature of micro-teaching. At present, 'feedback' in the supervision of student teachers is ordinarily based on a supervisor's recall and selective note-taking. His overall impressions provide the basis for subsequent analysis of the student teacher's performance. But subjective factors enter into his assessment as they do into the student's ability to recall details of the lesson and in the absence of objective criteria the student may covertly oppose the supervisor's evaluations and suggestions.

(1) The most simple source is the oral feedback of the laboratory supervisor. Experience has shown that the relatively non-threatening atmosphere in the laboratory creates better communication between the supervisor and the trainee, even if his feedback is subjective. The micro-elements of the laboratory help the supervisor in focussing and concentrating his observations, thus ensuring greater accuracy of feedback.

(2) Another source of feedback consists of questionnaires filled in by the pupils learning in the micro-lesson. These questionnaires – geared to specific skills with well-defined questions – provide the most important, although subjec-tive, feedback from the teacher's 'clients'. When teachers are used to the pupils' feed back and accept it with some ease, it is possible even to conduct short discussions with the pupils in which the teacher and his supervisor try to elaborate on the feedback provided by these questio-nnaires.

(3) Audiotape-recordings are an important source of accu-rate feedback. Recent technological developments have resulted in small, portable tape recorders, operated by batteries and relatively low-priced. This calls for expan-ding their general use in schools and particularly in micro-teaching laboratories. They are, however, limi-ted to verbal interaction in the class and "thus do not provide the 'whole picture'. A supervisor's comment, based solely on an audio-tape might be considered by the teacher as one-sided. In addition, the peculiarity which causes many people not to recognize their own voice on tape, disturbs sometimes its acceptance as a source of feedback.

(4) The most accurate and powerful source of feedback is the video tape-recording. Newly developed portable

video tape recorders consist of a small camera and a small television monitor. Classroom activities can thus be recorded with minimum disturbance to teacher and students. It provides instant and accurate feedback of classroom interaction (verbal and non-verbal) in the teacher's natural habitat and thus provides a basis for reliable analysis.

The effectiveness of video tape-recordings and playback techniques has been confirmed in a number of studies of teacher training and in related areas such as counsellor training and counselling, phychotherapy and human relations.

Safe Practice-grounds. Providing a safe practice-ground is another important feature of micro-teaching. A micro-teaching laboratory seems to be one effective answer, for it appears to posses all the inherent features of the real classroom. The student teaches the relevant subject-matter to genuine pupils (at whatever level is desired).

The Teaching 'Models'. The tapes or films of teaching 'models' are an important facet to the learning process in the micro-teaching laboratory, and provide the trainee with many opportunities to study desired patterns of teaching behaviour. There are, of course, many styles of good teaching and trainees will develop their own individual styles using these models as a guide.

The Research Laboratory. The micro-teaching laboratory simplifies the act of teaching and provides opportunities for controlled research to a degree never possible before. According to Alien and Ryan, the following areas of research seem to make the most effective use of the micro-teaching settings: (a) in-house studies designed to optimize the procedures and sequences in the micro-teaching situation; (b) research in modelling and supervising techniques; (c) task analysis of the teaching act and the investigation of the relationships between teaching behaviours and student performances; (d) aptitude treatment interaction studies, to try to provide optimal training procedures for teachers with different abilities, interests and backgrounds.

Current and Potential use of Micro-teaching. In a recent survey in the United States on the use of micro-teaching in teacher-education programmes, it was found that 141 of the 442 NCATE-accredited colleges and universities were using micro-teaching in the secondary education programmes, and about fifty reported the beginning of its use in-service training programmes.

Micro-teaching as an Innovation. While micro-teaching has been described as an innovation in teacher education, in fact, certain of its aspects have long been in use in various training situations.

The micro-concept which is based on long-established learning theory, today, underlies programmed learning and computer-assisted instructions. In both cases, it is assumed that learning is more effective if a complex skill is divided into its components and learned step by step before it is undertaken as a whole. Other concepts of learning theory such as feedback, reinforcement, or extinction were also adopted in the micro-teaching procedure. Observation learning through a 'model' is another example of well-established educational theory and practice. The developers of micro-teaching should be credited, however, with incorporating all these well-known principles into a systematic training system.

By adopting micro-teaching in a systematic and meaningful way, we can bring about a revolution in teacher education in India. Micro-teaching can be very useful both at pre-level as well as at in-service teacher education programmes. But this technique has to be used in an imaginative way. It requires a lot of hard work and insight.

Micro-teaching is not a gimmick or a fad. It faces a real situation with the minimum risk for both the student-teacher and the pupils. It is based on sound theoretical principles of prompt feedback of result and immediate opportunity to make corrections. A wide range of experiences could be provided with economy in time and resources. There is considerable freedom in how the micro-teaching format can be adopted to individual circumstances.

Micro-teaching can be altered to suit many circumstances. It is flexible. It can be used in internship or in-service training to strengthen a particular skill. It can also be used for demonstration purposes. Time may be manipulated. Micro-teaching is not dependent on any particular facilities of equipment. The usefulness of recording facilities has been acknowledged but the technique can be effective even without such equipment The most important ingredients are the people involved. Micro-teaching focusses on teaching behaviour. This is the heart of the problem of studying teaching.

The Advantages

Main advantages of micro-teaching may be summarised as:

(1) Micro-teaching is real teaching.

(2) Micro-teaching lessens the complexities of normal classroom teaching.

(3) Micro-teaching focusses on training for the accomplishment of specific tasks.

(4) Micro-teaching allows for the increased control of practice.

(5) Micro-teaching greatly expands the normal knowledge of results of feedback dimension in teaching.

Skills for Teaching

The Stanford Model listed the following general teaching skills.

(1) Stimulus variations,

(2) Set induction,

(3) Closure,

(4) Silence and non-verbal cues,

(5) Reinforcement of student participation,

(6) Fluency in asking questions,

(7) Probing questions,

(8) Higher order questions,

(9) Divergent questions,

(10) Recognising attending behaviour,

(11) Illustrating and use of examples,

(12) Lecturing,

(13) Planned repetition more, and

(14) Completeness of Communication.

Macleese states that the pupil teacher integrates these skills. Researches conducted by D.B. Young, Claus, Goodking, Wragg and others have shown that integration of skills takes place and it proves very useful. As we believe in the integration of skills when the pupil teacher goes to teach in the regular class, C.C. Wood (1968) says that video tape has a positive contribution to make in developing student teacher awareness of teaching acts. There is no doubt about the utility of video tape.

Stones and Morris have also highlighted the advantages of the video tape. But researches have been conducted and it has come to light that micro-teaching without videotape is also effective and successful. Alien and Ryan (1969) think that videotape is not an essential component of micro-teaching, although it strengthens the micro-teaching process.

Professor N. Flanders (1969) is of the view that procedure of micro-teaching can be as successful when video tape is not employed. C.J. Lawless has proved that micro-teaching is successful in the absence of video tape. Some workers have replaced tape-recordings in place of video tapes. All these are very useful experiments and findings for India where it may not be possible to get the advantage of video tape but the micro-teaching technique can be utilised successfully.

The Background

The term micro-teaching was first coined by A.W. Dwight Alien of the Stanford University in 1963. A number of experiments have been conducted in many institutions in the USA, UK and the Netherlands. In India also, a number of institutions have started work in the area of micro-teaching in recent years. The Lever Halrne Trust gave a five-year grant to the Sterling University in the UK for doing work on micro-teaching. Work is being done at the Exeter University by B.C. Wragg. A lot of work in this field has been done at the Purdue University by Dr Joe E. Shively, Aderehen P. Wan Mondtrans and Chery L. Read. A comprehensive biblio-graphy on micro-teaching has been prepared by W. Raymond McAleese of the University of Aberden and Derick Unwin of the University of Ulster. Perlberg Ayre and David C. Oberiant of the Department of General Engineering University of Illinois, have used micro-teaching techniques to improve engineering instruc-tion.

Micro-teaching Flow Chart

The procedure of micro-teaching in Tokyo Institute of Technology may briefly be described by using the following flow-chart.

Planning for 5 min. teaching
↓
Micro-Teaching (I)
5 min. each, 3 Teachers
↓ Video
Discussion with Video Play-back
3 Teachers
↓ ← Evaluation Sheet
Replanning →
↓
Micro-Teaching (2) 5 min.
↓
Self-Confirmation

Three volunteers from participants play the teachers' roles in front of VTR camera and other participants also take part of pupils' roles. After discussing how the teaching behaviours should be improved, three volunteers teach other participants again. The comparison is made between two teaching traits in each teacher on the evaluation sheet.

The Assessment

Critics of micro-teaching. Like other innovations micro-teaching too has both its supporters and critics. Earl Seidman has raised the point that "much emphasis is placed on training in teaching skills which presuppose the idea that the teacher's role is to control the students and to direct the class ...... if we treat our interns mechanistically, how will they treat their students?" Noam Chomsky, a scientific linguist at the Massachussetts Institute of Technology, has also questioned such Skinnerian type training, which is appropriate only to industrial workers who need to develop complex technical skills. Chomsky asks: "Is growing up and learning no more than the shaping of behaviour? If that is what education is all about, authoritarian figures shaping people, then may be we don't need it." Other critics of micro-teaching claim that while teaching a micro-class the teacher does not encounter the regular management problems common in large classes.

Utility of micro-teaching. Micro-teaching is not a gimmick or a fad. It faces a real situation with the minimum risk for both the student-teacher and the pupils. It is based on sound theoretical principles of prompt feedback of result and immediate opportunity to make corrections. A wide range of experiences could be provided with economy in time and resources. There is considerable freedom in how the micro-teaching format can be adopted to individual circumstances. Alien and Ryan see five main advantages of micro-teaching, especially if it becomes a routine part of the training of teachers. First, the faculty have to get together to agree on common purposes in its use.

Secondly, it becomes feasible to follow trainees' performance closely. Thirdly, the programme is individualised. Fourthly, evidence of suitabilities for teaching is ascertained, and fifthly, it is a useful research tool. In addition to these, it simplifies the complex-teaching process.

Micro-teaching can be altered to suit many circumstances. It is flexible. It can be used in internship or in-service training to strengthen a particular skill. It can also be used for demonstration purposes. Time may be manipulated. Alien and Ryan in their micro-teaching found no difference between four and seven minute lessons and they suggested longer sessions. Micro-teaching is not dependent on any particular facilities of equipment. The usefulness of recording facilities has been acknowledged. But the technique can be effective even without such equipment. Studies of Pangotra, Jangira and Singh have been completed without them. The most important ingredients are the people involved. Micro-teaching focuses on teaching behaviour. This is the heart of the problem of studying teaching.

Micro-teaching—An Aspect of Teacher Education Programme. It should be stressed here that micro-teaching is only an aspect of the teacher education programme. It is not intended to replace the theoretical foundations in the teacher education programme. It only attempts to strike a balance between theory and practice in the programme. Micro-teaching practice begins with the basic teaching skills and progressively provides the teacher with opportunities to practise and master high-order skills and instructional decision-making.

Adoption and Adaption of Micro-teaching. It should be borne in mind that howsoever excellent the innovation of micro-teaching may be, it should be adopted and practised according to the needs and conditions of the Indian teacher-education system. The number of untrained teachers, the number of student teachers admitted to colleges of education, the staff pattern, the curricular demand and the resources available in the colleges are to be taken into account. Absence of technological devices is also a deterrent to the introduction of micro-teaching. But the experts say that micro-teaching can be adopted even without technical sophis-tication, without a TV network or a taperecorder. The 'micro' and 'laboratory' elements are the really important ones. The only problem in developing countries, today, is to train teams of teachers, educators and supervisors who will be able to introduce this innovation in their colleges and school systems.

Micro-teaching in India. A number of educational institutions have started work in the area of micro-teaching. D.D. Tiwari was the first to take up this work in 1967 at the Government Central Pedagogical Institute at Allahabad. This was followed by G.B. Shah who tried an experiment in micro-teaching with the help of a tape recorder in the Faculty of Education and Psychology in 1970. Other names in the field who worked, are R.R. Chandasama, L.P. Singh, N.S. Sarkar and N. Pangotra. A major breakthrough was made at the Technical Teacher Training Institute, Madras where a studio for educational television programme was set up in which micro-teaching was introduced for the training of technical teachers. A major contribution to the micro-teaching as a teaching device was made in 1974 at the Technical Teachers' Trai-ning Institute, Chandigarh under the guidance of Dr. N.L. Dosajh. The Institute has published a number of research papers in the area of micro-teaching. The Royal Netherlands Government has provided a closed circuit television to this Institute. The Technical Teachers, Training Institute, Calcutta has started micro-teaching with the help of audiotape.

Perhaps the first book on micro-teaching in India was written by N.L. Dosajh under the caption '*Modification of Teacher Behaviour through Micro-teaching* (1977)'.

Apparatus Needed in Micro-teaching. Micro-teaching can be conducted with or without closed circuit television.

The following apparatus may be considered sufficient for a simple type of micro-teaching:

(a) Vidiocon camera preferably with a Zoom lens and Tripod.

(b) Videotape recorders.

(c) Two monitors.

(d) Recording tapes.

(e) Two clocks, a dozen lamps, about 100 yards of wire and switchgear.

Integration of Micro-teaching. Generally micro-teaching is integrated into the 'Student Teaching' programme. The following procedure is usually followed:

Lectures. Lectures on the theory connected with 'Student Teaching' are given.

Demonstration Lessons. Members of the Faculty give demonstration lessons to the teacher-trainees. Some good lessons are played on the video.

Diagnostic Lessons. The staff of the college evaluates the various teaching skills possessed by the trainees when they are asked to give diagnostic lesson. This enables the Faculty Members to diagnose the various areas (teaching skills) in which the teacher trainee is deficient and to take remedial measures to this end.

Micro-lessons for Practice. Micro-teaching is used as one of the devices for training teachers in 'Student Teaching.

The Simulation

Simulation may be defined as a role playing in which the process of teaching is enacted artificially and an effort is made to practise some important skill of communication through this. Under this, the student-teacher and the students simulate a particular role and try to develop an identity with the actual classroom environment. Thus, the whole simulated teaching programme becomes a training in role perception and role playing. Simulation is the basis of sensitivity training, socio-drama, role playing and psycho-drama.

Assumptions. It is assumed that certain underlying skills to teaching can be modified, described and practised like any other skill.

It is also assumed that through role perception the psychological appreciation of the classroom problems will grow and develop in the stu-dent teacher a basis for handling the problems in the class.

Use of Simulation. According to Stones, 'Simulation techniques for all their artificiality can often be preferable to putting students in the classroom to learn on their own or to lecturing to them about the classroom. In other spheres pilots trained in the 'artificial' circumstances of the link trainer, driving schools have their traffic simulators and medical students their cadaver's and this is eminently sensible. By the same token, classroom simulation removes the risk from the first steps of a neophyte and enables him to come to terms with the demands of a complex skill learning without the stress of the real situation. At the same time it is to be preferred to merely 'telling' the student, for much the same reasons as it is better to allow the beginning pilot to practise operating the dummy controls rather than telling him how to do it when he finds himself in the air."

Steps in Simulation. Flanders recommends the following steps:

(1) Letters A, B, C, D etc. are assigned to each person in the group and role assignments are rotated by letters so that each individual has a chance to be an actor or observer.

(2) The skills to be practised are discussed and topics of conversation that fit the skills are also suggested.

(3) Considerations as to who will start the conversation, who will intervene, who will stop the interaction and when it will be stopped, are decided.

(4) The procedure of evaluation, kind of data to be recorded and the method of recording etc. are decided.

(5) First practice session is conducted and the actor is provided with feedback on his performance. If necessary, the procedure of the second session is altered in order to improve the training procedure.

(6) If need arises, one should be prepared to change the procedure and the topic and move on to the next skill

so as to present a meaningful challenge to each actor to keep his interest as high as possible.

Teacher Training and Simulation. Cruikshank (1968) developed a teacher training system which is capable of presenting the student with upto thirty-one different simulated problems related to teaching. Following are the various steps:

(1) The participant is introduced into the situation i.e.. if he was a new teacher in a school.

(2) The participant is provided with information and opportunities to solve the problems of a beginning teacher.

(3) The participant is exposed to a variety of potential solutions to particular problems.

(4) The participant is given the opportunity of observing the results of his chosen line of action.

(5) The participant is introduced to the situation by film-strips.

(6) The participant is also given the materials that a teacher going to the school would actually receive things such as the school rules and regulations, curriculum handbook and record cards of all students in the class.

(7) The participant is, then, presented with thirty-one problems, ten in films and others in role playing situations, written incidents or combinations.

(8) After the presentation of each problem, the participant responds to an Incident Response Sheet.

(9) The participant, then, identifies the factors influencing the problems, locates the relevant informations, suggests appropriate alternative course of action, communicates and implements a decision.

(10) Small group discussions follow which consider the analysis and action taken.

(11) Small group discussions are followed by large group discussion.

(12) The objective of the discussions is to push the analysis of the teaching problem, and not to come up with the 'right' answer.

Simulators. The word simulator is associated with a single set of apparatus which by itself can represent to its operator a very large portion of the situation required in the use of a weapon system. Aircraft simulators are the best examples. The pilot, during the trial period, observes instruments and operates controls which simulate those of the real aeroplane with a high degree of precision.

Simulators are designed for procedures for adjusting electronic representation of motor skills, identification of targets or emergence signals, conceptual tasks involving reasoning and team functions. The simulator is deliberately designed to omit certain parts of the real operational situation.

(1) The beginner participants may face some difficulty in asking different kinds of question. A simple task such as "open" and "closed" questions may provide an introductory challenge.

(2) It is quite possible that during an exercise, the observer may record incorrectly.

(3) The most common error in serious skill training is the misconception that adults can play the role of pupils.

Various Problems

Flanders has suggested the following problems:

(1) The ability to ask open or closed questions at the appropriate time.

(2) The ability to ask a question which lifts the current level of abstraction or a question which lowers it.

(3) The ability to ask question from the areas in which concepts and logical connections have been expressed by the students previously.

(4) The ability to summarize what students have said previously.

(5) The ability to ask a question which may move the discussion to the next step in a logical sequence of problem solving.

(6) The ability to make the appropriate use of ideas expressed previously by the students.

(7) The ability to make constructive use of positive and negative feels of the students.

(8) The ability to provide reasons for using 'praise' or 'blame'.

(9) The ability to predict the consequences which follow from alternative actions.

(10) The ability to assist pupils to compare consequences of alternative actions through speculation before decisions are arrived at.

(11) The ability to guide constructive discussions.

(12) The ability to clarify the first steps needed to start work in ways that are in accordance with the interests and abilities of the pupils.

(13) The ability to organise pupils' ideas in terms of teaching objectives for reinforcing selectively those ideas which are in target.

(14) The ability both to demonstrate and explain rules of logic in class-room discourse.

(15) The ability to assist pupils to maintain consistency in the meaning of words and to assist to distinguish matters of fact, opinion and value.

To sum up, it can be said that simulation can be made a powerful tool in solving some of the problems that hinder effective teaching and it can also impart training of certain skills which are necessary for teaching and its effectiveness. Needless to mention that simulation exercises can be improved by a systematic experimentation around it. SSST (Simulated Social Skill Training) may be given a fair trial.

QUESTIONS

1. Explain the meaning of micro-teaching. What are its main propositions? State its main features.
2. State the meaning of simulation. What are its various steps?
3. Elucidate the use of SSST in the teaching of Social Studies.

11

Educational Technology

Patterns and Impacts

In addition to reading, vicarious experience can be gained from still pictures, films, filmstrips, resource persons, simulations, mockups, television, and the like. The more concrete and realistic the vicarious experience, the more nearly it approaches the learning effectiveness of the first level. Of course, unless the learner realizes that he is dealing with a substitute, his learning may not be comparable to that of real-life learning.

Interest in the role of the senses in learning was already there in educational circles when instructional media began their ascendency. It has long been recognized that the various senses condition the reception of messages in the communications act. Research done by Cobun (1968) indicated that:

1 per cent of what is learned is from the sense of test.

1.5 per cent of what is learned is from the sense of touch.

3.5 per cent of what is learned is from the sense of smell.

11 per cent of what is learned is from the sense of hearing.

83 per cent of what is learned is from the sense of sight.

Retention of what is learned is likewise related to sense experience.

Observation and research by Cobun tended to show, holding time as nearly constant as possible, that people generally remember:

10 per cent of what they read.

20 per cent of what they hear.

30 per cent of what they see.

50 per cent of what they hear and see.

70 per cent of what they say.

90 per cent of what they say as they do a thing.

Role of Media

Among the most significant forces for change in recent years is the technological sophistication we now possess, for this sophistication not only affects our lives in profound ways but also seems to hold tantalizing promise for increasing our efficiency in education (Kinder, 1973). The last 80 years have seen the development of steam-driven, high-speed rotary presses, advanced optics, films, wire and tape sound recordings, simple and complex duplicating and copying machines, radio, television, computers, and communication lasers.

This technological escalation has bestowed upon education proliferation of equipment and materials which can assist in the reorganization and redefinition of educational experiences. In the past, most teaching depended almost entirely on verbal communication between teacher and student, or written communication to the student from printed materials. Although, these communication channels continue to play important roles in the learning process, today's students are learning facts, skills and attitudes from pictures, television, recorded words, programmed lessons, and other media. Once technology enters the school building, dramatic renovations usually begin. With the technological magic touch a **simple** school-house turns into a systematized learning centre.

Today, many countries around the world use some form of technological media in education. In a few countries, the use is fairly widespread. Most technological devices and programmes, however, are structured around the needs of the teacher and are employed as teaching aids in the classroom. In other words, most educators are using technology to answer the question:

How can technology help the teacher? In a few areas, however, focus is on the needs of the student. There, educators ask the question: how can technology help the learner?

In the instances where the student is the centre of attention, technology is catalyst for educational change. Its absence would make a significant difference to the educational process, because technology is an integral part of a well-thoughtout system, not merely a teacher's aid.

Role of Computer

Educational technology can be classified into two categories, i.e., the hardware approach and software approach.

Hardware Approach

It is based on the application of engineering principles for developing electro-mechanical equipments for instructional purposes. This approach is the result of the impact of scientific and technological development during the present century. Hardware approach mechanises the process of teaching so that teachers would be able to deal with more students with less expenditure in educating them. Hardware devices include the following:

(1) Motion pictures

(2) Tape recorders.

(3) Television.

(4) Teaching machines.

(5) Computers.

Software Approach

This uses the principles of psychology for building in the learner a complex repertory of knowledge modifying his behaviour. It has originated from the pioneering work of Skinner and other behaviourists. The programmes which such a technology produces, are often called 'Software'. Software approach is characterised by task analysis, writing precise objectives, selection of appropriate learning strategies, immediate reinforcement of responses and constant evaluation. Newspapers, books, magazines, educational games, flash cards may also form part of software.

The Positive Side

Audio-visual aids or devices or technological media or learning devices are added devices that help the teacher to clarify, establish, co-relate and co-ordinate accurate concepts, interpretations and appreciations and enable him to make learning more concrete, effective, interesting, inspirational, meaningful and vivid. They help in completing the triangular process of learning viz., motivation-clarification-stimulation. The aim of teaching with technological media is 'clearing the channel between the learner and the things that are worth learning'. The basic assumption underlying Audio-visual Aids is that learning—clear understanding—stems from sense experience. The teacher must 'show' as well as 'tell'. Audio-visual aids provide significant gains in informational learning, retention and recall, thinking and reasoning, activity, interest, imagination, better assimilation and personal growth and development. The aids are the stimuli for learning 'why', 'how', 'when' and 'where'. The 'hard to understand principles' are usually made clear by the intelligent use of skilfully designed instructional aids.

Following are the main merits of the instructional aids:

1. They are potent motivators.
2. They lend reality to the classroom teaching and link instruction with real life.

3. They supply a concrete basis for conceptual thinking and hence reduce meaningless word responses of students.
4. They have a high degree of interest for the students as they are interested in things they can see, hear, touch, taste, plan, make, do and try.
5. They supply the necessary basis for developmental learning and hence make learning more permanent.
6. They offer a reality of experience which stimulates self-activity on the part of the students.
7. They develop a continuity of thought; this is especially true of motion pictures.
8. They contribute to increase retentivity as they stimulate the maximum response of the whole organism to the situation in which the learning is done.
9. They help in making right types of images which facilitate learning.
10. They contribute experiences not easily secured by other materials and contribute to the efficiency, depth and variety of learning. These aids focus attention, arouse interest, add to information, motivate to action and stimulate mental and physical activity.
11. New technological media like the T.V. and radio help in spreading education in remote areas.
12. They save time and make learning solid and durable.

Best Motivators. They are the best motivators. The students work with more interest and zeal. They are more attentive.

Fundamental to Verbal Instruction. They help to reduce verbalism which is a major weakness in our school. They convey the same meaning as words mean. They give clear concepts and thus help to brine accuracy in learning.

Clear Images. Clear images are formed when we see, hear, touch, taste and smell as our experiences are direct, concrete and more or less permanent. Learning through the senses becomes the most natural and consequently the easiest.

Vicarious Experience. It is beyond doubt that the first-hand experience is the best type of educative experience. But it is neither practicable nor desirable to provide such experience to pupils. Substituted experiences may be provided under such conditions. There are many inaccessible objects and phenomena. For example, it is not possible for the pupils living in India to see the person of Eskimo. Similarly, it is not possible for an average man to climb the Mount Everest. There are innumerable such things to which it is not possible to have direct access. So, in all such cases, these aids help us.

Variety. Mere chalking and talking do not help. Audio-visual aids give variety and provide different tools in the hands of the teacher.

Freedom. When audio-visual aids are employed, there is great scope for children to move about, talk, laugh and comment upon. Under such an atmosphere the students work because they want to work and not because the teacher wants them to work.

Opportunities to Handle and Manipulate. Many visual aids offer opportunities to students to handle and manipulate things.

Teaching Aids

While all these aids are becoming more and more popular day by day, there are still some problems to be faced and solved. These are:

Apathy of the Teachers. The teachers are yet to be convinced that teaching with words alone is very tedious, wasteful and ineffective.

Indifference of Students. The judicious use of aids arouses interest but when used without a definite purpose they lose their significance and importance.

Ineffectiveness of the Aids. Due to the absence of proper planning and the lethargy of the teacher and without proper preparation, correct presentation, appropriate application and discussion and the essential follow-up work, the aids have not proved their full usefulness. A film like a good lesson has various steps—Preparation, Presentation, Application and Discussion.

Projected and Non-Projected Aids

Projected Aids		*Non-Projected Aids*			
Projected Aids	***Graphic Aids***	***Display Boards***	***3-Dimensional Aids***	***Audio Aids***	***Activity Aids***
1. Films	1. Cartoons	Blackboard	Diagrams	Radio	1. Computer-Assisted Instruction
2. Filmstrips	2. Charts	Bulletin	Models	Recordings	2. Demonstrations
3. Opaque Projection	3. Comics	Flannel Board	Mock-ups	Television	3. Dramatics
4. Overhead Projection	4. Diagrams	Magnetic Board	Objects		4. Experimentation
5. Slides	5. Flash Cards	Peg Board	Puppets		5. Field Trips
	6. Graphs	Specimens			6. Programmed Instruction
	7. Maps				7. Teaching Machines
	8. Photographs				
	9. Pictures				
	10. Posters				

Classification of Audio-Visual Aids

Audio Materials	*Visual Materials*	*Audio-visual Materials*
(1) Language laboratories	(1) Bulletin boards	(1) Demonstrations
(2) Radio	(2) Chalk boards	(2) Films
(3) Sound distribution system sets	(3) Charts with recorded sound	(3) Printed materials
(4) Tape and disco recordings	(4) Drawings etc.	(4) Sound filmstrips
	(5) Exhibits	(5) Study trips
	(6) Filmstrips	(6) Television
	(7) Flash cards	(7) Videotapes
	(8) Flannel boards	
	(9) Flip books	
	(10) Illustrated books	
	(11) Magnetic boards	
	(12) Maps	
	(13) Models	
	(14) Pictures	
	(15) Posters	
	(16) Photographs	
	(17) Self-instructional	
	(18) Silent films	
	(19) Slides	

Financial Hurdles. The Central and State Governments have set up Boards of Audio-Visual Education and have chalked out interesting programmes for the popularization of teaching aids but the lack of finances is not enabling them to do their best.

Absence of Electricity. Most of the Projectors cannot work without the electric current.

Lack of Facilities for Training. More and more training colleges or specialised agencies should be opened to train teachers and workers in the use and usefulness of the these aids.

Co-ordination between Centre and States. Good film libraries, museums of Audio-visual education, fixed and mobile exhibitions and educational 'melas' should be organised both by Centre and the States.

Language Difficulty. Most films are in English. We should have these in Hindi and other important Indian languages.

Not Catering for Local Needs. No attention is paid in the production of Audio-visual aids to the sociological, psychological and pedagogical factors.

Improper Selection of Films. Films are not selected according to the classroom needs. Today, the problem is not whether visual aids should have a place in education. Their place has been recognised long ago. The problem, now, is that of extending the benefits of these aids to all teachers and all children. The future can be bright if there is proper planning on the part of the Government and co-ordination between producers, teachers and students. Useful and effective aids can be produced after getting the reaction of the audience and doing research work in the field. A great deal is being done already but a lot more still remains to be done.

The Blackboard

Significance of Blackboard. Blackboard is a unique device which in spite of newer and better devices in vogue, is irreplacable as well as indispensable. It is the oldest and the best friend of a teacher. It is a mirror through which students visualise all about the teacher's mind, his way of explaining, illustrating and teaching as a whole. It is the cheapest and the most valuable teaching device and continues to be the *'sine qua non'* of our educational system. It is the most universally used aid. Writing on sand and clay was the ancient form of blackboard writing.

The use of blackboard in class teaching creates an informal atmosphere and motivates learning. Teaching no longer confines to any one instructional device. It is a help to 'planning', to 'crystallizing' main points and to 'summarising' and 'reviewing' results. Blackboard being a simple means of dealing with the whole class as a unit, it is extensively used during the course of a lesson.

Uses of the Blackboard. Following are the uses:

1. The teacher can illustrate his lesson on the blackboard and draw the attention of the class to salient features in the lesson.
2. The lesson can be phased and summarized in the right manner. Abstract statement can be clarified in the exposition stage and a summary containing important points can be given in the recapitulatory stage.
3. Questions and problems when planning class work or approaching a new subject can be listed by the teacher on the blackboard.
4. Pupils' interest in class work can be stimulated by blackboard writings and drawings.
5. It can be put to wide and varied uses. A teacher can use it for graphs, maps, graphic statistics, sketches and various types of drawings.
6. It provides a lot of space for decorative and creative work.
7. The teacher can erase writings and drawings and start afresh.
8. It helps the "teacher to focus the attention of his students on the lesson. It takes heed of varying capacities and rates of grasp of the students.
9. A teacher can review the whole lesson for the benefit of the class with the help of the blackboard.

Types of Blackboards

Fixed Blackboard. Fixed in the wall facing the class and normally made of wood or concrete cement.

Blackboard on Easel. A portable and adjustable blackboard put on a wooden easel can be taken out of the classroom while taking classes in the open.

Roller Blackboard. Made of thick canvas wrapped on a roller mostly used for teaching higher classes.

Graphic Board. It has graphic lines and is used for teaching mathematics, science and statistics.

Magna Board. A board which enables teachers to make three dimensional demonstrations with objects on a vertical surface. Small magnets are used to hold suitable objects fixed wherever they are put on this vertical surface.

Chalk Boards of Different Types

1. Paint-coated pressed wood.
2. Dull finished plastic surface.
3. Vitreous-coated steel surface.
4. Ground glass board.

Chalk Boards of Different Colours and Colour Chalks

Colour of the Blackboard	*Colour of the Chalk*
1. Green chalk board	White or Yellow chalk
2. Grey board	Yellow
3. Red chalk board	Green, Yellow
4. Orange chalk board	Blue or light Green
5. Yellow chalk board	Blue
6. Rose chalk board	Purple, dark Blue
7. Black chalk board	Any colour

Effective Use of Blackboard. Following points may be kept in view while using the blackboard:

1. Blackboard should be kept clean so that writing on it could be easily read by the students from all parts of the room.
2. Writing on the blackboard should be legible.
3. Letters and drawings should be large enough to be seen from all parts of the room.
4. Writing should be started from the top left corner.
5. Writing should be in straight rows.
6. Extreme lower corner of the blackboard should not be made use of as writing on it cannot be seen easily.
7. Material on the blackboard should not be covered by standing in front of it.
8. Only salient points of the subject-matter should be written on the blackboard.
9. Diagrammatic visual presentation involving many processes should be prepared before the beginning of the lesson.
10. It should be ensured that blackboard is well lighted by natural or artificial means.
11. Everything needed for the blackboard should be got together before the class begins i.e., collection of chalk, rulers, T. Square, Compass, Projector etc.
12. While writing on the blackboard, the teacher should ensure that the class is attentive.
13. Duster and not hand or handkerchief should be used in cleaning the blackboard.
14. Occasionally students may be asked to write or draw diagram on the blackboard.
15. Teachers should develop the ability to draw freely on the black-board. The map or chart or diagram that grows

before the very eyes of the students is much more useful and valuable than a well finished map, chart or diagram.

16. It should be ensured that the blackboard is periodically serviced.

The Charts. A chart is a combination of pictorial, graphic, numerical or vertical material which presents a clear visual summary. The most commonly used types of charts include outline charts, tabular charts, flow charts and organisation charts. Other types of charts are technical diagrams and process diagrams. Flip charts and flow charts are also being used. Readymade charts are available for use in teaching in almost all areas in all subjects. But charts prepared by a teacher himself incorporating his own ideas and lines of approach of the specific topic are more useful.

Purposes of Charts. Charts serve the following purposes:

1. For showing relationship by means of facts, figures and statistics.
2. For presenting material symbolically.
3. For summarising information.
4. For showing continuity in process.
5. For presenting abstract ideas in visual form.
6. For showing development of structure.
7. For creating problems and stimulating thinking.
8. For encouraging utilisation of other media of communication.
9. For motivating the students.

Effective Use of Charts

1. Teacher-made charts should be preferred.
2. Students should be involved in the preparation of charts.
3. Charts should be so large that every detail depicted should be visible to every pupil in the class wherever he is sitting.

4. Charts should display information only about one specific area in a subject.
5. A chart should not contain too much written material.
6. A chart should not contain too many details.
7. A chart should give a neat appearance.
8. When a chart is to be used in the classroom, the teacher should make sure that there is provision for hanging the chart at advantage point.
9. The teacher should have a pointer to point out specific factors in the chart.
10. Straight pins, staples, pegboard clips, gummed hangers, paper-clips, folded making tapes may all be used for fastening charts without damaging them.
11. Charts should be carefully stored and preserved for use in future.

Types of Charts. The following is a list of basic types of charts in terms of arrangements and the kinds of ideas which they may express:

1. The narrative chart, an extended left-to-right arrangement of facts and ideas for expressing: (a) The events in a process such as shoe making, oil cracking, or the like, (b) The events in the development of a significant issue to its point of resolution or to present status (sometimes a time limit) Example: the events leading to the separation of the Bangla Desh from Pakistan, the events leading to the establishment of the idea that an individual should be free and that he should have a voice in his own government and the events leading to increased regulation of business by government, (c) Technological improvement over a period of years such as improvement in transportation, communication, manufacturing etc.
2. The tabulation chart, a left-to-right, top-to-bottom arrangement of facts and ideas for expression: (a) Numerical

data for making comparisons, (b) Lists of products, mountains, rivers, or the like in selected areas.

3. The cause and effect chart, usually a limited left-to-right arrangement of facts and ideas for expressing: (a) Relationship between standard of living and such factors as economic system, availability of natural resources, level of technological advancement, (b) Relationship between a culture and neighbouring cultures, (c) Relationship between rights and responsibilities, (d) Relationship between a complex of conditions and change or conflict, (e) Relationship between the elected and the electors, (f) Relationship between community workers and the community which supports them.
4. The chain chart, a circular or semicircular arrangement of facts and ideas for expressing: (a) Transitions, such as the transition from raw materials to useful products, (b) Cycles, such as the water cycle.
5. The evolution chart, a left-to-right arrangement of facts and ideas for expressing: (a) Changes in specific items from beginning to date, perhaps with projections into the future. Example: origin of the automobile and its subsequent development, early basic homes and changes in basic homes to date, (b) Change in standard in food consumption, length of work, weak purchasing power of a rupee, or the like.

(Adapted from 'Social Studies Instruction in the Secondary School' by Richard E. Servey).

Map Study

Significance of Map Study. In social studies, the learning of many geographical, historical and economic concepts becomes unreal, inadequate and incomplete without map media. A resourceful teacher by motivating the pupils will turn the fear of map into the genuine love for them. This, however, pre-supposes the invariable uses of maps at every possible opportunity by the teacher in the classroom, and the possession of individual atlases by the pupils. Every student should also know certain elementary aspects of map preparation such as copying, enlarging and reducing, symbolizing, colouring, gardening and preparation of map. Most of the students develop a version to maps because they do not know skills relating to map preparation.

Meaning of Map. A map is an accurate representation plain surface in the form of a diagram drawn to scale, the details of boundaries of continents, countries etc. Geographical details like location of mountains, rivers, altitude of a place, contours of the earth surface and important locations can also be represented accurately with reference to a convenient scale with suitable colour scheme.

Identification of Various Aspects of Maps

1. Understanding and interpreting the key of index.
2. Understanding the lines—boundary lines, lines of communication, lines indicating the rivers, contours, meridians and parallels.
3. Understanding the colours, tints, shadows, symbols in a map or globe.
4. The top of every map is not north, but the direction of northern pole is north.
5. Globe is the only real map. All the flat surface maps are distorted representations of earth in one way or other.
6. Distinction between the various types of maps such as relief, political, distribution maps, etc.
7. Understanding of the position of earth in the universe. Many students suffer from a notion that the earth leans in June towards the Sun northwards and in December southwards and thus the seasons are formed. Earth never dances that way. The student shall understand that the inclination of earth is constant and the leaning effect changes due to its rotation around the sun.

Variety of Maps

1. *Relief maps (regional and the world).* This requires the knowledge of colours, contours, symbols and the other connected ethics of map making.
2. *Historical maps.* Maps in history reveal the changing times, the growth and decline of various kingdoms of man's life. Knowledge of lines of boundaries and other symbols is necessary. Every history map shall contain some important relied aspects also.
3. *Distribution maps.* Generally, the student shall associate with the following types of distribution maps:
    1. Vegetation maps
    2. Population maps
    3. Economic maps
    4. Statistical maps
    5. Dot maps
    6. Pictorial maps
    7. Language, race and other human division maps, etc.
4. *Geographical maps.* Contour maps, weather maps, seismological maps, archaeological maps, rainfall maps, geological maps, etc.

Richard E. Servey gives the uses of maps in social studies as under:

Maps can be used in a wide variety of ways to express many different statements, some of which are listed below:

A. With colour as a basic symbol, maps may be used to express:

1. Land-use patterns
2. Topography
3. Political divisions

4. Political relationship
5. Economic relationship
6. Cultural relationship
7. Religious relationship
8. Population density
9. Climate, or aspects of climate
10. Distribution of resources.

B. Through the use of conventional or invented symbol, maps may be used to express:

1. Any of the ideas listed for colour, but with substitutions of crosshatching or visual textures.
2. Production, total of selected items.
3. Distribution of fauna and flora.
4. Clothing, shelter, and basic foods in various areas, total or selected.
5. Population.
6. Military power.
7. Routes of all kinds.
8. Centres of commerce.
9. Communities of various sizes.
10. Points of historical interest.

C. Three-dimensional maps most adequately express topography and land-use patterns.

D. Rearranged maps (maps in which location and size of nations and continents are distorted to express significant relationships) are particularly good for showing:

1. Political relationships.
2. Economic relationships.
3. Cultural relationships.
4. Religious relationships.

The Globes. Knowledge of map is unreal without the knowledge of globe, the true map. It is the true representative of earth's physical personality.

Need for Globe Study in Social Studies. If social studies is a study of man and his environment globe gives a true idea of the total environment at a glance in a classroom situation. It is through globe a child can understand the concepts of time, space, wind's planetary relations and proportion. Hence, every school shall have globes. Four types of globes may be kept in every school. (1) Political globes, (2) Physical globes, (3) Washable projection globes, (4) Celestial globes.

Atlases. Atlases are of great value in the learning process of social studies. Students should be trained in the use of index and to understand the implications of projections. Every school shall have a big atlas. The Readers Digest "Great Atlas" is one such which may create the pride of atlas possession.

Preparation of Relief Models. Relief Model is a three-dimensional representation of earth's surface. This gives a better idea about the relief aspects to the pupils than the plain surface maps. There are many types of relief maps with many methods of preparation. The following two types of relief maps may be attempted in schools: (1) Relief maps on the ground, and (2) Relief maps on hardboard. Greater the involvement of pupils in these projects better the results.

Incentives. Every school should think of introducing certain incentives to cover up the deficiencies in map study.

1. Awarding scores to the maps drawn by the pupils.
2. Holding best map competitions – classwise.
3. Assigning group projects in map and globe preparation.
4. Supplying atlases in the school library.
5. Providing apparatus and the equipment.
6. Carrying field trips for elementary surveying.

Films for Education

Broadly speaking, a film is a multiple media of communication. It presents facts in a realistic way, dramatizes human relations, arouses emotions and transmits attitudes. It is quite effective as a technique of telling a story. It may be used for the communication of ideas, attitudes and experiences to the masses of people outside the classroom. It is very effective in adult education. An educational film has been described as the greatest teacher because it teaches not only through the brain but through the whole body. It has a very powerful influence on the minds of children and in shaping their personality. The main aim of educational films is to elevate and educate them according to the patterns and principles set by the society. A good educational film should help the students to develop a sense of citizenship. A film on national integration can be prepared to help inculcate ideas of oneness and unity. 'Live and Let Live' can be the theme. A variety of topics—historical, biographical and of current interest can be covered.

The Children's Film Society established in 1955 with the specific aim of undertaking and promoting the production of educational films has been doing good work. The society has set up a National Centre of Films for Children affiliated to the International Centre of Films set up at Brussels under the sponsorship of UNESCO. Some of the important films a Social Studies Teacher can make use are:

1. Scout Camp
2. Guru Bhakti
3. Ganga Ki Lahren
4. Bachon Se Batten
5. Gulab Ka Phool
6. Ekata
7. 26 January
8. Char Dost
9. Jaldeep.

Major sources of Educational Films. **These sources are:**

1. **Children's Film Society, New Delhi.**
2. **Central Film Library, National Institute of Audio-visual Education, Indraprastha Estate, New Delhi.**
3. **British Council in India, Rafi Marg, New Delhi.**
4. **Burmah Shell Film Library, New Delhi.**
5. **Ministry of Information and Broadcasting, Parliament Street, New Delhi.**
6. **Indian National Commission for Cooperation with UNESCO, Ministry of Human Resources Development, Department of Education, Government of India, Shastri Bhawan, New Delhi.**
7. **United Nations Information Centre, New Delhi.**

Broadcasting for Education

The potential of the radio as an instructional aid is being recognised more and more all over the world. R.G. Rejnolds writes, "Radio is the most significant medium for education in its broadest sense that has been introduced since the turn of the century. As a supplement to classroom teaching, its possibilities are almost unlimited. Its teaching possibilities are not confined to the five or six hours of the school day. It is available from early morning till long after midnight. But utilising the rich educational and cultural offerings of the radio, children and adults in communities, however remote, have access to the best of the world's stores of knowledge and art. Some day its use as an educational instrument will be as common place as textbooks and blackboards."

Frederic Wittis has rightly remarked, "I like to think of education by radio as a timely, vital and dramatic thing; a system of learning on acquiring more information; a means of widening one's horizons or enriching one's life and breaking down prejudices through inspiration and not perspiration; an education by desire and not by discipline; a pattern of swiftly changing pictures, events with keen interpretations, not statistics and formula; a moving panorama of the world in which we live right now, while we are living in it not a dreary drill of textbooks and tests. In short, I feel that one of broadcastings' most helpful contributions to education and one of its real responsibilities to itself and its listeners is the popularising of education itself."

Role of Electronic Media

Availability of Direct Stimuli. Learning can be accomplished more effectively by televised instruction than by conventional methods. Proper use of television's illustrative technique can provide a more direct impact than a conventional lecture or text-book. This is accomplished through the direct pictorial interpretation of fact or theory, utilising static or dynamic visualisations. Pictures provide stronger and more direct stimuli to personal thought and understanding than to words.

Consistency in Teaching-learning. Communication by speech is a learned skill, seeing and the thought stimuli provoked by sign begin shortly after birth and comprise the base of experience on which sensory reaction and knowledge are built. Through the use of visual media, consistency is built up into the instructional system and thus it is more reliable for the student.

Economically viable. Utilisation of video-assisted learning systems and internal video feedback techniques hold promise for meeting the pressure of information requests, while at the same time maintaining favourable cost benefit ratios especially if we allowed the use of INSAT.

Services of Super Teacher. Through television the 'Super lecturer' or 'Master teacher' is available at a number of places simultaneously without the expense of time and toil for travel.

Education of a Greater Number. Television is capable of providing the best possible instructions for the greater number of students.

Multiplication and Magnification. Television is an instructional tool that makes possible multiplication and magnification of distance and time factors and the storage of accomplished and tested instruction. Multiplication implies the exact reproduction of an instructive situation with transmission to an unlimited number of students, for example, the magnification and distribution of 'Live' surgical techniques and the magnification of minute biological reactions, specially in circumstances where normal observation would be difficult.

Television, a complex tool for the possible development of excellent instruction, can be effective only if properly used by good craftsmen. The key to efficient, inspirational and practical educational television is cooperation among a progressive administration, a dedicated and sincere faculty and an educationally aware and technically knowledgeable staff. No other medium of instruction relies as heavily for quality on the interaction and interdependence of the team of experts: the manager, the educator, the artist and a number of other persons to be selected as much as for their ability to cooperate with others as for their competence in their respective fields.

It is of great importance that TV instructors are auditioned. The instructors appearing on the television must be capable of accepting and assimilating criticism which they would not ordinarily receive in the classroom.

The relationship between the instructor and the production expert determines the quality of presentations. The instructional expert, normally a qualified academician, too often tends to regard the production experts as the 'technician' without any academic stature. This tendency should be curbed before any worthwhile production can take place.

Television is a visual method and to attempt the production of a good instructional programme without a versatile artist is to attempt to produce dairy products without the source of milk.

Organization of the total effort should include, besides instruction and production specialists, an expert in programme system analysis whose responsibility would be to analyse the educational needs of the educational institutions and to reco-mmend the most efficient use of the medium.

An educational psychologist should be an integral member of the team for testing and evaluating the result of the instructional methods as well as for advising on methods to be employed. A great deal of research is necessary to theorise E.T.V's impact on learning processes.

Like books, films, blackboards, and laboratory equipments and maps, it also can serve the teacher to communicate to the student. But it is a very sophisticated 'monster' aid and requires careful preparation for use and higher prerequisite for understanding. Apart from this the computer does some of the teachers' work.

Computer-assisted instruction has two major levels of impact on the teacher. First, the teachers' ability to work in an efficient way is increased, because the strenuous works of correcting work books, comparing exercises, maps etc., can be given to the computer. Second, the computer makes the teacher to be more critical and active, because the work is synthesised and regulated by the computer.

To the student it gives immense opportunities for learning more and to rationalise the thinking. The learning will become sharp and not speculative. The serious student involved with facts, ideas and logics, will find fast sequences in learning. The most important factor is that the computer is a 'flexible' teacher not like 'rigid' human teacher. There, with a level of flexibility, the computer will give alternatives to the learner so that depending upon learning capacity and imaginative power, different options are available to the student.

Computer-oriented instruction has more application in Geography. Particularly maps and aerial photographs, weather changes can be easily taught through the computer using simulation techniques. Synthesization and updating information of economic facts can be readily achieved by the computer.

QUESTIONS

1. What do you understand by audio-visual aids? How are they useful in the teaching-learning process?
2. Explain the importance of audio-visual aids in the teaching of Social Studies.
3. Explain any three aids that may profitably be used by the teacher of Social Studies in different classes.
4. Discuss the importance of excursion in the teaching of Social Studies.
5. State the importance of pictures in Social Studies. What type of pictures can be useful?
6. "Writing on the blackboard is an art". Elucidate this statement.
7. What is the importance of the following aids in the teaching of Social Studies? What precautions should be taken in their use?
   (a) Radio
   (b) Film
   (c) Television.

12

Preparation of Curriculum

Organisation of the subject matter for different stages and classes in social studies is an important problem. It has to be organised in such a way as it is taught effectively and in a coherent way. It is, therefore, very essential that organisation of the subject matter must be comprehensive and continuous. Generally, three approaches are adopted for organising the subject matter in social studies. They are:

1. Unit Approach.
2. Concentric Approach.
3. Topical Approach.

Unit Systems

The unit approach is based on the growing acceptance of the Gestalt-Organismic – Field Theories of learning which emphasise the 'wholeness' nature of learning. This approach is contrary to the older atomistic conception of learning according to which learning was a matter of adding one small item of knowledge to another bit by bit. The new approach is based upon the assumption that effective learning takes place in an environment in which the goals are clearly perceived and every phase of the operational procedure is viewed as a relational part of the total learning situation. The underlying assumption is that the learner reacts to the situation as a whole and not to parts in isolation.

Few terms in modern educational usage have been more extensively used with as much disagreement as to meaning as has the term 'Unit'.

According to Bossing, "A Unit consists of comprehensive services of related and meaningful activities so developed as to achieve pupil purposes, provide significant educational experiences, and result in appropriate behavioural changes."

The Dictionary of Education defines a unit as "an organisation of varied activities, experiences and types, learning around a central problem or purpose, developed cooperatively by a group of pupils under teacher leadership, involves planning, execution of plans and evaluation of results."

James High defines unit approach in 'Teaching Secondary School Social Studies' as, "It is more than a mere technique and is often called the unit approach rather than method. The primary requisite is a point of view that will allow the imaginative instructor to arrange and organize all available and pertinent information around a nuclear idea and then select and provide references, aids and activities that will enable his students to master the basic material."

H.C. Morrison has explained the 'Unit Method' in detail in his book 'The Practice of Teaching in Secondary School' published in 1926. The unit method is very popular and frequently used in the USA.

According to Morrison, 'Unit is a comprehensive and significant aspect of the environment of an organised science and art'.

According to Wesley, 'Unit is an organized body of information and experience designed to effect significant outcomes of the learner'.

Jarolimek John defines unit "as a means of organising materials for instructional purposes which utilises significant subject matter content, involves pupils in learning activities through active participation intellectually and physically and modifies the pupil's behaviour to the extent that he is able to cope with new problems and situations more competently."

Richard Survey has pointed out in Social Studies Instruction in Elementary School as, "A teaching unit in social studies is a comprehensive instructional plan specifying the 'what', the 'how' and 'when' of teaching a big idea."

According to East S. Johnson, "Unit is a segment of experience which is cut out for study, within it, i.e. method employed. It is my understanding that every unit is a 'project'. It is a project in the sense that one projects enquiry into it. Furthermore, every unit has a topic, theme or careful tendency or whatever name you choose to call it, otherwise it could have no unity. Every unit is a 'contract' in the sense that the student enters upon a contract or obligation to study how the things which it contains are related, how they work, how cause and effect are identified and related and how a conclusion is reached. Every unit is also a 'problem,' a problem of significance and meaning in some unknown or less than thoroughly known phase of human experience."

Hanna, Hageman and Potter state, "A unit can be defined as a purposeful learning experience focused upon behaviour of the learner and enable him to adjust to a life situation more effectively.

Main Features

A unit is a purposeful learning activity or experience.

A unit is around a central problem.

A unit has a significant content.

A unit is comprehensive enough to have scope and unity.

A unit is developed cooperatively by a group of pupils.

A unit is developed under the guidance of the teacher.

A unit involves pupils in learning intellectually and physically.

A unit modifies the pupil's behaviour to the extent that he is able to cope with new problems and situations more competently.

A unit emerges out of the pupil's experience.

A unit provides opportunities for creative experiences.

A unit is flexible and provides opportunities in adopting instruction to individual differences of children.

A unit is a logical useful division.

A unit is evolutionary or functional.

Factors at Work

A good teaching unit has nine elements but the sequence of those elements is not fixed. Following sequence is generally followed:

Overview. This implies the consideration of the needs of the students while formulating the objectives of teaching unit.

Inventory or Background. This element is concerned with exploring the entering behaviour of the students. The teacher is required to establish the behaviour repertoire by linking the new knowledge with the previous knowledge of the students.

Presentation. This element is concerned with providing new experiences to the learners. It includes an analysis and presentation of the elements of teaching units in a logical sequence so that they are helpful to the students. With a view to encourage students' participation in teaching, question-answer strategy is employed.

Motivation. This element of the teaching unit is concerned with the creation of motivational situations to facilitate learning.

Summarization. This element of the unit is concerned with providing a summary of the unit.

Drill. This element provides an opportunity to the students for Drill or practice which enables them to retain longer what is learnt.

Review. This implies giving the salient features of the unit orally.

Organisation. This element involves giving assignments to the students to organise their learning experiences of their own.

Evaluation. This element of the teaching unit consists of ascertaining how far the teacher has been successful in achieving the objectives of the lesson, i.e. to what extent students have grasped the content and developed meaningful behaviour.

A good teaching unit possesses the following characteristics:

A teaching unit consists of meaningful elements.

A teaching unit arranges all elements in such a manner as the students can understand the whole.

A teaching unit provides the starting point of teaching activities.

A teaching unit provides the ending point of activities.

A teaching unit has a broad and comprehensive structure.

A teaching unit has a practical form rather than theoretical.

A teaching unit provides for various activities so as to create appropriate learning structures by the teacher.

A teaching unit provides for the interaction of the teacher-taught.

A teaching unit includes appropriate techniques of reinforcement.

A teaching unit presents the basis for evaluating the performance of the students.

A teaching unit reveals the forms of teaching activities and selects appropriate teaching strategies, tactics and teaching aids.

A teaching unit is economical from the point of view of time and energy.

A teaching unit achieves the learning objectives.

The Categorisation

Units may be classified into four types:

1. Subject-matter Units
2. Experience Units
3. The Adaptive Units or Units of Adaptation
4. The Resource "Units

Subject-matter Units. In these units emphasis is more on the subject-matter than the learner. The wholeness or integration is achieved through large bodies of informationor subject-matter to be acquired or achieved. It has three types as follows:

The Topics Unit. It is like the traditional topical organisation of the subject-matter. It differs from that only in degree. It is not recommended by modern educators as teachers in this approach are apt to include too much or too little and thereby confuse the students.

The Generalization Unit. This is based on the understanding of some principle. For example a principle of Utility could be selected in economics as the central factor.

The Environment Unit. This was developed by Morrison of University ' of Chicago and is, therefore, also known as the Morrison Unit. Morrison defined it as "A comprehensive and significant aspect of the environment, of an organised science, of an art or of conduct, which when learned results in adaptation in personality." An environmental unit is organised around an important aspect of the environment or culture!

Experience Units. These are based upon the experiences of the learner on certain life situations or problem situations. The learner fully reacts to situation he is confronted with. The learner's needs, purposes and interests determine these experiences. Need, purpose or interest is the binding and motivating force. This results in greater effort, knowledge and understanding on the part of the learner. Experience unit is of three types as: (a) Student-interest unit, (b) Student-purpose unit, (c) Student-need unit. An important limitation of the student interest is that all areas of curriculum cannot be planned on this basis. The learner may not be interested in all the areas of the curriculum. Student-purpose and student-need units cannot be planned in advance. They have to be continuously planned as they develop.

The Adaptive Units. In the words of Jones of the University of Pennsylvania who is the originator of this unit, "a unit consists of a group or chain of planned co-ordinated activities undertaken by the learner in order to obtain control over a type of life situation." The central point in the adaptive unit is that it is the 'general ability' that should be developed to meet specific life situations, resulting in greater adjustment or adaptation or integration of the individual. The development of acquisition of skills, habits, knowledge, each as a separate aspect of learning does not result in unification or integration of the individual.

The Resource Units. A resource unit like the 'subject matter type' or of the 'experience type' is not planned for a specific group of pupils in a particular school and for a definite time. It is concerned with a broader field and, in fact, it serves as a guide for teachers working at different places. This unit is generally built by a group of teachers who operate in a workshop guided by specialists and helped by the extensive library facilities. Once built up, ' it is mimeographed and made available to other teachers of the concerned subject. A resource unit serves as a teacher's guide in planning his programme. It includes: (i) Statement of objectives concerning the theme, (ii) Problem, (iii) The approach or initiation, (iv) content of subject matter basic to the area of study, (v) Direct and related experiences, (vi) Organising and summarising experiences, (vii) Evaluation of learnings, (viii) A collection of instructional resources.

System and Outcome

The centre of interest usually offers an opportunity to cover a considerably wide area. For instance, a child in the first class, is interested in knowing more and more about his own school. Obviously 'school' is his centre of interest. Therefore, for him, 'school' may be a suitable unit of work. The topic provides both intellectual and manual work. Also, it offers opportunities for him to work individually and in co-operation with his class-mates. This unit of work is broken up into a few sub-units, each covering an important aspect of the main problem or a topic, in which a child is profoundly interested. Thus the unit can be conveniently broken up into sub-units such as (a) The School is our Home, (b) How do we come to School? (c) Annual Day of the School, and (d) To be a good boy or a girl at Home and School.

In other words, a unified course in Social Studies consists of a series of problems or units of study, drawn from the major areas of the daily living. Information from all subjects contributes to the solution of the problem. It thus cuts across the subject boundaries and presents a content in a composite and united form, centred around children's typical interests.

The choice of the unit of study or of unit work is based on the following criteria:

(a) The unit is related to the current needs and problems of the society.

(b) It is appropriate to the physical and mental development of the children, their needs and interests at the particular age level.

(c) It is conducive to achieve life-like, practical and creative learning. The organisation of the subject of Social Studies into a series of a unit of work offers the best transition from a more verbal learning of a practical approach. The unit of work offers many opportunities for learning through activity and provides for constant correlation with the physical, social and cultural environment, and even with crafts, wherever possible. A unit of work, moreover, is realistic and functional in nature.

Chain of Tasks

The sequence of the Social Studies programme in the syllabus is based on the studies of child growth and development. These suggest that children should first deal with direct experience and with the simpler aspects of their own environment. Then, they are prepared to progress gradually, to its more remote and complex aspects.

Another pedagogical consideration in determining the grade-placement of various units of work, is to group the units of work for each grade, so as to develop a central theme, or a big idea, throughout the year. Thus an attempt is made to develop, also, the grade-themes for each grade or class.

The sequence of the grade-themes, again is based on the principle of widening children's mental horizon, gradually, from the immediate to the remote and from the simple to the complex aspects of our living. In fact, an attempt is made to fit every unit in a sequence both horizontal and vertical.

For instance, transport is one of the major areas of our daily living. The problems listed under this are (a) How do we come to school? (b) How do people travel in town and village? (c) Avoiding road accidents, (d) Undertaking a rail journey, (e) How do goods come from abroad? and (f) The age of aeroplanes or a shrinking world.

The units, in the order they are stated, represent a vertical sequence from grade to grade. They are in conformity with the pedagogical principles as such 'from immediate to remote and 'from simple to complex'.

Concentric Approach

This is based on the psychological principle that children come to know things in the first instance as 'wholes' and gradually learn to analyse them. The subject matter in social studies at each succeeding stage gradually increases in difficulty but the developing and growing child seems to be ready for comprehending each new aspect. The approach provides for adequate repetition for fixing events. This approach resolves, to some extent, the problem of adaption of the teaching material to the age and understanding of the student. In the first year, the review of the entire subject-matter is very sketchy, every subsequent year means the provision of greater detail. In the initial states, thinking is at a simpler level. As the pupil advances in age and understanding he develops his capacity of thinking in abstract terms and greater detail. The learning sequence progresses from the simple to the more detailed sequence.

Merits

1. It proceeds from 'simple to complex' and 'whole to parts'.
2. It arouses interest and revision becomes easy.
3. It follows a simpler path.
4. It covers the course during the course of a few years.
5. It takes into consideration the mental growth of the child.

Demerits

1. Repetition is sometimes cumbersome. Some facts are repeated again and again.
2. The presentation lacks novelty and freshness. A sense of boredom and dullness is inherent as the children go through the whole course more than once.
3. This approach makes it difficult to develop time and space sense in the pupils.
4. A passing reference to the topic is not helpful in understanding the complex problem.
5. Very capable teachers are needed for following this approach.

Topical Approach

Topical approach implies the revolving of the contents of social studies around a series of topics connected together. Topics of study suitable for the age, ability and interests of students make up the entire syllabus. These topics are also called 'linked' lessons.

Each topic stands by itself. According to the topical approach, particular topics are taken as the central theme of work in social sciences.

This approach takes different forms. The teacher may announce a topic. The students tell what they know about the topic, ask question, raise doubts and take part in lively discussions. The teacher notes down the questions which the students are not able to answer.

The teacher notes the questions, selects the questions according to the mental growth of the students and answers are provided by the students and the teacher in a cooperative way. Learning takes place spontaneously as the students are motivated.

A teacher may introduce the topic with the assistance of a material aid. Topics can be picked up from daily routine, life situations and environment.

Merits. Topical approach has the following merits:

1. Integrated knowledge is imparted to the pupils.
2. Learning is related to life and environment.
3. Pupil's interest and motivation remain aroused.
4. Correlation of different subjects takes place.
5. The approach helps the pupils to understand the facts in their development setting.
6. The approach can be adopted according to the age, ability and aptitude of the children.

Demerits. Limitations of this approach are as follows:

1. Approach is rather difficult to be adopted.
2. This approach pre-supposes good library facilities.
3. This approach requires very competent resourceful teachers.
4. Appropriate instructional materials are not readily available.

Many a Method

The Education Commission, 1964-66 observed, "The social studies syllabus may be organized in different ways, and both the integrated approach which seeks to combine the knowledge and skills provided by the separate subjects of history, geography, economics and civics, and the traditional method according to which these subjects are treated as separate disciplines, have their own place in a balanced school curriculum. "At the lower primary stage, the integrated approach is desirable. Instead of giving the pupils miscellaneous and unrelated bits of information in history, geography and civics, it is far better to provide a coordinated programme of social studies centering round the study of man and his environment. In the upper classes of the primary school, the content of social studies may still be organised as an integral whole in connection with the treatment of certain topics, but the pupils should be gradually introduced to an appreciation of history, geography and civics as separate subjects. In the secondary school, these subjects will be studied as separate disciplines and form the basis of specialised studies in social sciences at the higher secondary stage."

QUESTIONS

1. Explain briefly the approaches to the organisation of curriculum in Social Studies.
2. Elucidate the merits and limitations of unit approach to the teaching of Social Studies.

13

Selection of Books

Curriculum is the pivot and the hub around which all activities in the school revolve. It is the sum-total of experiences that the child receives in and outside the classroom through the study of different subjects, through community relationships, through library, workshops, sports and games etc. It is a means of enabling the child to adjust himself to his environment. It is the 'warp and woof' of the process of education.

Curriculum in Social Studies is that part of the school curriculum which includes subject matter and activities that enable the child to acquire an understanding of human relationships, knowledge of the environment, dedication to the basic principles and values of the society and a commitment to participate in the process through which the society is maintained and improved.

Main Syllabus

Social Studies is to serve as core-curriculum which is evolved as a part of efforts of the forward looking educators to develop a more functional and significant programme of general education for all young children. It is intended to provide the 'irreducible minimum' regarded as necessary to everyone to be able to understand the modern society and live effectively in it is intended to equip the student with the fundamental and foundational knowledge for social living. It is similar for every one whatever future plan in life the student chooses to take. The primary purpose of the core-curriculum is to let a person become 'a good human being' first and good artist, doctor, engineer, technician, scientist etc. afterwards.

Social Studies as core-curriculum aims at enabling a child not only to adjust himself but also to improve his social, cultural and economic environment in active cooperation with others.

Social studies curriculum may be considered as a tool in the hands of the artist (social studies teacher) to mould his material (the pupil) in accordance with the nature of the Society and the Child in his studio (the school).

Old Courses

It was considered as a bundle of subjects.

New Courses

This includes the following:

Reading. Books, magazines, pamphlets, newspapers, maps, charts graphs etc.

Writing. Essays, articles, reports, notes, summaries etc.

Seeing. Pictures, paintings, photographs, drawings, filmstrips, slides, dramatics, processes, sceneries.

Listening. Stories, lectures, conversations, discussions, speeches etc.

Talking. Asking and answering questions, participating in debates, conversations etc.

Creating. Drawings, paintings, clay modelling etc.

Playing. Dramatics, rhythm, games, dances.

Observing. Working of civic bodies, village panchayats, state and national assemblies.

Practising. Map drawings, chart making, graph preparing, civic skills, farm operations, tools etc.

Problem Solving. Reflecting, experimenting, generalisations, Concluding etc.

Human Relationships. Student-teacher, student-head, student-student, teacher-teacher, teacher-head, teacher-community, student-community—which make up the Social climate. A Social Studies Curriculum must regard the child as an individual and growing by his own activity, living in his own environment and preparing himself for adult life, not by imitating the adult but by living as fully as possible in the environment.

Syllabus for Schools

The elementary course in Social Studies should aim at achieving the following general objectives:

1. It should encourage students to explore, and observe systematically their social and cultural environment.
2. It should help school children to understand the evolution of the community around them. This may be done by tracing mainly the different forces and influences that were, and are still, at work.
3. It should invite pupils to find out and collect for themselves more and more relevant facts about the different problems that confront them. This should serve as a basis on which they could form, as they grow, an objective judgement on various issues which arise in their daily lives.
4. It should provide the young with numerous opportunities for group work as a part of their learning process. This may include activities such as discussing and solving their problems collectively, and also, planning

and executing different projects, in a democratic atmosphere. All this should result in giving them enough practice in discipline and cooperation, that are implied in self-government.

5. It should kindle among the growing citizens of tomorrow a passion to truth, and social justice. The social justice should, however, also cover respect for every individual—his views, worth and contribution.
6. It should make children conscious of their rights and duties in a democratic society, and encourage them to undertake responsibilities. Its purpose is to enable them to contribute their best to the well-being of the society as a whole.
7. It should develop, among the school children, the spirit of intergroup and inter-communal understanding and harmony. This should lead to the appreciation of the underlying unity of our culture, or a way of our life, in all its diversity.
8. It should foster a sense of true patriotism in every child. The concept of patriotism, however, should include as pointed out in the Secondary Education Commission Report; (a) a sincere appreciation of the social and cultural achievements of our country as a whole—both in the past and at present; (b) a readiness to recognise our weaknesses frankly, and to work for their eradication; and (c) an earnest resolve to serve the country to the best of one's ability, harmonising and subordinating individual interest to broader national considerations.
9. It should lead the students to appreciate the contributions of different cultures, groups of individuals, which have helped the advancement of our present day civilization on a global scale. The purpose of it is to impress upon the growing citizens of tomorrow that patriotism needs to be supplemented by a lively realisa-

tion of the fact that we are all members of 'One World' and must be prepared to discharge the responsibilities of promoting international understanding, cooperation and peace.

The National Council of Educational Research and Training (NCERT) has outlined the need for the inclusion of Social Sciences (NCERT has not used the term Social Studies) in these words. The study of Social Sciences as component of general education is of critical importance in facilitating the learner's growth into a well informed and responsible citizen. It should aim at developing in him/her an understanding of his/her physical and social environments, both immediate and remote, in terms of time and space, and an appreciation of the cultural heritage of India and various cultures of the world. The study of the present physical and social environment should help him/her in developing an understanding of the interaction of man with his physical and social environment and with the institutions—social, economic and political—through which human beings interrelate with one another and function in the society. The study of social sciences should also aim at enabling him to see the present in the perspective of past developments.

Similar to the study of physical and natural environment in science education, the study of social environment in social sciences should have three aspects, namely, learning about the social environment, learning through the social environment and learning for the social environment. This would mean that a pupil will learn, for example, about the social customs, cultural heritage, history of society etc. through observation, exploration and scientific study of social phenomena and events, and will thereby develop genuine interest in, and an urge for, preservation of what is good in our culture and improvement of existing socio-economic cultural set-up.

Social sciences is perhaps the singular curricular area which can prove to be the most effective tool for providing education in the context of all the core components indicated in the NPE-86. Special care should, hence, be taken in designing the curriculum in social sciences so as not to overlook any of the core components.

Initial Level

Although pre-primary education naturally does not deal with the study of social sciences, social development of the child is a major objective to be achieved at this stage of education. To attain this objective, a variety of activities and programmes are directed at providing ample opportunities for a child to interact with other children and with his physical and natural environment. Education at this stage aims at, along with other things, developing in the child desirable social attitudes and manners which would encourage him for healthy social participation and sensitize him to rights and privileges of others. The child is encouraged for independence, dependability and self-expression.

Secondary Level

In Grades I and II, the child should be introduced to the environment as a whole without making any clear-cut distinction between natural and social elements that go into its making. It should be called environmental studies. In Grades III-V, while the environmental focus should continue, the physical and social aspects of the environment should be introduced into social studies as a broad and composite area of study, parallel to general science. The social studies at this stage should widen the child's mental horizon from his/her home, school and neighborhood to the state, country and the world. Stories and narratives about major aspects of our cultural heritage and great personalities, events and developments that have acted as major influences in shaping the life of man in India and elsewhere may also be a part of the curriculum.

Upper Level

At the upper primary stage, the study of social sciences should comprise the study of history, geography, civics and contemporary issues and problems. The learner at this stage should be initiated into the study of India's past in all its major aspects such as social, cultural and scientific development. He/she should also be helped to appreciate diversities in ways of living and interdependence of various regions of India and the world. He/she should know the civic and political institutions and understand contemporary social and economic conditions and problems. Social skills and civic competencies, and a national perspective would thus equip him/her to participate in the task of social and economic reconstruction.

School Level

At the secondary stage, the study of social sciences should comprise elements of history, geography, civics and economics to promote an understanding of contemporary India. He/she should be introduced to the stages of development of human civilization and to the historical forces and factors that have shaped the modern and the contemporary world. His/her understanding of contemporary historical perspective of India's heritage and the struggle for freedom should be enhanced. The other social science subjects should help him/her understanding Indian society, polity and economy and the social, economic and political challenges facing the country. The study of social sciences at this stage should also develop his/ her understanding of contemporary world problems and of India's role in relation to problems like world peace and international cooperation, decolonization and safeguarding of human rights.

The teaching of history should be objective and free from any communal, parochial and other prejudices. The perspective of the past should help in understanding the contemporary developments. Independent work by the learners through challenging assignments and project work should be encouraged. They should be introduced to the method of geography through practical work. Group activities such as organizing youth parliament, seminars and discussions should be increasingly used to encourage the learners participation. The study of newspapers and the use of newspaper clippings in teaching-learning are of particular importance in promoting an understanding of contem-porary events and problems. The study of economic activities, institutions and problems should be used to promote economic literacy among the learners.

Basic Principles

The Principles of Curriculum Construction are as follows:

Child Centered Curriculum. The curriculum is primarily an aid in the process of adjusting the child to the environment in which he will have to organise his activities later. This process of active mutual adjustment in which the child and his world act and react on each other goes on spontaneously from the very beginning of the child's life long before he comes to school, and continues throughout his life. In the course of this mutual interaction, the child begins to gain experience of various kinds – social, geographical, historical, manual, mathematical and so on. He watches the phenomena of sunrise and sunset, the spreading flush of dawn and the gradual falling of dust, the clouds, the rain, the fields and the trees, and all these constitute the basis of his knowledge of Geography. He sees various kinds of buildings, dresses, specimens of arts and crafts of previous days, he comes across pictures of old times; he sees different kinds of vehicles plying side by side in his town or village. These are many observations of similar kind bring to his notice the fact of change, the gradual process of evolution as it has been going on during the ages. In other words, he comes to acquire, in however rudimentary a form, consciousness of the processes of History. One can go on multiplying such instances. This would, however, suffice to make it clear that the starting point of all knowledge is the experience acquired by the child in the course of his every day life as he comes into contact with the world of nature and the world of society in the midst of which he has to work out his purposes. No school can be an effective instrument of education which fails to utilise this storehouse of direct, vital, first-hand experiences acquired by the child in the course of school life in the "real" world which is not a world of abstract symbols and books but one full of practical and interesting realities.

The Conservative Principle. It has been stated that nations live in the present on the past and for the future. This means that the present, past and the future needs of the community should be taken into consideration. The past is a great guide for the present as it helps us to decide what has been useful to those who are living now. This point has been explained in the "Handbook of Suggestions for Teachers" as "It is, in fact, being increasingly recognised that the various subjects of the curriculum represent certain forms of skill and certain branches of knowledge which have proved to be of importance in the experience of the race, and which have to be taught to each succeeding generation. From this point of view it is the function of the school to preserve and transmit the traditions, knowledge and standards of conduct on which our civilization depends."

This principle will be of help only when we carefully select as to what things of the past are likely to help us in the present. All the things of the past may not suit us. It is, therefore, essential that we should select only those subjects and activities which are required by the present generation.

This principle has been criticised by some educationists on the ground that it looks to subjects and not the pupils. It is contended by its antagonists that in these, days when it is accepted that education and schools, and therefore curriculum should be child-centred, this principle does not take us very far. It may be replied to such critics that to condemn every thing of the past is not a sound policy and especially in a country which has had a glorious past and which showed the path of knowledge to other countries. Another point to be stressed is that there must be a base to stand upon and if the base is durable, it must be accepted. Thirdly it would be wrong to say that in the past the child was entirely ignored. However, as stated above, the principle of selectivity should be adopted in the selection of the curriculum on the basis of the past.

The Forward-looking Principle. While discussing the previous principle, we have pointed out that in the present, future needs and requirements of the community should be given their due place. Children of today are the future citizens of tomorrow. Therefore, their education should be such as enables them to be progressive-minded persons. Education should give them a foundation of environment where change is needed.

The Creative Principle. In the curriculum those activities should be included which enable the child to exercise his creative and constructive powers. The objective of education is to discover and develop the special interests, tastes and aptitudes. Raymount says, 'The first promptings to anyone of the intellectual interests may fade away and become practically irrevocable unless opportunities be then and there forthcoming. None of the child's native gifts should escape our notice and so perish of inanition. In a curriculum that is suited to the needs of today and of the future, there must be a definite bias towards definite creative activities.

The Activity Principle. The curriculum should be thought in terms of activity and experience, rather than of knowledge to be acquired and facts to be stored. Growth and learning take place only where there is activity. 'Experience' rather than 'instruction' is to meet the needs of the various stages of the growth. In the words of John Dewey, "The general movement is away from the old overreliance on verbal instruction, formulated subjects and learning from books and in the direction of more varied and many sided individual activities in keeping with child's real interests."

Play-ground, shops, workrooms and laboratories not only direct the natural active tendencies of youth but they involve intercourse, communication and cooperation.

Abbot and Wood Report has also stressed the activity principle, "It is vitally important that young children should not be required to sit still for long periods at a time. A young child needs rest, it is true, but he must play, he must explore, and he must be physically active if he is to derive a daily satisfaction out of his attendance at school. In short, he needs experience more than instruction."

The curriculum must ensure the activity of the body and mind. It should be the centre of the curriculum. All modern methods of teaching, i.e., Kindergarten, Montessori, Project, Basic etc., are based on this principle of activity.

Principle of Preparation for Life. This is the most important principle in the construction of the curriculum. Education must equip an individual for life. Hence, curriculum must include those activities which enable the child to take his part effectively and amicably in the activities of the community when he becomes an adult. We have to prepare him in such a way that he is capable of facing the various challenges of the complex problems of the future.

Principle of Maturity. Curriculum should be adopted to the grade of the pupils and to their stage of mental and physical development. In the early childhood, 'wonder' and 'romance' predominate. So subjects and activities which present the elements of 'wonder' and 'romance' should be included at this stage. At later stage, they are interested in practical things. So at the Junior Secondary Stage, the curriculum should provide for practical problems. At the next stage that is the Senior Secondary Stage, students are interested in generalisations and accordingly curriculum should provide such activities. The child at this stage is keen to discover, to find out and discuss new facts. The curriculum should harness the adventurous spirit of the growing child.

The experiences provided should be within the comprehension of the students.

Principle of Individual Differences. Individuals differ in taste, temperament, skill, experience, aptitude, innate ability and in sex.

Therefore, the curriculum should be adopted to individual differences. It should not be rigid.

Principle of Vertical and Horizontal Articulation. On the one hand each year's course should be built on what has been done in previous years and at the same time should serve as basis for subsequent work. It is absolutely essential that the enure curriculum should be coordinated.

Principle of Linking with Life. The community needs and characteristics should be kept in view while framing the curriculum.

Principle of Balance. The curriculum should be framed in such a way as every aspect of life, i.e. economic relationships, social activities, occupations, spiritual life, is given due emphasis.

Principle of Loyalties. The curriculum should be planned in such a manner that it teaches a true sense of loyalty to the family, the school, the community, the town, the province, the country and the world at large. It should enable the child to understand that there is unit in diversity.

Principle of Flexibility. Curriculum should take into consideration the special needs and circumstances of the pupils. Curriculum of the girls cannot be identical with that of boys. The special needs of both the sexes should be given their due consideration.

Principle of Core or Common Subjects. There are certain broad areas of knowledge, skill and appreciation with which all children must be made conversant and these should find a place in the curriculum. This is more important at the higher secondary stage where there are diversified courses. These subjects are to be common to all groups, they are known as core subjects. Mother tongue or regional language, social studies (general course), general science including mathematics and one craft are expected to be the core subjects.

Principle of Leisure. The curriculum should prepare the child for the use of leisure time. The capacity to enjoy leisure greatly determines a man's capacity to work. If leisure is spent in gambling, drinking and reading obscene literature, it will hamper progress not only of an individual but also the nation as a whole. The school curriculum should, therefore, prepare the would-be-citizens to use their leisure time effectively.

Principle of All-round Development of Body, Mind and Spirit. All kinds of experiences should be provided to the students so that the child may develop his all powers.

Subject Teaching

Primary Stage. The Curriculum for the Ten Year School has observed as under:

> "The primary concern of the school at this stage should be to develop the necessary social skills, values and attitudes that would enable the child to contribute his mite, as he grows, towards the development of the society to which he belongs. During the five years of primary school the child's mental horizon would be gradually widened from the home to the school and the local community to the world. In the process, the child would begin to appreciate the geographical elements of his environment. Various human activities, which help him to understand how the gifts of nature are processed to produce goods for serving the various needs of man, would also be studied. He would also get an idea of the social and cultural life in different parts of the country as well as of some different ways of living in certain parts of the world. Stories and narratives about personages and events that have contributed to our national heritage and human heritage will also be studied. In addition to these, the child would get ample opportunities to develop socially desirable habits, attitudes and values besides becoming broadly acquainted with the functioning of political and social institutions."

Middle Stage. For the organisation of content in social sciences, comprising history, geography, civics and economics, in the next two stages of school education, three different approaches can be visualized.

History, geography and civics may be introduced as separate disciplines in the middle classes and carried over as such to high school classes, while economics may be introduced at the high school stage as a separate discipline.

History and civics may form one group and geography and economics other group, and these two groups may be introduced right in Class VI and carried up to Class X.

The contents of History, Geography, Civics may be identified and economics may be identified in an integrated manner for all the five years taken together.

While the first two approaches are common today and do not need any elaboration, except that they contribute to the isolation of the disciplines amongst themselves and disciplines from problems or situations, in the third approach it would be necessary to identify essential units in each subject into two cycles of three years and two years. The units thus identified for the first cycle of three years may be integrated and arranged sequentially between and within subjects in the form of a common syllabus for Social Science. For the next two years of education a similar exercise may be done treating the earlier cycles as the base. Some old units may be taken at a greater depth while new ones may be introduced in each subject so as to lead to a slightly more advanced integrated syllabus in these subjects. While selecting units from individual subjects care may be taken to preserve the general structure of the discipline and include those facts and principles which are useful to a growing adolescent and serve as a base for a systematic study of the subject subsequently. The scope of different subject areas as visualized at the middle and lower secondary stages is given below.

History: History at the middle stage should acquaint the pupils with the growth of Indian society from prehistory times to the present. It is necessary to change the emphasis from dynastic history and political details to social economic conditions and the growth of various aspects of culture in different parts of the country. At the same time, a broad perspective of the history of mankind as a whole should also be provided.

The organisation of the syllabus and t. .e selection of the content may be based on what is known as the 'patch' approach. In the light of the requirements of general education, it is not necessary to give a continuous chronological account of the history of India in the sense that every decade or century of Indian history is covered. Representative periods or 'patches' in chronological order, dealt with in all their important aspects may be given. This may be combined with the 'topical' approach in that in a particular 'patch', a few aspects would be selected to be studied in greater detail than other aspects.

It is suggested that the class-wise distribution of the Indian history syllabus may be as follows: Class VI – Ancient India; Class VII – Medieval India, Class VIII – Modern India. Along with this, with each of these major periods of Indian History, a broad perspective of the contemporary history of mankind as a whole should be provided.

Curriculum Approach: Civics should aim mainly at imparting training in civic life rather than mere scholarship. The civics programme should contain such socially imperative knowledge as would not only impart an understanding of civic processes but also provide training in the development of the civic competencies and civic abilities.

The course envisages the study of local government and the Indian Constitution in Class VI and VII, respectively; and in the last year, i.e., in Class VIII, the students would study the actual problems that are facing India today. In the course, some practical aspects of citizenship education and the elements of economics should also be incorporated to adopt a functional and integrated approach.

Though many of the activities and topics of study included under this scheme may be organised by the teacher in the class or school, it is suggested that the training would be more fruitful if the students are taken out of the class-room and involved in real life situations.

Geography at the middle school stage has to perform two distinct functions: (i) introduction of the students to geography as a school subject so as to develop their interest in the same, and (ii) reinforcement of values, attitudes and general understanding that would promote the objectives of citizenship education. Although these two functions have been listed separately, in practice, they are not exclusive of each other. -' At the middle school stage, the course would necessarily be more descriptive and, within the broad framework, would concentrate on imparting knowledge about India in the context of the world, which we have to share with other peoples, characterized by their diverse ways of living. It should bring home to the pupils the interdependence of the various regions of the country and the world. They should begin to appreciate that it is only through sharing with others that the peoples of the world can really enjoy the blessings of the mother earth.

For successful living in a developing society where socio-economic changes are occurring rapidly, it will be helpful if some rudimentary understanding of the economic forces that influence the citizens' daily life is given even at the middle stage. From this point of view, it appears desirable to introduce some elementary knowledge of consumer economics, such as earning and spending controls, price rise and the effects of increasing population, in a very simplified form.

A systematic course in the history of mankind from pre-historic times to the present day should be introduced for Classes IX and X. This does not mean a chronologically continuous narrative but the selection of 'patches' that have a certain unity and distinctiveness alongwith many diversities. The main basis of the selection of these 'patches' may be the successive stages of distinct social formations that existed in different parts of the world in specific chronological periods. The main focus of this course should be on the study of social systems in their rise and growth and their replacement by new forms, and on scientific and cultural development. The historical Africa and the America, should be covered. The selection of the content should be based on the specific histories of individual countries only where these histories have a significant bearing on the general history of mankind and represent new trends which became relevant to the history of mankind as a whole.

Alongwith the above, there should be a course in depth on certain aspects of Indian history, particularly the social, economic and cultural development and the factors that have a close bearing on the understanding of contemporary India.

Civics: In Classes IX and X, the two major objectives of teaching civics should be: (i) to promote an active and intelligent citizenship, and (it) to develop an intelligent understanding of the structure and working of the social and political institutions. In addition to this an understanding that the UNO is playing a significant role in strengthening world peace and cooperation should also be promoted.

From this point of view, the course in Class IX should include the meaning and scope of civics, community life, forms of government, rights and duties and democracy in action. In Class X, the students would study the structure and functions of political and social institutions in India and the role of UNO in maintaining world peace. Some basic elements of sociology should also be introduced.

Economics: At the terminal stage of general education, the subject of geography should shift its emphasis from the more descriptive to the somewhat analytical and conceptual in its presentation. This should bring it closer to the philosophy and spirit of general education. A few selected detailed studies from world geography and the economic geography of India should also be undertaken, besides a brief analytical study of all the different aspects of the same.

Geography: The approach of teaching of economics at the lower secondary stage should emphasize not so much the principles of economics as the current problems and issues that affect the everyday life of the man. While doing so, some light should, of course, be thrown on the principle of economics as well. Such an introductory course would, it is hoped, lay down the necessary foundations for a more systematic and rigorous course in Classes XI and XII.

The course should include a brief review of the economic conditions of India at the start of British Rule. This should prepare the ground to understand the need for the economic development of India through the National Plans and help to appreciate their objectives. As a part of his introduction to economic institutions, child should be introduced to the role of money and financial institutions. The current economic problems such as poverty, rising prices, agricultural stagnation, etc. would be discussed. The course would throw some light on the future economic prospects of the country on the basis of its potential resources and the performance shown as far.

Role of Committee

Environmental Studies (Class I and II)

Our family: Life, structure and functions.

Our home: Shelter, facilities, love.

Our school: Teachers, building, learning.

Our neighbourhoods: Life, work, cleanliness, space.

Our earth: Features, vegetation, water, minerals.

Our sky: Lights, heat, weather, stars.

Man's life: Interesting imaginative stories.

Ecological Science

Class III

1. *The world we live in:* Continents, oceans, our country in the world.
2. *Life in the district:* Setting, occupation, festivals.
3. *Life in our state:* Location, relief, vegetation, resources, occupations, communications.
4. *Life in our country:* Food, clothing, occupations, languages, festivals.
5. *Institutions which help us:* Panchayats, cooperatives, centres, education, transport

Class IV

1. *India – Physical Divisions:* Mountains, plains, rivers and plateaus.
2. *India – Resources:* Human and national (soil, water, minerals).
3. *India – Transport and communications:* On land, water and air; post and telegraph and telephone.
4. *The people of India:* National symbols and festivals, one country.
5. *Indian heritage I:* Monuments, music, dances, religions, scripts, languages, handicrafts, festivals.
6. *Indian heritage II:* Stories of famous rulers, reformers, writers, scientists, saints.
7. *Our freedom struggle:* Briefly through some of the more prominent leaders.

Class V

1. *The globe and map of the world:* Hemispheres, equator, poles, tropics, arctic circles.

2. *India and neighbouring countries:* Man's ways of living life and occupations in some distinctive areas of the world, e.g. Tundra, Savanna, Desert, Equatorial, Mediterranean.
3. *Our shrinking world:* Transport and communications, land, sea, air, radio, television, newspapers, cinema, satellites.
4. *How we govern ourselves:* The state and central governments, fundamental rights, directive principles, duties of a citizen.
5. *The United Nations:* Cooperation among nations, work of UNICEF, WHO, UNESCO, India in the UN.
6. *The changing world:* Stories of scripts, numbers, trade, money, discoveries and scientists, Columbus, Galileo, Newton, Einstein.
7. *Great men:* Secretes, Lincoln, Lenin, Tolstoy, Mahatma Gandhi.

HISTORY (Class VI – Ancient India)

1. *Prehistory:* Man as a nomad. Discovery and use of metals. Invention of the wheel, Farming.
2. *The Harappan Culture:* Cities, Occupations, Religion, Script.
3. *Life in the Vedic Age:* Settlements – Economic and political life – Religion.
4. *Rise of Magadha:* Kingdoms and Republic, Emergence of towns, Jainism and Buddhism.
5. *The Mauryan Empire:* Persian and Greek invasions, Chandragupta Maurya, Ashoka – administration.
6. *India from 200 B.C. to A.D. 300:* Satavahanas, Cholas, Pandyas, Cheras, Shakas, Kushanas.

7. *The Age of the Guptas:* Administration, Trade, Religion, Art, Science.
8. *India from A.D. 500 to A.D. 800 Harsha:* The Deccan and South India, Art and Architecture.
9. *India and the World:* Rise of Islam, The Arabs in India, India's contacts with other countries.

HISTORY (Class VIII)—Medieval India

1. *India from A.D. 800 to A.D. 1200:* Kingdoms of south. Religion, Architecture. The struggle for Kanauj, Turkish Invasions, Religion, Art and Architecture.
2. *The Sultanate of Delhi:* Mamluks, Khaljis, Tughlaqs, The Bahamani and Vijayanagar Kingdoms, Sufi and Bhakti movements.
3. *The Advent of the Mughals and the Europeans:* Kingdoms in the Deccan, Renaissance in Europe, Voyages of discovery.
4. *The Mughal Empire:* Akbar-Jahangir and Shahjahan, Aurangzeb, Rise of the Marathas, Art, Architecture, Literature.
5. *Decline of the Mughal Empire:* Invasions, Rise of Independent states.

HISTORY (Class VII)—Modern India

1. *India in the Eighteenth Century:* Expansion of the Maratha Power, Society and Polity.
2. *The Rise and Growth of British Empire in India:* The Carnatic wars, the British conquest of Bengal, British paramountcy.
3. *Administrative Structure of the British Empire in India:* Civil, Judicial, Revenue system.

4. *Impact of British Rule on Indian Economy and Society upto 1875:* The village economy. Industry and Trade, Educational and Social Reform.
5. *The Revolt of 1857:* Cause, Nature, Results.
6. *Reorganisation of the British Empire in India:* The Act of 1858 Civil Services, Policy of 'Divide and Rule'.
7. *Changes in Economy and Society after 1858:* Agriculture and Railways, Plantations, Industries, Economic Conditions; Social Life, Education, Social and Religious Reform movements, cultural awakening.
8. *Rise of Indian Nationalism and the Struggle for Freedom:* The Indian National Congress, Partition of Bengal, The Gandhian era, Civil Disobedience, The INA, Quit India Movement
9. *Achievement of Independence:* Immediate Problems.

CIVICS (Class VI—Our Civil Life)

1. *Development of the Community:* Scheme, Cooperatives, Community Development.
2. *Local Government (Rural):* Need, Structure and Functions.
3. *Local Government (Urban):* Structure and Functions.
4. *District Administration:* Law and Order, Civic Amenities.
5. *Preservation of Property of the Community:* Public property, its preservation, historical monuments.
6. *Project Work:* Opportunities to develop abilities which are essential for any active citizen in India, Problems.

CIVICS (Class VII—Our Constitution)

1. *Chief Features of our Constitution:* Basic Principles, National Government, State Governments, Rights, Duties, Directive Principles, National Symbols.

2. *Law-Making Process:* Parliament, State Legislature, How Laws are made.
3. *Executing Laws:* President, Prime Minister and the Council of Ministers, Governor, Chief Minister and the Council of Ministers, Public Services.
4. *Interpreting Law:* Supreme Court, High Courts and Subordinate Courts.
5. Project Work.

CIVICS (Class VIII—Independent India—Achievements and Challenges)

1. *Our National Goals:* Democracy, Socialism, and Secularism, International Cooperation.
2. *Strengthening our Democracy:* Citizenship in a democracy, Literacy in India.
3. *Social and Economic Reconstruction:* Poverty, Population, Unemployment Casteism.
4. *Five-Year Plans – Achievements and Failures:* Agriculture, Industries, Rural Life.
5. *Defence of the Country:* Armed Forces, Territorial Army, Border Security Force, N.C.C., A.C.C., Citizens and Defence.
6. *India and the World:* Need for cooperation, co-existence, the United Nations.
7. Project Work.

GEOGRAPHY (Class VI)

1. *The Earth as a Globe:* Distance and direction on a map. The earth and the solar systems. Rotation and Revolution. Latitude and Longitude.
2. *Africa – Land and People:* Land, Climate, Vegetation and Wild Life, Equatorial Lands, Savanna Lands, Sahara Lands, and the Mediterranean Lands.

3. *Asia – Land and People:* Land, Climate, Vegetation and Wild Life, The People, Pakistan, Nepal, Bhutan Bangladesh, Burma and Sri Lanka.

GEOGRAPHY (Class VII)

1. *Atmosphere and Hydrosphere*: Air-Temperature Pressure and Winds.
2. *Australia – Land and People:* Land, Climate, Vegetation and Wild Life, The People.
3. *South America – Land and People:* Land, Climate, Vegetation and Wild Life, The People.
4. *North America – Land and People:* Land, Climate, Vegetation and Wild Life, The People, Canada, the United States.
5. *Practical Work:* Observation and keeping records of sunrise and sunset. Stars and constellations, studying – Local maps, Landforms in the neighbourhood.

GEOGRAPHY (Class VIII)

1. *Lilhosphere and Landforms:* The crust of the earth. Rocks.
2. *Europe – Land and People:* Land, Climate, Vegetation and Wild Life, The People, France, the United Kingdom and Germany.
3. *The Soviet Union* – Land, Climate, Vegetation and Wild Life, The People.
4. *India – Physical Setting:* Relief, Climate, Vegetation and Wild Life.
5. *India – Its Agricultural Resources:* Soils, Irrigation, Crops, Methods of Farming.
6. *India – Minerals and Industries:* Iron, Coal, Petroleum, Bauxite, Manganese, Textiles, Sugar, Oil refinery. Heavy industries, Small Scale and Cottage Industries.

7. *India – Transport and Population:* Internal, and external, Land – water and air. Population – distribution and density.
8. *Practical work – Weather Study:* Daily weather, observation and recording.

HISTORY OF MANKIND (Class IX and X)

1. *Pre-history:* Stages of evolution and development – Paleolithic and Neolithic.
2. *First Civilizations (Bronze Age):* Egypt, Mesopotamia, India, China.
3. *Ancient Civilization (Iron Age):* Contribution and influence of Ancient Greece, Rome, India and China – rise of world religions.
4. *The Medieval Europe and Asia:* Developments in Europe, West Asia, India and China, Feudalism.
5. *The Renaissance and Rise of Nation States:* Rise of towns and cities, learning, discoveries and exploration, scientific development, Nation States, colonization.
6. Capitalism, Industrial Revolution.
7. *Revolutionary and Nationalist Movements:* American, War of Independence, Nationalist and Democratic Movements.
8. *Imperialism (up to 1914):* Important causes and results.
9. *The Socialist Movement:* Growth and socialist ideas and movements, Russian Revolution.
10. *World after World War II – United Nations Cold War:* Technological development.
11. *World after World War II – United Nations, Cold War:* Technological development.
12. *Emergence of Asia, Africa, Latin America:* Importance of the Third World, developing countries.

13. *The Contemporary World and India:* International peace and cooperation, new economic order.

CIVICS

1. Man as a social being
2. Man as a citizen
3. Local self-government
4. State and national government
5. Rights and duties of a citizen
6. Democracy in India
7. India as a nation: unity in diversity
8. Social and economic challenges before our country
9. India and the World
10. India and the United Nations
11. Project work

GEOGRAPHY

(General Geography of the World with special reference to India)

1. *Landforms:* Continents, mountains, plateaus, plains, Landforms in India.
2. *Climate:* Climate zones in the world and in India.
3. *Natural Regions of the world:* Tropical, temperate, cold lands.
4. *Natural Resources:* Soil, vegetation, animals, minerals, and water in world and in India.
5. *Major Occupations:* Primitive, pastoral, agricultural, industrial.
6. *Agriculture:* Principal agricultural areas, crops and practices in the world and in India.

7. *Minerals and Power:* Major minerals and mining areas, water and nuclear power.
8. *Industries:* Important areas and location, heavy and light industries, production and output
9. *Transport and Communications:* Land, water, air.
10. *International Trade:* Commodities, import-export, foreign exchange.
11. *Population of the World and India:* Distribution, density, control of population.
12. *Case Studies:* Life of the people in various parts of the World and in India.

Pragmatic Approach. The Patel Committee took note of the prevailing criticism levelled against the over-loaded curriculum as prescribed under the new scheme of education popularly known as New Pattern or 10+2+3 pattern of education. It rightly suggested the deletion of some material which was hardly needed in social studies. The Committee emphatically observed, "We are of the view that one area in which the present scheme is overloaded is 'Social Studies' or 'Social Sciences'. The Committee, therefore, recommended the inclusion of courses in History, Civics and Geography and exclusion of subjects like Economics, Commerce and Psychology in the pattern of general education for classes IX and X.

Curriculum According to the Maturity Level. Curriculum of Social Studies and Social Sciences is psychologically sound as it has taken into consideration the level of maturity of the students. Social Studies are to be taught as a part of the study of environment in classes one and two, social studies as an integrated subject in classes 3 to 5 and separate discipline at middle and high school stage.

Syllabus Frames. The Committee has suggested frames and topics and not detailed contents of the syllabus. It has been left to the Education Departments, Examination Boards and Schools to decide the details of the schools content, in relation to their particular needs and in keeping with the facilities available.

Curriculum Related to the Community. The curriculum takes care of the specific needs of the community. Significant social and economic problems form an important part of school curriculum.

Well-knit Curriculum. The curriculum for each class is fairly connected. For instance, Indian and World history has been taken up in the form of biographies and stories at the primary stage, a detailed description at the middle stage.

Flexibility of the Curriculum. Care has been taken to ensure that the contents of the curriculum are so arranged and kept flexible so as to suit the needs of individual learners. The curriculum Us capable of catering to the requirements of a wide range of learners and learning circumstances. It is suggestive and illustrative rather than prescriptive or restrictive.

Self-contained Courses. The courses are self-contained as well as lay the foundation of the subsequent stage. The curriculum provides for a minimum but sufficient broad knowledge for those who may not continue their education after the secondary stage.

Development of Basic Skills. The contents of the programme have been planned in such a manner so as to provide adequate opportunities for the development of basic understandings, skills and attitudes needed for the realization of the ideals of democracy, secularism and socialism.

Promotion of Understanding. There is sufficient scope for the development of right attitude of national and international understanding.

Emphasis on Sources of Learning. The curriculum does not consider classroom as the only place or source from which students learn. It rightly states that the environment and society are also sources from which children acquire understandings, skills and attitudes. It provides scope for the arranging of educational programmes in such a way that all these factors are fully utilized. The curriculum focuses attention on the practical aspects.

The curriculum, integrated as it is, with its many and varied objectives and comprehensive programmes, concerning the whole area of experience—the family, the community, the nation and the world—is aptly suited to bridge the wide gulf between the schools and the outside world. It provides for sufficient scope for the students to be able to understand how society has come to its present form. They will also be able to interpret intelligently and rationally the matrix of social forces and movements in the midst of which they are living. Adequate emphasis has been laid on making the knowledge as relevant to life as possible by weaving the content around day-to-day problems. Attempts have been made to make knowledge functional and relevant. To broaden the outlook, developments in other parts of the world too have been put in proper perspective.

QUESTIONS

1. Explain the significance of curriculum. State the value of Social Studies as Core-curriculum.
2. 'Traditional Curriculum was in terms of certain subjects', elucidate the concept of Social Studies curriculum in this context.
3. Point out the need for the inclusion of Social Studies at different stages of education.
4. Throw light on the principles which should govern the construction of the curriculum in Social Studies.

14

Significance of Books

Authors have given different definitions of a textbook. 'A true textbook', according to the American Textbook Publishers Institute...' is one especially prepared for the use of pupil and teacher in a school or a class, presenting a course of study in a single subject, or closely related subjects.'

Webster's dictionary defines textbooks as "a manual of instruction, a book containing a presentation of the principles of the subject used as a basis of instruction...."

Becon defined textbook as "a book designed for classroom use, carefully prepared by experts in the field and equipped with the usual teaching devices".

A more comprehensive definition is given in the third edition of Encyclopaedia of Educational Research. It states, "In the modern sense and as commonly understood, the textbook is a learning instrument usually employed in school and colleges to support a programme of instruction. In ordinary usage, the textbook is printed, it is non-consumable, it is hardbound, it serves an avowed instructional purpose, and it is placed in the hands of the learner."

Textbooks of social studies should serve the following purposes:

1. The over-all purpose of teaching social studies should pervade all social studies textbooks.
2. Social studies textbooks should assume special responsibility towards the promotion of national goals like democracy, socialism, secularism and national integration.
3. Social studies textbooks should promote moral values.
4. Social studies textbooks should give a balanced picture of the life of man and interaction between man and the environment.
5. Social studies textbooks should reflect and help in the realisation of the specific objectives of teaching social studies in the grade for which the textbook is meant.
6. Social studies textbooks should take into consideration the objectives at the secondary stage.
7. Social studies textbooks should be based on the charac- terisitcs of children. They should provide for the needs of the children at different levels of intelligence.

The Utility

Assistant Master in Print. A textbook is content plus instructional technique. This technique is aimed at enabling the content understandable to the people even in situations where they are not helped by the teacher.

A Structured Framework. A textbook is essentially based on some pre-determined syllabi which circumscribe the limits of a textbook besides setting the standard at which it has to be written. It clearly spells out and interprets the syllabus both for the students and teachers.

Instrument of Some Instructional Objectives. As an important tool of instruction, a textbook is an instrument for the achievement of pre-determined objectives.

Important Tool for the Teacher. A textbook assists the teacher to plan his daily lesson, prepare assignments and organise class activities.

Constant Companion of a Student. A textbook guides the students in learning – in the school and at home. A student uses it continuously and constantly. This feature distinguishes it from a general and reference book which a student consults once a while. Each word of the textbook has not only to be read by every student but he is also expected to understand it.

Self-teaching Device. A textbook enables a student to learn through his own efforts. A textbook provides an opportunity to a student to reflect and evaluate. A student can find the specific information he needs in a book without listening to extraneous material that comes before and after it. He can move ahead as quickly or as methodically as his individual capacities for comprehension permits.

Logical and Comprehensive Material. A good textbook by providing in a systematic and comprehensive form, sets a standard of minimum essential to be achieved by students of all categories. For a teacher, it provides essential knowledge at one place. All teachers are not in a position to dig up facts. A textbook, therefore, can be a constant standby of the Social Studies teacher.

Transmitter of Culture. It serves as potential media of mass communication. It has a positive role to play in bringing about desirable cultural change by discarding certain values and customs and introducing radical changes.

Revolutionising Society. A textbook is used not only for preserving the cultural heritage but also revolutionising a society, its values , beliefs and social system.

Rallying Point. By providing a common ground few both the teachers and the students, it focuses attention on the same issues, events sequences and circumstances.

A Laboratory. A textbook enables a student to reinforce the learning, to do assignments at home, to prepare for the examination and to seek guidance and reference for further studies. It provides a common basis on which the process of reading, analysing, outlining and summarising can be mastered.

Basis for Almost all the Methods. Almost all the methods of teaching like the Assignment, Unit Method, Discussion and the Project Method can be used with advantage with the help of a textbook.

Definite Information. A textbook is a storehouse of basic and definite information needed for learning experiences of different kinds. The use of the textbook can help the pupils to sum up all the ideas of the unit, acquaint them with the vocabulary, help them learn enough about the topic to be able to proceed intelligently.

Educational Interaction. A textbook plays a crucial role in generating educational interaction in the classroom between the teacher and the learner, and also between the learner and other co-learners as a result of which learning occurs in a group.

Syllabus 'de facto'. A teacher defines and delimits his content of teaching. He uses the textbook as a prime instructional aid to generate a variety of educative experiences through group-work and individual assignments.

The Shortcomings. Demerits of textbooks are stated below:

1. They tend to dominate the educative process. They have influenced the purpose, character and scope of the curriculum. They have dominated the method of instruction and the evaluating process. They have narrowed down the scope of the curriculum.
2. They do not provide for direct experience. The students get readymade knowledge and, therefore, fail to assimilate it properly.

3. They introduce uniformity and rigidity for definite achievements and kill all initiative and spirit of both the pupil and the teacher.
4. Textbooks are great hindrance in the new methods of teaching like the Heuristic and the Inductive. The students get readymade answers and this defeats the very purpose of introducing new methods.
5. There is every danger that the textbooks maybe used for the purpose of indoctrination of the ideas and beliefs of the party in power. In fact, textbooks have been used in many countries for the propagation of Fascist and Communistic ideas. They are a potent instrument in the hands of the party in power to inculcate narrow nationalism and racial prejudices.

How to Use Textbooks. A textbook should be treated as a means and not an end in itself. It should be borne in mind that it is a useful means to help in study. The student should never have the impression that a textbook constitutes a boundary and this task is simple to learn what it contains and no more. A textbook should serve as a basis of his learning. A textbook does not provide the last word on the subject. A textbook is not to usurp the functions of a teacher. It is to supplement his work and not supplant it.

Can We do Away with Textbooks? We may not accept the sovereignty of a textbook but it must be admitted that a good textbook is an indispensable means or tool in the teaching-learning process, whatever scheme is adopted. It is neither desirable not feasible for most of the teachers to do without textbooks. The only point is that a textbook should be used very skillfully and intelligently. It should be treated, as an obedient slave' and not 'a commanding master.'

The Education Commission 1964-66 described the values of the textbook as an effective tool of learning and of diffusion of improved teaching methods in these words, "A good textbook written by a qualified and competent specialist in the subject, and produced with due regard to quality of printing illustrations and general getup, stimulates the pupil's interests and helps the teacher considerably in his work. The provision of quality textbooks and other teaching and learning materials, can thus be an effective programme for raising standards. The need to emphasise it is all the greater because it requires only a relatively small investment of resources. Moreover, a quality book need not cost appreciably more than one that is indifferently produced."

Significant Aspects

These may broadly be classified under two heads:

A. Academic B. Physical

Academic

I. Selection of content.
II. Organisation of content.
III. Presentation of content.
IV. Verbal Communication (Language).
V. Visual Communication (Illustrations).
VI. Assignments, Exercises etc.
VII. Prelims and back pages.

Physical

VIII. Size and Format of the textbooks.
IX. Printing lay-out.
X. Durability.
XI. Price.

Subject Matter

(1) *Relevant content.* The content should be relevant to the instructional objectives of Social Studies.

(2) *Coverage of the course.* The content should be adequate in respect of each topic.

(3) *Adequate content.* The content should be adequate in respect of each topic.

(4) *Authentic content.* The content should be accurate and authentic.

(5) *Up-to-date content.* The content should be up-to-date.

(6) *Continuity and balance.* The continuity and balance among the various topics covered in the book should be maintained.

(7) *Integrated content.* The selected topics should be properly integrated from the preceding to the succeeding class or stage.

(8) *Linking with life.* Considerable material drawn from practical life situations and day-to-day life of the community should be included in the book.

(9) *Division into units.* The subject-matter should be divided into proper chapters and units.

(10) *Division into sections.* The matter should be properly divided into sections and paragraphs.

(11) *Psychological approach.* The approach followed in the book should be suitable to the needs of the students.

(12) *Coherence in the subject-matter.* There should be sufficient coherence and sequence in the organisation of the subject-matter.

(13) *Flexible organisation.* The organisation should be flexible enough to submit to changes in accordance with the change in the instructional plans.

Attractive Presentation

(14) *Attractive and appropriate title.* The titles of the chapters should be appropriate.

(15) *Motivating presentation.* The presentation should motivate children for further study.

(16) *Interesting and creative approach.* The matter should be presented in a creative and interesting manner to sustain interest.

(17) *Adequate terminology.* The presentation should provide an adequate coverage of the terminology relevant to the syllabus.

(18) *Adequate provision for replication.* It should provide adequate reinforcement of new items of learning through replication and application.

(19) *Provision for suitable suggestions for teachers.* The presentations should provide some suggestions and implications for adoption of effective teaching methods and instructional strategies by the classroom teacher.

Ways of Communication

(20) *Appropriate vocabulary.* The vocabulary should be appropriate for the class level.

(21) *Short and simple sentences.* The sentences should be simple and short.

(22) *Correct spellings.* The spellings should be correct.

(23) *Correct punctuation.* Should be punctuated correctly.

(24) *Grammatically correct language.* The language used should be grammatically correct.

(25) *Proper use of technical terms.* The technical terms should be used properly, and suitably explained wherever necessary.

(26) *Clear illustrations.* The illustrations should be correct and authentic.

(27) *Purposeful presentation of illustration.* The illustrations should be purposeful and appropriately placed in the textbook.

(28) *Adequate illustrations.* The illustrations should be adequate, proper in size and suitably captioned.

(29) *Supplementation of text.* The illustrations should supplement the text.

(30) *Variety of illustrations.* There should be variety in illustrations.

The Tasks

(31) *Adequate exercises.* The exercises should be adequate to test the various purposes like recapitulation, consolidation, etc.

(32) *Wide coverage.* The exercise should cover the significant content.

(33) *Scope for projects.* The projects provided should help in achieving various purposes of teaching of social studies.

(34) *Scope for projects.* The projects provided should help in achieving various purposes of teaching of social studies.

(35) *Real projects.* The projects should have a close resemblance to actual life situations.

(36) *Challenging exercises.* The exercises should promote the spirit of enquiry and motivate the students for further study.

(37) *Graded exercises.* These exercises should suit the special needs of the gifted as well as slow learners.

Important Chapters

(38) *Appropriate title page.* The title page should give the necessary information, i.e., suitable title, author's name, publisher's name, place of publication and year of publication etc.

(39) *Suitable preface.* Preface should give an idea about the scope and central theme of the book.

(40) *Effective introduction.* Introduction should explain the scheme and purpose of the book.

(41) *Correct table of contents.* The table of contents should be given correctly.

(42) *Bibliography.* Bibliography should be given in adequate language.

(43) *Suitable glossary.* Glossary should be given in adequate language.

(44) *Index.* Index should be given where possible.

Other Aspects

(45) *Suitable size.* The size should be suitable from the viewpoint of age group of students.

(46) *Suitable volume.* The size should be suitable in relation to the volume of the book.

(47) *Suitable length.* The length of the line should be such as can be conveniently read by the students.

(48) *Suitable type.* The type size used for chapter title, subtitles, footnotes, exercises etc. should be suitable for the age-group of the students.

(49) *Appropriate margin.* The left-hand, right-hand, top and bottom margins should be appropriate.

(50) *Aesthetic outlook.* The margins should provide an aesthetic look to the page of the book.

(51) *Appropriate spacing.* Spacing between lines, and paragraphs should be appropriate.

(52) *Durable paper.* The paper should be durable enough in view of the age-group.

(53) *Life of the book.* The paper should be durable enough in accordance with the expected life of the book.

(54) *Suitable price of paper.* The quality of the paper should be in accordance with the cost of the book.

(55) *Suitable binding.* The binding should be durable keeping in view the volume and functional life of the book.

(56) *Attractive binding.* The binding should be attractive.

(57) *Price suited to the economic background.* The price should be suitable in view of the econoimc background of the students.

(58) *Reasonable price.* The price should be suitable keeping in view the printing layout, size and durability of the book.

Committees' Report

Class I-IV/V

Textbooks. We have referred earlier to the obsession with literacy resulting in the dominant position of textbooks in our system of education. This has assumed serious proportions in that we have not the uncommon spectacle in cities, at least, of young children carrying loads of books to and from school because of the emphasis given to book learning by parents and teachers.

We are of the view that except in the case of Language there is no need for textbooks in Class I-II; in Class III-IV/V there should be one textbook for Language, one book in Mathematics and one for the Environmental Studies.

Teacher's Guidebooks and Teaching Aids. Teacher's guidebooks and teaching aids, we believe, are necessary and these should cover the whole range of activities for all classes and that in the preparation of guidebooks the principle of correlation should be the basis.

Class VI to VIII

Textbooks. We realise that there will have to be textbooks for each of the areas of study, but the number of these can be reduced by having one book for Science and one in which Civics and History are combined.

We are of the view that the number of pages in each textbook should be reduced to the minimum and that the language used should be easily understood by children of this age-group.

Class IX and X

History, Civics and Geography. We are of the view that the one area in which the present scheme is overloaded is in 'Social Studies' or 'Social Science'. In some of the courses prescribed by Examining Bodies under one or other of these headings, the subjects included are History, Civics, Geography, Economics, Commerce and Psychology.

We agree with the conclusion of the Kothari Commission that History, Civics and Geography only should be taught in this area of the curriculum and that such correlation as in natural and possible should be introduced.

We have, therefore, recommended definitely that a course in History, Civics and Geography should be included in the scheme as, we believe, that such a course will, with the other areas of study, be sufficient to provide a broad-based general education.

The Ishwar Bhai Patel Committee have given Syllabus Frames in most subjects and not detailed syllabuses. The Frames give the main topics in each subject and it will be for the States, Local Authorities, Education Examination Boards and Schools to plan and Fill in the details.

The Committee observed, "We believe that uniform courses of study designed to serve the needs of average schools cease to be meaningful as there is a large variety of schools in each state and there are many variable factors, such as the quality of teachers, facilities available and the needs of children to be taken into consideration.

A single rigid scheme of studies for all schools may prove to be beyond the competence of some schools and may not provide a sufficient challenge to other schools.

The content of the courses, finally framed, must be capable of being taught or studied within the time allotted per week as given in the scheme. We believe that in each subject, only the main ideas should be introduced; these should be few and important and that in teaching they should be thrown into every possible combination so that the children will make these ideas their own and understand their application. In the words of a distinguished educationist, "We enunciate two educational commandments: 'Do not teach too many subjects' and gain 'What you teach, teach thoroughly'."

We believe that the main concepts in each subject should be studied and that unnecessary details, which overload the syllabus, instead of developing knowledge, inevitably lead to the memorising of scraps of information, never interconnected, never utilised.

Another value of providing syllabus frames only lies in the fact that the limits of knowledge to be expected at the end of the ten-year period will be clear to those responsible for framing courses at the higher secondary stage.

Freedom to Develop Textbooks. We are also of the view that by not giving details of the courses, but only the main topics, it will be possible for Education Authorities to perpare textbook material to suit the needs of schools under their control.

We recommended that NCERT should concentrate on the production of instructional material and the State Governments, Education/Examination Boards, School and other Educational Agencies should be free to adapt and develop this material to suit their particular needs.

Significance of Supplementary Material. Supplementary material is of potential value for social studies teaching. Textbooks cannot satisfy all aspects of critical and inspirational knowledge and may be even lacking details with regard to current contemporary affairs. Textbooks cannot cope with the material of fast changing social events. Textbook, with rare exceptions, are not self-explanatory and the students stand in need of elaboration. Elaboration is possible through advanced works, reference books and source books, etc. Similarly, autobiographies and biographies serve as inspirational sources. Well written historical plays, short stories and speeches on related subjects are very helpful. Pamphlets prepared by local, state and national societies provide admirable material for students.

Supplementary material should be a vital factor in all the work of social studies. Following advantages are gained from the proper use of collateral supplimentary source and fiction reading:

1. Development of good reading habits.
2. Colourful understanding of the past.
3. Development of an intelligent and critical attitude.
4. Stimulating independent judgement.
5. Training in independent reading and thinking.

Bining and Bining point out the merits of supplementary material as "During the period of adolescence, when interest can readily be aroused, when good habits can be developed, when attitudes can easily be built up, when the capacity for forming ideals is strong, and when the mind is wide open to impressions, the natural desire for reading should be skilfully directed and the foundations laid for the wise use of books.

Five Types of Readings. These are as given below:

1. Reading for understanding.
2. Reading for memorisation.

3. Reading for the purpose of locating specific information.
4. Rapid reading for expanding general knowledge.
5. Reading for pleasure.

Most supplementary reading can be classified under the last three categories, major share going to fourth category of rapid reading.

Various Types of Supplementary Material. It may be categorised as under:

1. Autobiographies and biographies.
2. Historical fiction.
3. Magazines.
4. Newspapers.
5. Plays.
6. Poetry.
7. Travel and other stories.
8. Work books.

Autobiographies and Biographies. Autobiographies and biographies of great persons throw a flood of light on the social, economic and political conditions prevailing in their period. They also serve as source of great information.

Historical Fiction. It has been observed that historical fiction, by recreating the past, serves as a stimulus to the imagination, provides opportunities for the exercise of critical faculties and offer endless opportunities of extending human sympathy.

Historical fiction also serves as a source of entertainment. It also provides inspiration. 'Anand Math' of Bankim Chandra Chatterji is very useful for creating a sense of unity and national pride in the people. 'Bande Matram' of Bankim Chandra Chatterji, which became the anthem of the struggle for national freedom is enshrined in this very novel. Historical novels in different languages are very useful as supplementary material for creating interest in the past and widening the horizons of the understandings of the students.

Magazines. Many magazines contain interesting and latest material on different matters which can supplement classroom information. They enable the students to keep themselves abreast of the latest developments in various fields.

Newspaper. Newspapers help in bridging the gap between information contained in the books and changing developments in movements, trends, ideas and changes in politics, international relations and economic and civil life. Special and Sunday issues such as Republic Day and Independence Day are full of important events. Articles on new researches in various fields can enlighten the students. It is, therefore, very essential that from the very begining of their school career, students are made newspaper-minded. Newspapers serve as a wonderful supplementary material as they contain a reservoir of resources and illustrations. They help in closing the gap between information contained in the books and changing developments in politics, economic, social, industrial and international fields. Special features, the editorials, the cartoons, etc., all can enlighten the students.

Current events can serve as a starting point to stimulate interests. Many news items link the present with the past.

Travel Stories. Travel accounts of the Buddhist Chinese travellers like Fahien, Hieun Tsang and Itsing who visited India provide a comprehensive account of the social and cultural life of the people living during that period. Their accounts are considered a great valuable source of information as they spend a few years in India and travelled widely. Similarly, travel accounts of the Arab sailors, merchants and visitors who visited India during the medie-val period provide interesting accounts. Alberuni and Ibn Batuta have furnished valuable descriptions of the period. Achievements of the rulers of the Vijayanagar Empire have found an important place in the travel accounts given by the Portuguese and the Indian Travellers.

Work Books. Work books are based on the principle of 'Learning by Doing'. They play a vital role in leading to the concretisation of the concepts presented in textbooks. Work books provide opportu-nities to the students to apply knowledge gained through text-books. Pictures of the different scripts of different countries and of the tools and weapons motivate the students to learn more. Projects in social studies which have as part of their fulfilment the construction and manipulation of things are sometimes very valuable.

Supplementary material is intended to achieve the following objectives:

1. It aims at helping the students acquire additional information.
2. It aims at widening the horizons of the students.
3. It aims at enriching the knowledge already acquired through the text-books.
4. It aims at enabling the students to develop study habits.
5. It aims at motivating them to write articles and speeches, etc.
6. It aims at serving as a means of bringing out the relationship between the present and the past.
7. It aims at enabling the students to form an acquaintance with historical literature.
8. It aims at making the teaching of social sciences more inspiring and interesting.
9. It aims at enablinhg the students to make the best use of their leisure time.
10. It incidentally helps the students form the conception of how social sciences material are built up, if used effectively, not only utilises instruction but also provides a new meaning to leaching and learning.

The Guidelines

1. While suggesting supplementary material, the teacher should bear in mind the mental capacity of his students. Only those materials should be suggested which the students can grasp.
2. As far as possible, only those materials should be suggested which the students can get easily from the school library or local sources.
3. Suggested supplementary material should be within the easy reach of the pocket of the students if it is not available in the school library.
4. There should be no element of compulsion in supplementary reading. The teacher would do well to keep in mind the suggestion of Johnson in this regard, "there should be no set questions to answers, no problems to solve, no looking forward to any report, but complete freedom to read because he likes it or to stop reading because he dislikes it."
5. Language of the supplementary material should be simple so that it may maintain the interest of the students.
6. For motivating the students, the teacher should maintain a small library in the classroom or a reserved shelf in the library or hall so as to make it easily available to students.
7. The students may be motivated to keep their own record of supplemntary reading done as, (a) Name of the book, (b) Author's name, (c) Publisher's name, (d) Newspaper or the magazine read by them, (e) Extracts taken.
8. Supplementary material should be well illustrated.
9. Supplementary material as the name implies should only supplement the textbook and not replace it.
10. Supplementary material should be authentic and not a distortion of facts or politically motivated.

QUESTIONS

1. State the use of textbook method in the teaching of Social Studies.
2. Explain the essential characteristics of a good textbooks.
3. "A textbook should be used as a servant and not master." Explain this statement.
4. Can we do away with textbooks? Illustrate this.
5. Explain the need for supplementary material in the teaching of Social Studies. How can we make the best use of this material?

15

Planning the Lesson

Bossing explains the meaning of lesson planning in these words, "Lesson planning is the title given to a statement of the achievements to be realized and the specific means by which these are to be attained as a result of the activities engaged in day-by-day under the guidance of the teacher." This definition tends to focus the teacher's attention upon:

1. Outcomes or results in terms of the pupil.
2. Definite processes and procedures with a recognition of activity as the basis of learning.
3. The pupil in the foreground and the teacher in the background as guide and director only of the learning activity.

The Format

According to Bossing, "Lesson planning is essentially an experience in anticipatory teaching. It is living through in advance, mentally and emotionally, the classroom experience as the teacher visualizes it. The eager faces, the questions that will arise, the difficulties the pupils will encounter, the way these difficulties are to be met all these the teacher will experience in imagination. This is the first essential of good planning. It is here that the teacher can bring into play the subtle power of well-developed imagina-tion. The more vivid, the better, so long as it is fully ringed with realism." The teacher must possess the following four qualities to plan effectively:

1. A broad understanding of the subject-matter, materials and activities that will provide the nucleus for the class-room experience.
2. An intimate knowledge of the environmental forces that have played upon the life of the class collectively and individually.
3. A thorough comprehension of the psychology of the mental process with an understanding of the realisation of the laws of learning leading to the anticipated classroom situation.
4. Teaching technique to meet the general and specific needs of a learning situation.

The Procedure

Planning is essential not only in teaching but in all spheres of human activity. Probably, there is no type of work where the results of poor planning are so devastating as in teaching. R.L. Stevenson said, "To every teacher I would say, 'Always plan out your lesson before-hand but do not be slave to it'." Bagley has put it thus, "However, able and experienced the teacher, he could do never without his preliminary preparation." To be effective, every intelligent worker plans out his work. A surgeon diagnoses the case, prepares his surgical instruments before he puts the patient on the operation table; a lawyer makes attempts to anticipate and prepare for every move in the court, an engineer prepares his blue print before he actually starts the construction work of a bridge or a building; the house mistress plans the details of the daily meals; the sales manager gives careful attention to every step in a proposed selling campaign. So must a teacher plan and prepare his work.

A lesson plan indicates the aims to be realised by teaching a lesson, the methods to be employed and the activities to be undertaken in the class so that it is kept engaged for the realisation of the aim. A lesson plan is actually a plan of action. It includes:

(i) The working philosophy of the teacher.

(ii) His information and understanding of his pupils.

(iii) His comprehension of the objectives of education.

(iv) His knowledge of the material to be taught.

(v) His ability to use effective methods of education.

The lesson plan affects the teacher's skill, intelligence, ability and his personality. Following are the chief functions of planning:

1. It delimits the field of work of the teacher as well as of the students and provides a definite objective for each day's work.

2. As the goal is determined, the teacher gets impetus to realise his goal.

3. It tends to prevent wandering from the subject and going off the way. It serves as a check on the possible wastage of time and energy of the teachers and students. It makes teaching systematic, orderly and economical.

4. Planning helps the teacher to organise and systematise the learning process. The activities in the lesson are well-knit, inter-connected and associated. The continuity of the educative process is ensured.

5. Planning helps in avoiding needless repetition.

6. Planning helps the teacher to overcome the feeling of nervousness and insecurity. It gives him confidence to face the class.

7. Lesson planning gives opportunities to the teacher to think out new ways and means of making the lesson interesting and to introduce thought-provoking question.

8. Lesson planning ensures a definite assignment for class and availability of adequate materials for the lesson.

Four Types of Planning. These are given as under:

(a) Planning of the work of the year in a definite manner and in units.

(b) Planning of each unit.

(c) Daily lesson planning.

(d) Planning shared with pupils.

Planning—Old and New. The modern emphasis is on providing learning experiences. We have repeatedly emphasised that good and effective teaching is 'causing students to learn'. It must stimulate the child to think and motivate him to learn further. The teacher is there to create learning situations and organise them in such a way that the child feels the inner urge to know, to think and to do. Therefore, the modern education makes the work of planning all the more important. Planning was not so elaborate and difficult in the traditional system of education which simply glorifies the subject-matter and fails to develop desirable habits, attitudes and skills. The present stress is on development of the abilities of the students, their attitudes, their experience and capacities. It is, therefore, inevitable for the modern teacher to plan his lessons very skilfully and carefully.

Different Steps in a Lesson. R. Schorling in 'Student Teaching' suggests the following steps in planning a good lesson:

1. Select the most appropriate aims.
2. Provide the illustrative materials available.
3. Include crucial questions.
4. Consider the level of the ability and interests of the pupils.
5. Consult courses of study and grade requirement.
6. Select the best procedures.
7. Tie the lesson with previous ones.

8. Take into consideration knowledge already possessed by pupils.
9. Include an appropriate assignment.
10. Consider supplementary materials in making the assignment.
11. Emphasise the main points of interest.
12. Arrange a logical order of activities that would lead towards a realization of the aim of the lesson.
13. Provide for adequate summaries.
14. Make the plan flexible enough to allow the teacher to leave it temporarily and follow pupil interests.
15. Budget the time devoted to phases of the lesson.
16. Provide a means for evaluating the results of the lesson and the teaching.

Broad Ideas

1. Suitable subject-matter should be selected.
2. The selected material should be presented in an organised, orderly and effective manner.
3. The children should actively participate in the lesson.
4. The outcomes of orderly procedure and achievement of objectives should be evaluated.

Main Considerations

1. What are the needs, difficulties, problems and interests of the students?
2. In what way can the requirements of the subject-matter be made suitable to the capacity and growth of the students?
3. What preparations have the students made for attacking the subject?

4. What are their experiences of the past which can be of assistance in the present situation?
5. How can the subject-matter be presented economically and effectively?
6. What type of material aids should be prepared and used in the lesson?
7. What incidents should be related?
8. What comparisons can be drawn and what similarities can be shown?
9. What type of application work should be used to fix, to clear up and to make real the grasp of the students of the general principles of the lesson?
10. What methods should be used to make the students participants in the lesson?

Generally speaking, the following are the characteristics of a good lesson plan:

1. A lesson plan should preferably be written and should not remain at the oral or mental stage. Panton writes, "The teacher is strongly advised, at least in the early stages, to make a written note of his preparation. Memory, sometimes, proves a treacherous servant, especially when his attention is divided." It is advisable, however, not to teach from notes. "Excessive reliance upon these may undermine the teacher's confidence so that he can never do without them. If, however, the teacher has occasion while teaching to refer to his notes, it is better for him to do so openly than to take a surreptitious peep at them. He loses nothing in the eyes of the children by the former method whereas by the second, he is likely to be misjudged by his pupils." Writing lesson plan helps in clarifying thoughts and in concentration.
2. The lesson plan should clearly state the objectives, general and specific, to be achieved.

3. It should be linked with the previous knowledge. The plan should not let the lesson remain an isolated one. It should have its basis on the background of the class. It should grow out of what the pupils have already learnt.
4. It should show techniques of teaching. It should state clearly the various steps that the teacher is going to take, and also various questions that he will ask.
5. The illustrative aids to be used should be shown in the lesson plan.
6. The materials of instruction or subject-matter should be carefully selected and organised.
7. To motivate the lesson, there must be a provision for audio-visual aids.
8. The plan should be divided into units, but care should be taken to see that the lesson remains an integrated whole arid every unit develops from the previous and submerges into the next one.
9. The children must be given enough scope to be active. It should not make them mere passive listeners.
10. The plan should be prepared in such a way as it does full justice to all the students of varied capacities and provides for individual differences.
11. It should show certain routine things. The plan should indicate the duration of the period, the period itself, average age of the students, subject and the class.
12. It should be flexible. The plan is a means and not an end. It is wrong to follow it slavishly. It is an instrument and should be used as such. The teacher should be prepared to change his teaching methods from those as referred to in the plan, if need be.
13. The lesson plan should include the summary of the whole lesson which is to be built up on the blackboard with the help of the students.

14. The plan becomes more useful if it lists reference material.
15. Care should be taken to suggest only those books or other materials which are available in the library.
16. It should include assignments for children.
17. A good lesson plan must provide for self-criticism.

QUESTIONS

1. "Careful lesson planning is the foundation of all good teaching." Examine this statement.
2. "A lesson plan is a servant and not a master." Explain this statement.
3. State the characteristics of a good lesson plan and prepare a lesson plan on any topic in Social Studies for class VIII.
4. Why is it necessary to plan a lesson? What principles should be taken into consideration for planning a lesson?
5. Explain the steps in lesson planning.
6. List the specific aids that you would use in the following lessons:
   - (a) Indus Valley Civilisation
   - (b) Buddha's life
   - (c) Ashoka's efforts for the spread of Buddhism
   - (d) Glorious Age of the Guptas
   - (e) Akbar's religious policy
   - (f) First War of Indian Independence, 1857.

16

Question Development

"Good Exercise", writes F. Theodore Struck, "by their very nature, are educative, and they have a very prominent place in all kinds of learning." Questioning plays an indispensable part in 'learning', teaching', and 'testing'. If used in the right way, at the proper time, questions lead to new realms of understanding; they serve as means of organizing knowledge, or correlating the results of educative experiences; of tying together units of learning; and of integrating personality. One who questions faultlessly teaches effectively, is not without meaning. Salmon holds that a bad questioner is a bad teacher; he may be a good lecturer. In the words of Rybum, "It is no exaggeration to say that the success of a teacher in any particular lesson, and in teaching in general, depends upon his ability to question well." According to Raymont, "The acquisition of a good style of questioning may be laid down definitely as one of the essential ambitions of a young teacher." The art of questioning is the most potent weapon in the educational armoury of the teacher. It has been well said:

"I keep six honest serving men,

They taught me all I know,

Their names are what and why and when,

And how and where and who."

Classification of Questions

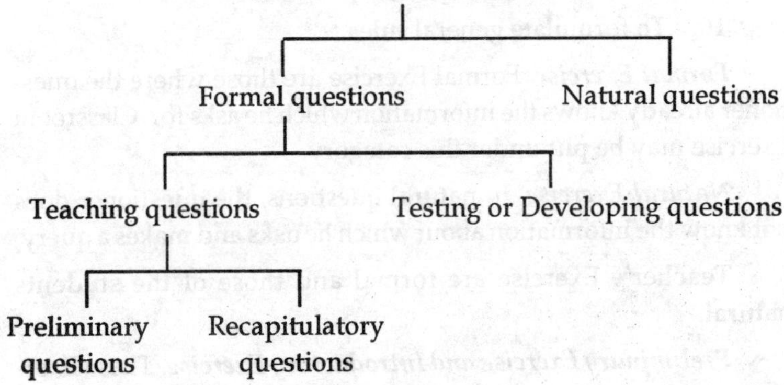

The Objectives

1. To test the previous knowledge of the students.
2. To enable them to recall something.
3. To enable them to recognise something.
4. To enable them to think over something.
5. To enable them to reason about something.
6. To elicit something from students.
7. To stimulate interest and effort on the part of students.
8. To keep the children mentally alert.
9. To promote initiative and originality.
10. To stimulate the curiosity of the students.
11. To ascertain whether they are following the lesson or not.
12. To link new knowledge with old.

13. To revise the lesson and thus fix the facts in the minds of the students.
14. To secure the co-operation of the students.
15. To diagnose the weak points of the students.
16. To formulate general rules.

Formal Exercise. Formal Exercise are those where the questioner already knows the information which he asks for. Classroom Exercise may be put under this category.

Natural Exercise. In natural questions, the questioner does not know the information about which he asks and makes a query.

Teacher's Exercise are formal and those of the students natural.

Preliminary Exercise and Introductory Exercise. These Exercise are generally asked at the beginning of the lesson. The purposes are:

(i) To test the previous knowledge of the students.
(ii) To link the new knowledge with the already learnt knowledge.
(iii) To motivate the child and arouse his curiosity.

These Exercise enable the teacher to test the readiness of the student's mind. Questioning at this stage enables the teacher to follow the maxim "From known to the unknown".

Exercise should be relevant to the topic. Their number should be very small, say three or four.

Recapitulatory Exercise. Such Exercise are generally put at the end of a lesson or at the end of each section of the lesson. Such questions serve two purposes:

(1) To enable the teacher to know if the children have picked up the ideas he wanted them to learn.
(2) To serve the purpose of revision and to give students a good opportunity for practice.

Developing Exercise. These questions are said to be the backbone of the lesson. They are used:

(i) to develop a particular line of thought;

(ii) to lead the pupils to discover facts for themselves;

(iii) to formulate new generalizations in an inductive way;

(iv) to focus attention on important points;

(v) to develop knowledge step by step;

(vi) to enable the students to use their powers of observation, of comparison and concentration;

(vii) to break the narrative in order to ensure that the class is following; and

(viii) to make the inattentive students attentive ones.

A great skill is required on the part of the teacher to ask developing questions. The teacher has to lead the students to think and discover facts for themselves. While narrating a story, the teacher should not ask question.

Various Types

(1) Comparison or contrast. Example: What is the difference between wealth and capital?

(2) Decision for or against. Example: Do you consider it correct to call Chandragupta Maurya as the first Emperor in India?

(3) Application in new situations. Example: Suggest measures to remove illiteracy in your village or town.

(4) Classification. Example: Are the following free goods or economic goods—air, sun-shine, machinery, gold, food?

(5) Relationship between cause and effect. Example: What is the relation between population and economic prosperity?

(6) Example or illustration. Example: Describe cases when prices rise with the decrease in the supply of some commodities.

(7) Statement of aim. Example: Why is the author interested in the study of problem children?

(8) Criticism. Example: Do you think Ashok was justified in following the policy of 'Non-violence'?

(9) Inference. Example: From the data given, which place do you consider to be more hotter?

(10) Discussion. Example: Discuss the most important proposals for bringing down the prices.

(11) Definition. Example: Define elasticity of demand.

(12) Recall. Example: What do you consider the three most important inventions of the last century?

(13) Summary. Example: What were the causes of the downfall of Mughal Empire?

(14) Observation. Example: Observe this experiment.

(15) Formulation of new questions. Example. What questions did occur to your mind?

Different Approaches

The teacher should bear in mind the following points in this connection:

1. The question should be asked first and then the student asked to answer it. The main advantage in asking the question first is to set the whole class thinking to find out the answer. On the other hand, if a particular student is asked to stand or sit, as the case may be, and then the question is put to him, other students may not show much interest.
2. Exercise should be evenly distributed. No child should be neglected. At the same time Exercise should not be

given in a regular order round the class. Generally there is a tendency to put either too many questions or too less to the students sitting at the back or in the front. Such a tendency should be avoided.

3. Plenty of time should be allowed for pupils to think out the answer. However, the time allowed will depend upon the nature of the question.
4. The inability of a child to answer a question should be accepted. The teacher should avoid to waste a lot of time in trying to get an answer out of a child who cannot answer. A skilful teacher recognises when the case is hopeless and the child is unable to answer the question in spite of his best efforts.
5. A volley of question asked in a rapid-fire manner is upsetting.

Questioning, an Art

1. The language of the question should be simple.
2. Exercise should be graded. They should neither be too easy nor too difficult. If the problem is too easy, the child will not take any interest in it. If it is too difficult, he will get discouraged.
3. Exercise should not be ambiguous, lengthy and vague. They should be clear, brief and to the point.
4. They should be suited to the ability of the children to whom the questions are put.
5. Exercise should be relevant to the topic.
6. Exercise once asked should not be repeated unless the teacher is sure the class has not followed it.
7. The teacher should try to vary the form of his questions.
8. Two questions should not be asked in one.
9. Exercise should be interesting as far as possible.

10. Exercise should be framed in such a way that these do not encourage guess work. The teacher should not generally admit answers like 'yes', 'no', or other single words.
11. Exercise should be of developing nature. Every question should grow out of the response of the previous one. Exercise should be in a sequence so that lesson may develop properly.
12. Suggestive questions such as "Was Sardar Patel an Iron man"? should be avoided as they fail to encourage mental activity.
13. Leading questions such as "Do you know that Subhas Chandra Bose was the founder of the Indian National Army?" should not be asked.
14. Echo questions such as "Mahatma Buddha was born at Lumbini. Where was Mahatma Buddha born?" should not be asked.
15. Avoid phrases like "Can any one answer this question?"
16. Euestions should be addressed to the entire class.
17. Exercise should be asked in a pleasing manner.
18. Exercise should be put in such a way that every student thinks that he will be asked to answer whether he is good or weak.
19. Adequate time should be allowed to answer.
20. Exercise should be addressed to the whole group and not to individuals.

Conclusion. The chief characteristics of questioning is to lead the child to discover new facts for himself, by guiding him through easy process of thinking or of reasoning.

The Teacher's Attitude to Pupils' Exercise. Following facts should be kept in mind:

1. The students should be encouraged to ask question.

2. Relevancy in Exercise should be insisted upon.
3. The teacher must insist on courtesy. Several pupils should not be allowed to ask question at the same time. Everyone should be asked to listen to a question.
4. Pupils' Exercise may be may be made the starting point for a small project.
5. The teacher should be frank enough to admit his inability to answer a question when he does not know the answer. However, in due course, he should be able to answer that question. For the sake of prestige in the eyes of the students, he should not give a wrong answer.

Judicious Blending of Talking and Questioning. Questioning is not a one-way traffic. There is an ample scope for the teacher as well as the students to put Exercise. The teaching-learning process is effective only when the teacher as well as the pupils are active and co-operative. The aim of the teaching-learning process is to enable the child learn in such a way that it enables him to adjust himself to the environment. As both the teachers and the pupils are attempting to realize the same goal, it is evident that they must be active and not passive.

Skill for Answers

The same care and skill in dealing with pupils' answers, as in questioning them, should be shown. After all, what for do we ask question? Not for the sake of question! The aim is to motivate children, to create interest, to test what the child knows and what he does not know, to encourage and stimulate thinking and fact-finding and to clear ambiguities and doubts. The quality and the nature of the answer reveal whether the purposes of questioning are fulfilled or not. Rather it may be put that questioning is a means to teach something that is revealed through the answers. Exercise and answers may be compared with the blades of scissors. Both are indispensable in the teaching-learning process as both the blades are required to cut a piece of cloth.

Answers reveal the deficiency of the students as well as the teachers. They are the touchstone to test the effectiveness of the teaching-learning process. If the answers are not satisfactory, it clearly indicates that either there is something wrong with the teaching process or with the learning process. Either the teacher has not taught in the proper manner or the students have not understood the subject-matter. Therefore, answers provide an important tool to make necessary changes in the teaching-learning process.

Classification of Answers. A close analysis of the various types of answers shows that these can be put under the following six categories:

(i) Right and correct answers.

(ii) Correct but incomplete.

(iii) Partially correct and partially wrong.

(iv) Wrong but intelligent.

(v) Ridiculously wrong.

(vi) Mischievous.

How to Deal with Answers. No hard and fast rule can be laid down for dealing with various categories of answers. Ward and Rascoe write in this connection, "There are no rules. It is unwise to pass over all wrong answers as it is unwise to deal with all. Some are genuine, misconceptions, which the teacher must clear up at that time or later on, others are imperfect and incomplete answers, genuine also, which must be rounded off, others are haphazard or stupid and should be treated with contempt or else with such brief but emphatic words of disapproval as the teacher may have a command." The following are the different ways of dealing with answers.

Appreciation. The teacher should always appreciate the answers of the students as appreciation will encourage the students to think further. Even if the answers are wrong but teacher feels that the child is making genuine attempts, due appreciation should be given.

Analysis of Wrong Answers. When the answers given by most of the students are wrong, the teacher should try to analyse their causes. The causes may be as under:

(i) Defective or difficult language used by the teachers.

(ii) Defective explanation of the subject-matter taught.

(iii) Inattentiveness on the part of the students.

(iv) Lapses of memory.

(v) Toughness and complexity of the subject-matter. In such cases, the teacher should accept the responsibility and should not feel shy of teaching the subject-matter again.

Encouragement of Children. When the answers are partly right and partly wrong, the students should be encouraged to analyse themselves the nature of their mistake. The teacher may ask further Exercise to analyse the nature of the mistake. When all the factors which are responsible for wrong answer, or answers are not clear to all the students, they may be asked to build up the real answers once again. It is unwise on the part of the teacher to be impatient and to make the necessary completion or correction himself.

Treatment of Wrong Answers. When a particular student gives a wrong answer, the teacher should not pass on till he gets the right answer without explaining why the first answer is wrong. The child must be made to understand why his answer is wrong. He is not likely to gain anything from the right answer if his doubts remain unexplained.

Answers Carrying Some other Version, other than Expected by the Teacher. The teacher should accept and appreciate correct and complete answer although it may differ from the answers as expected by the teacher. There are a few intelligent students in every class who believe in novelty and do a lot of extra-reading. The difference in approach should be explained by the teacher.

The Form of the Answers According to the Nature of the Lesson. Whether the answer should be in bits or incomplete sentences depends upon the nature of the lesson. Complete sentences may not be insisted upon in arithmetic, science and in some cases in history or geography. But in a language lesson where the aim is to develop the power of expression, the teacher should insist upon complete sentences. No general rule can be laid down. It is up to the teacher to decide the form of the answer. But it must be stressed that whatever be the form answers should be in a clear, simple and concise language.

Answers based on Right Understanding. The teacher must make sure that the answers as given by the students are really based on genuine mental activity. Parrot fashion words, though they may have senses, are not based on any thought or understanding on the part of the child. The teacher must go deeper and ensure that the child really knows what he says.

Answers Given in Unison. Answers given in unison should be discouraged. Such answers lack educational value and, therefore, should be disallowed. Assertive students should be given their due only. They should not be allowed to usurp the right of others who are slower or are perhaps making a mistake. Students should not be allowed to interrupt others while they are answering Exercise.

Observance of Courtesy. The teacher should see that the ordinary courtesy is observed in answering Exercise. The students should stand or sit and address in the proper way.

Encouragement to Shy and Submissive Students. There are always some students who feel shy and become nervous when Exercise are put to them. Though they know the answers quite all-right, yet they remain mum. The teacher should, in all such cases, give more encouragement and appreciation.

Repetition of Good Answers. Good answers of the students should be referred to the class, got repeated, preferably by another pupil. The teacher should avoid to repeat a correct answer himself, unless he wants it to be specially stressed.

Discouragement to Irrelevant Answers. The students should be made to realize the cause of the irrelevant answer, the teacher should study thoroughly that the irrelevant answer is not due to some mischief on the part of the student.

Development of the Summary of the Lesson with the Help of the Answers. The answers given by the students at the recapitulatory stage may be used to develop a summary of the lesson. All the answers in brief may be written on the blackboard and the students encouraged to develop an integrated summary with the help of these answers.

Conclusion. Correct, clear and thoughtful answers result from clear thought-provoking Exercise. The better means of evoking responses from the students are sympathy, patience and encouragement rather than impatience, harshness or snubbing them. Right and correct answers imply that the teacher is using right and correct methods of teaching and the students are learning in an appropriate manner. It may, therefore, be concluded that the pupil's answers to the questions are equally important if not more than the questions of the teacher in teaching-learning process.

Exercise properly planned, carefully worded, evenly distributed, scientifically and psychologically asked, honestly answered and intelligently followed up are very profitable and in fact indispensable in the effective teaching-learning process. Colvin gave recognition to questioning in these words, "The efficiency of instruction is measured in a large degree by the nature of the questions that are asked and the care with which they are framed. No teacher of elementary of secondary school subjects can succeed in his instruction if he has not a fair mastery of the art of questioning."

QUESTIONS

1. Elucidate the importance of questioning in Social Studies.

2. Give a few examples of introductory, developmental and recapitulatory questions in history.
3. State the different types of question.
4. Explain the techniques of asking questions.
5. How should a teacher deal with the answers of the students?
6. Describe the art of questioning.

17

Measurement and Evaluation

The importance can hardly be minimised. The examinations have been in existence since times immemorial. "To close down examinations would be to give the signal for educational saturnalia", observed Sir Michael Sadler.

Similarly, J.C. Mathur emphasises the value of examinations when he writes, "Even in the idealised picture of society portrayed in H.G. Well's Utopia, examinations find an important place."

The Secondary Education Commission has also observed, "Nevertheless examinations and especially external examinations have a proper place in any scheme of education. External examinations have stimulating effect both on the pupils and on the teachers by providing well defined goals and objective standard of evaluation. To the pupil the examinations give a goal towards which he should strive and a stimulus urging him to attain that goal in a given lime thereby demanding steady and constant effort. This makes the purpose clear and the method of approach definite. He is judged by external and objective tests on which both he and others interested in him can depend. And, finally, it gives him a hallmark recognised by all."

The Procedure

1. To evaluate the achievement of the students.
2. To help in diagnosis.
3. To help in prognosis.
4. To act as motivators.
5. To measure the efficiency of the teachers and of the school.
6. To give uniformity of standards.
7. To measure fitness for admission to higher courses.
8. To help in selection by competition.
9. To help in guidance.
10. To acquaint the parents with the progress of their wards.
11. To measure personality.

The Effects

1. A bane of educational system.
2. A begetter of rivalry and strife.
3. A blood sucker.
4. A dead hand of education.
5. A glorification of memory.
6. A growing tyranny.
7. A necessary evil.
8. A presumptuous attempt to gauge the depth of human ignorance.
9. An enemy of true education.
10. An incubus.
11. An obstacle to learning.

The Demerits

1. Examinations lack definite aim.
2. There is a major element of chance.
3. Examinations lower educational standards as the entire energy of students and teachers is spent in preparing for the examination. Stress is laid on spoon feeding and not on understanding.
4. Examinations tempt the students to adopt unfair means to gain success.
5. Subjective attitudes of examiners influence marking.
6. Examinations put heavy strain upon the students who burn the mid-night oil near the examination days.
7. Failures in examination leads to frustration and even to suicides in some cases.
8. Examinations ignore the development of personality of the students.

Examination System

Evaluation has to be very comprehensive in a system of education which aims at the many-sided development of the personality of a child. "The school of today concerns itself not only with the intellectual pursuits but also with the emotional and social development of the child, his physical and mental health, his social adjustment and other equally important aspects of his life-in a word, with an all-round development of his personality", writes the Secondary Education Commission. In the light of these objectives of the system of education, comprehensive programme of evaluation would include:

1. Evaluation of the academic subjects.
2. Evaluation of the skills.
3. Evaluation of the physical development.

4. Evaluation of the moral development.
5. Evaluation of the social development.

In the words of Lestcr D. Crow and others, "Evaluation is a broader term than measurement. Evaluation not only is concerned with the determination of learning results but it also involves value judgment of the desirability of those results. It is a continuous process in which various techniques to testing or measurement can be utilised. Evaluation is a co-operative activity in which the principal, the teacher, the pupils and the parents participate."

One of the best definitions of evaluation is given by Clara M. Brown, "Evaluation is essential in the never-ending cycle of formulating goals, measuring progress towards them and determining the new goals which emerge as a result of new warnings. Evaluation involves measurement which means objective quantita-tive evidence. But it is broader than measurement and implies that considerations have been given to certain values, standards and that interpretation of the evidence has been made in the light of the particular situation."

H.H. Remmers and N.L. Gage point out, "It is the felt need that has caused the shift from the term 'measurement' — implying mathematically precise mensuration of knowledge — to the term 'evaluation' which widens the areas to be studied to include subjective opinions and qualitative changes as well as objective and quantitative changes to include changes in attitudes, appreciations, and understandings as well as acquisitions of knowledge and skills."

Evaluation is a process by means of which changes in behaviour of children are studied and guided towards goals sought by a school.

Wiles defines as, "Evaluation is a process of making judgements that are to be used as a basis for planning. It consists of establishing goals, collecting evidence concerning growth or lack or growth toward goals, making judgments about the evidence, and revising procedures and goals in the light of the judgments. It is a procedure for improving the product, the process, and even the goals themselves."

Chester T. McNernly observes, "The purpose of any programme of evaluation is to discover the needs of the individuals being evaluated and then to design learning experiences that will solve these needs... Evaluation is an important and delicate process not only from the standpoint of determining the needs and growth or programmes of individuals but also from the standpoint of what it does to the individuals being evaluated... An evaluation cannot adequately be made by using a single check list, an isolated anecdotal record, or a battery of examinations; a complete evaluation will require the use of many techniques."

Thomas H. Briggs and Joseph Justman write that evaluation is "a process by which the values of an enterprise are ascertained." Further they write, "Evaluation should be conceived primarily in terms of educational purposes which the programme of supervision is intended to serve."

(i) If the purpose is to stimulate teachers to improve their techniques of classroom instruction, evaluation must concern itself with ascertaining the extent to which such improvement is being effected.

(ii) If the purpose is to enrich and vitalize the course of study, evaluation must seek to determine whether the pupils are really deriving greater educational value from the "enriched" and "vitalized" programme than they did formerly.

(iii) If the purpose is to re-establish faculty 'espirt de corps' and school morale, the objectives of evaluation will be as to assess in various ways the degree of improvement in personal and professional attitudes, in human relations, and ultimately, therefore, in efficiency of teaching and learning.

(iv) If an important purpose of the supervisory programme is to promote greater educational attention to individual needs of pupils, evaluation will necessarily concern itself with estimating the success with which guidance procedures, differentiated programme of study, courses and units of learning experience, individualised teaching and learning procedures, and other educational measures designed to achieve greater satisfaction of individual needs are operating.

Shane and McSwain conceive evaluation, "as a process of inquiry based upon criteria cooperatively prepared and concerned with the study, interpretation, and guidance of socially desirable changes in the developmental behaviour of children .... It is a process within the child as a result of which he responds to the psychological interpretation he makes of his school-community environment."

Nature of Evaluation

The concept of evaluation implies a checking or assessment of what goes on. This is done so that actual facts of a situation may be ascertained and remedial action taken where necessary. Since a detailed analysis helps to isolate the factors which may contribute to the malfunctioning of the whole system, evaluation can perform a vital diagnostic role by suggesting corrective action at every stage of preparation, instead of having the system with all its errors proceed blindly to its final end. Evaluation used specifically for this purpose of correcting an ongoing process, rather than only for final product assessment, is one of the most important contributions of systems thinking to programmes in education. Formative or continuous evaluation, (providing feedback which enables adjustment of the programme to meet intermediate objectives), results in a better chance for the programme to achieve its final objectives.

Purpose of Examination

1. Evaluation appraises the status of and changes in pupil behaviour.
2. Evaluation discloses pupil's needs and possibilities.
3. Evaluation aids pupil-teacher planning.
4. Evaluation expands the concepts of worthwhile goals beyond pure achievement.
5. Evaluation serves as a means of improving school-community relation.
6. Evaluation familiarizes the teacher with the nature of pupil learning, development and progress.
7. Evaluation relates measurement to the goals of the instructional programme.
8. Evaluation facilitates the selection and improvement of measuring instruments.
9. Evaluation appraises the teacher's competence.
10. Evaluation appraises the supervisor's competence.
11. Evaluation serves as method of self-improvement.
12. Evaluation serves as a guiding principle for the selection of supervisory techniques.

New Trends

Fairly exhaustive techniques have been designed by educationists to evaluate the various aspects of a child's growth. Following are the commonly used techniques.

1. Intelligence tests.
2. Achievements tests.
3. Aptitude tests.

4. Personality tests.
5. Test of attitude and bahaviour.
6. Rating scales.
7. Questionnaires and check lists.
8. Interview.
9. Anecdotal records.
10. Autobiographical method.
11. Pupil's diary.
12. Case history.
13. Sociometric techniques.
14. Projective techniques.

For the development of an effective evaluation programme the teacher must be acquainted with:

(i) the objectives of the subject as a whole and of specific units.

(ii) the relationship between objective, instruction and evaluation.

(iii) the varied purposes of evaluation i.e., diagnosis, guidance, grading, classification, etc.

(iv) the elementary theory and practice of measurement.

(v) the techniques and tools of evaluation-their preparation and uses.

(vi) the follow-up procedure to utilize the 'feedback' in the classroom.

The above discussion leads us to conclude that formulation of the objectives of teaching Social Studies at a particular stage of education is the foremost task. Everything that a teacher does must be based upon the kind of behaviour he wishes to result from his teaching.

Main Aspects

Schemically the concept of educational evaluation may be presented by showing the relationship among objectives, content subject-matter, learning activities and evaluation procedures (testing).

The inter-relationships of these four aspects of evaluation clearly indicates that the process of evaluation is a continuous one and involves continual appraisal of objectives of the teaching-learning process and of the testing procedures used by the classroom teacher.

Major Functions

1. To make provision for guiding the growth of individual pupils.
2. To diagnose the weaknesses and strength of pupils.
3. To locate areas where remedial measures are needed.
4. To provide a basis for a modification of the curriculum and courses.
5. To provide a basis for the introduction of experiences to meet the needs of individuals and group of pupils.
6. To motivate pupils towards better attainment and growth.
7. To test the efficiency of teachers in providing learning experiences and the effectiveness of instruction and classroom activities.
8. To improve instruction.
9. To bring out the inherent capabilities of a pupil, such as attitudes, habits, appreciation and understanding, manipulative skills in addition to conventional acquisition of knowledge.

Objective Type Tests

Matching Test. Under column A, names of some of religions and under column B, names of their founders are given. Write down the correct names under column C.

A	*B*	C
Christianity	Mohammad	
Islam	Buddha	
Buddhism	Mahavira	
Jainism	Christ	

Multiple Choice Test. Below are given a few questions. Against each are given a number of answers. One of these is correct. Underline the same.

(a) Who was Kalidasa? (King, poet, scientist)

(b) During whose reign Fahien visited India? (Harsha Vardhana, Ashoka, Chandragupta)

(c) Where was the capital of Kanishka? (Ujjain, Patliputra, Parushpur)

True/false Test. Certain statements are given below. Against each statement are mentioned two words, e.g., true and false. Underline the correct one.

1. Ahimsa is practised in its extreme form in Christianity. (True/False)
2. The Holy Bodh tree is situated at Sarnath. (True/False)

Simple Recall Test. Write in one word the answer of the following:

(a) What is the per capita income in India?

(b) What is the per capita income in the UK?

(c) What is the exchange value of the Indian rupee in terms of the dollar?

Best Answer Test. Put mark against the best answer.

Alexander did not proceed further because

(i) he did not know the route.

(ii) his forces refused to go further.

(iii) he was defeated by some king.

Completion Test. Fill in the blank by appropriate word(s) in the following:

(i) To be a thing must have scarcity, utility and ....

(ii) .... in the currency of UK.

Classification Test. In each line, underline the word that does not belong there.

Example: Harbour, trade, exports, import, mountains.

(a) Tulsidas, Kabir, Surdas, Napoleon.

(b) Calcutta, Madras, Bombay, Delhi.

(c) Cat, horse, cow, tree.

Construction of New Type of Tests. (1) Prepare a list of all the topics falling within the scope of the examination. (2) Keep in view the most significant items in each topic. (3) Put easy questions first, then moderate and, in the end, the most difficult ones. (4) Put definite questions; brief and free from the ambiguity; (5) Do not put suggestive statements. (6) Put items which should have only one correct answer. (7) Include different types of objective tests, e.g., multiple choice, matching, etc. (8) Give reasonable time to the students to answer the paper. This suggests the following time: Recall type – 4 to 8 items per minute. (9) Give very clear instructions.

Some advantages have been mentioned by Percival Symonds and they are discussed as under:

First Advantage. "The new type examinations are more objective in their scoring, since the responses of pupils are controlled, and since there can be no doubt as to the correctness or incorrectness of their responses."

They are free from the personal factor of the teacher. The mood of the examiner in no way affects scoring. Each question must have only one possible answer. 'Contrast the achievement of Mahmud Ghaznavi with Mohd. Ghori is a legitimate thought-provoking assignment in the essay type of examination, but there is a great scope for a variability in marking.

Second Advantage. "They may be very comprehensive and can be made to cover a great deal more material than the old type of examination. Since the pupil does very little writing, he can devote his time to thought and can thereby answer a great many questions than when he has to write his answers out at length."

Chance element is very predominant in the essay type of examination. Only a limited number of question are set out of the wide field that has been covered. It is not uncommon to find students preparing fifteen or twenty questions in a subject and securing very high marks and students preparing forty questions but failing miserably. How does it happen and how could it be avoided? The answer is very simple. This happens simply because the number of question set in the paper is so small that quite a major portion of the course covered remains untested. On the other hand, a large number of question which are set in a new type of test eliminate the element of chance and cover a wide field of course.

Third Advantage. "They are very easy to score as compared with the older type of examination. Notwithstanding the fact that the tests are more comprehensive, they may be scored in less time and with less labour. This is in itself a sufficient reason to make them attractive to all teachers."

A key of the various questions may be prepared and then anybody can mark the question papers.

Fourth Advantage. "Pupils like them. There is no question as to the accuracy of marks they receive. There is no chance for the teacher to show favouritism or personal bias. The pupils, relieved of much writing, find these tests less tiring."

The pupils like the new type of tests because they think that marking will be fair and judicious. Even the students may be asked to mark the papers themselves if key is supplied to them. The general complaints of leniency of marking in one case and hard marking in the other are eliminated.

Fifth Advantage. "They are more educative for the pupils. Let your pupils score their own tests directly after they take them by exchanging papers with their neighbours. It is then that their interest is at white heat. After the papers have been scored, the questions may be discussed. The pupils readily see where they need further study."

Besides the five advantages given by Symonds, we might add some more.

Sixth Advantage. The new type of tests discourage cramming and encourage thinking, observation and scrutiny.

Seventh Advantage. They are more reliable. Same results will be secured whoever may be the examiner. An essay type of question paper cannot give the same results if it is given to different examiners.

Eighth Advantage. Objective test can be standardised by applying before hand to a large number of students of the same age group before the actual examination. On the basis of the results of these standardised tests, the authorities of a particular institution can compare the standard of their institution with other institutions of the same area.

Developing Questions

Symonds gives two main limitations of new type examinations.

First Limitation. The pupil does not have an opportunity to show his ability to organize his thought He has nothing to do except check over the truth and falsity of statements or fill in the missing words or incomplete sentences. Pupils miss the valuable experience of making comparisons, giving explanations or giving definitions. They are not asked to summarize the material or to make applications of principles, and, of course, these are valuable abilities which we do not want to neglect.

Second Limitation. "These new types of examinations are not diagnostic in that they do not tell where the pupil's reasoning process goes wrong or where he stops reasoning altogether and starts guessing."

Besides, the following limitations may also be noted:

Third Limitation. It is commonly said that new type of tests fail to check cramming. Once the test is standardised, the teachers will coach their pupils on the test thus making it utterly useless. There is every possibility that 'keys' or 'guides' to these tests may find their way in the market. General knowledge guides have already made their entry in the market.

Fourth Limitation. It is often argued that use of new type of tests is very expensive.

Fifth Limitation. Like the essay type tests, these also fail to test the character-building aspects.

The Old vs New Type Tests

1. The number of question in the essay type or old type is very small, generally five or six questions in a paper.

   There are a large number of question in the new type tests.

2. Answers required in the old type of tests are large. The answers are so short in the objective tests as can be written in a word or two or at the most in a sentence.

3. Essay-type questions are usually broad, general and indefinite. The examinees are at a loss to know how much they will have to write as answers.

   Objective questions are specific, narrow and definite.

4. In essay-type tests personal factors like bias, temperament, whims etc. of the examiner influence marking.

   Scoring becomes objective in the new type of tests.

5. In the answer of the essay test, there is scope for partial credit. Answers may be partially wrong and right.

   In the new tests, there is no provision for partial credit. Answer must either be right or wrong and hence full or no credit.

6. In the essay tests examinees have to devote a long time. questions can be answered in a short time in the new tests.

7. In the essay tests, questions are selected at random and the entire course is not covered. Some chapters or questions are completely ignored.

   The entire course can be covered by comprehensive questions.

8. Essay tests put premium on expression. Students hardly find any time to think over the question.

   New tests put premium on thinking.

9. Pupils having linguistic skill are at an advantage in the essay tests. New tests are advantageous to the intellectually smart students.

10. It takes a short time to frame questions in the essay tests. It takes a long time to frame questions in the new tests.

11. Students find it easier to prepare essay questions. They can safely omit many portions of the subject-matter in the essay tests.

Students have to devote a longer time to prepare new type tests as they have to go through the entire course for clear conceptions.

12. Essay tests are very suitable for testing composition and skills and knowledge of the subject. New tests are not suitable for testing composition and skill as well as appreciation of the subject.

13. In the essay tests, there is great scope for 'guessing' questions. Students prepare themselves from 'Made Easy' books. In the new type there is scope for guessing answers.

14. Essay tests take a longer time in examining scripts. Short answers take less time to examine scripts.

15. Printing cost is small in the case of essay tests.

    Since there are many questions, printing is costly in the new tests.

16. Answer scripts cost much as answers are very lengthy in the case of essay tests.

    Answers being very short and usually can be written on the question paper itself. This makes the answer scripts less costly.

17. There is less scope for adopting unfair means in the case of essay type tests by the students in the examination hall.

There is enough scope for adopting unfair means in the new tests.

E.W. Menzel observes that whether old-type or new-type, we should observe among others the following principles:

1. It will be general and comprehensive enough to test thoroughly the pupil's mastery of the desired skills or grasp of a subject-matter. It will make it impossible for a pupil to get a good mark just because he got a few 'lucky Exercise' and will not fail a good pupil just because of a few

'unlucky Exercise'. Very few examinations in India are adequate in this respect.

2. It will reliably grade the pupils into at least six to ten (or more) different classifications according to their ability.
3. It will be as objective as practicable. Some questions of a discussional nature can be given to advantage but there should also be some work which pins pupil and examiner down to answers which can be quite objectively scored. Even in the essay type of examination, the objectivity can be greatly increased with study and care.
4. Other things being equal, the test which examines most intensively or extensively in the least time and with the least fatigue on the part of the pupil is the best.
5. The test should encourage creative and self-reliant work and discourage mere mechanical rote-memory work.
6. The test should encourage the pupil to put forth his best effort.
7. The test should convincingly reveal to the pupil his deficiencies and encourage him to remove them.
8. The test should examine exactly what it pretends to examine and not handicap pupils for deficiencies in unrelated subjects. The more a test tries to examine in subjects extraneous to the avowed subject, the less efficiently it examines its own.
9. The standards of a test should be based on actual performance and not upon mere opinion of what a standard should be or on an arbitrary percentage work.
10. The more a test makes it possible to compare the performance of a certain group of pupils to that of other pupils the more revealing it is.
11. Keep in mind that no test is infallible. The daily work of the pupil and an observation of his habits of work are

equally important in appraising the work and ability of a pupil.

12. Keep in mind that poor results on the part of a group of pupils indicate a faulty test or one that is not graded to the ability of the pupils or deals with matters the children have not been taught.

Behavioural Objectives

B. S. Bloom has shifted the emphasis from content to the objectives in the examination and evaluation system. He advocated that tests should be objective-centred rather than content-centred. Each test should evaluate one specific objective. He made efforts to write objectives in behavioural terms. In describing the behaviour that is required of a student when he demonstrates his mastery of the subject or the skill, it is important to identify in very clear terms, exactly what he will do. This involves stating how he will recognise the cue or situation which will cause him to commence action or behaviour, as well as how he will recognize that the action has been successfully accomplished.

Instructional Objectives in Economics

1. To acquire the knowledge (information) of facts, terms, concepts, convention, trends, principles and generalizations, assumptions, hypotheses, problems, processes etc. in Economics.
2. To develop an understanding of facts, terms, concepts, conventions and trends, principles and generalizations, assumption, hypotheses, problems, processes etc. in Economics.
3. To apply the acquired knowledge and its understanding to unfamiliar situations.
4. To acquire the practical skills essential for the study of economics.

5. To develop interest in the subject and problems related to the economic life of the people.
6. To develop desirable positive attitudes necessary for developing a broader outlook.

• **Instructional Objective No. 1.** To acquire the knowledge (information) of facts, terms, concepts, conventions and trends, principles and generalizations, assumptions, hypotheses, problems, processes, etc. in Economics.

Behavioural Outcomes. To demonstrate the achievement of the above objective the pupil:

(a) recalls facts, terms, concepts, principles, trends etc.;
(b) recognises facts, terms, concepts, principles, trends, etc.; and
(c) reads information from various forms of representation of data, i.e., maps, charts, diagrams, graph, etc.

• **Instructional Objective No. 2.** To develop an understanding of facts, terms, concepts, convention, and trends, principles and generalizations, assumptions, hypotheses, problems, processes etc. in Economics.

Behavioural Outcomes. To demonstrate the achievement of the above objective, the pupil:

(a) discriminates.
(b) classifies.
(c) compares and contrasts.
(d) identifies relationships.
(e) detects the points of emphasis and the trends of arguments.
(f) cites illustrations.
(g) detects errors and fallacies and rectifies them.
(h) explains (analyses or gives meaning or clarifies or elucidates).

(i) gives reasons or advances arguments.

(j) interprets data presented in different forms.

• **Instructional Objective No. 3**. To apply the acquired knowledge and its understanding to unfamiliar situations.

Behavioural Outcomes. To demonstrate the achievement of the above objective, the pupil:

(a) analyses the unfamiliar situation or problem:

  (i) finds out what is given and what is required.

  (ii) recalls knowledge relevant to the situation.

  (iii) judges sufficiency or insufficiency, adequacy of data or any other evidence for solving the problem.

(b) establishes relationships.

(c) suggests alternative methods for solving the problem.

(d) selects the most appropriate method of attack.

(e) draws inferences and makes generalizations.

(f) makes predictions regarding the probable outcome of a given situation.

• **Instructional Objective No. 4.** To acquire practical skills essential for the study of Economics.

Behavioural Outcomes. To demonstrate the achievement of the above objective, the pupil:

(a) draws maps, charts, tables, diagrams, graphs, etc. from the given data.

(b) translates data from one form of presentation to another.

(c) prepares models.

• **Instructional Objective No. 5.** To develop interest in the subject and problems related to the economic life of the people.

Behavioural Outcomes. To demonstrate the achievement of the above objectives, the pupil:

(a) voluntarily studies literature related to economics and tries to know about the inherent issues and problems.

(b) spends leisure in trying to know about economic problems and issues and exerts in finding solutions to them.

(c) closely observes economic processes and changes at local, national and international levels.

(d) discusses and is able to communicate various aspects of everyday economic problems and their implications.

Application Based questions

1. Which of the following factors proved to be of the greatest help in the growth of Buddhism in North India in the Sixth Century B.C.?
   - A. Use of the language of the masses
   - B. Royal patronage
   - C. Buddha's dynamic personality
   - D. People's aversion to excessive and expensive Vedic rituals.
2. Hinduism differed from Buddhism and Jainism in respect of
   - A. law of Karma
   - B. purification through penance
   - C. doctrine of rebirth
   - D. belief in God.
3. According to the teaching of Buddha the best way to end miseries in lifs was to
   - A. help one's fellow beings
   - B. be a good scholar
   - C. live a life of austerity
   - D. keep a balance between austerity and indulgence.

4. The main cause of the almost complete disappearance of Buddhism from the land of its birth was
   - A. loss of royal patronage
   - B. the conquest of India by Muslims
   - C. the assimilation of the principles of Buddhism in Hinduism
   - D. the corruption in the Viharas.
5. Which of the following religious practices would have the approval of the Buddha if he were to come to life today?
   - A. construction of places of worship
   - B. rigid performance of religious ceremonies
   - C. respect of and compassion towards living being
   - D. insistence on asceticism.
6. Asoka convened the Buddhist Council at Pataliputra because he wanted to
   - A. counteract anti-Buddhist propaganda started by Brahmins
   - B. speed up the propagation of Buddhism
   - C. put an end to the schism in Buddhism
   - D. make preparation for sending missionaries abroad.
7. Hiuen Tsang was awarded the tide of 'Master of Law' because he
   - A. paid a visit to India
   - B. wrote an account of Harsha's reign
   - C. propagated Buddhism in India
   - D. studied at Nalanda University.
8. The best testimony to prove Harsha's scholarship is his
   - A. writing of the drama 'Ratnavali'

B. encouragement of scholars

C. developing Nalanda University

D. diffusion of Sanskrit learning.

9. Though similar in many ways Harsha differed sharply from Asoka in respect of

   A. tolerating other religions

   B. leaning towards Mahayana sect of Buddhism

   C. organising a smooth administration

   D. extending the boundaries of empire.

10. The main purpose of Hiuen Tsang's visit to India was to

    A. get access to authentic Buddhist scriptures in India

    B. visit holy places in India

    C. collect Buddhist relics

    D. meet adventurers in new lands.

11. Which one of the following traits of character proved to be of greatest harm to Mohammad Bin Tughlaq?

    A. fondness for administrative experiments

    B. little concern for human life

    C. indiscriminate financial generosity

    D. religious tolerance.

12. The chief factor responsible for Mohammad Bin Tughlaq's conquest of Warrangal was

    A. his superior military strength

    B. his well-planned strategy

    C. lack of preparation on the part of Warrangal

    D. the betrayal by Warrangal army chiefs.

13. Mohammad Bin Tughlaq succeeded in driving the Mongols from Afghanistan by

    A. sudden military encounters

B. creating rifts in their army

C. giving bribes to their soldiers and officers

D. inciting agitation among the Afghanis.

14. Mohammad Bin Tughlaq transferred his capital from Delhi to Daulatabad because

A. Daulatabad had a central and strategic position

B. Bahauddin had risen in revolt against him

C. Delhi had grown overcrowded

D. Daulatabad afforded better climate.

15. The difficulties of Mohammad Bin Tughlaq can be mainly assigned to

A. his hasty decisions

B. the non-cooperation of his officials

C. paucity of finances

D. opportunistic attitudes of his nobles.

16. Mohammad Bin Tughlaq inflicted untold miseries on his subjects because

A. he was cruel by nature

B. his subjects defied his orders

C. the sultan sometimes suffered from insanity

D. the people accused him of patricide.

17. Asoka was called the Sage-King because he

A. advocated non-violence

B. paid respects to the priests

C. lived a pure and simple life

D. undertook religious tours.

Source: *Simple Unit Tests in History* (1982), NCERT, New Delhi.

Short Answer Questions

1. Mention any two distinctive features of the town planning of Mohenjo Daro.
2. Mention the findings which indicate direct trade relationship between the people of the Indus Valley and Mesopotamia.
3. What similarity do you find between the sources of information of the Indus Valley and Mesopotamian civilisations?
4. In what manner can the Indus Valley civilisation be regarded as more impressive than other contemporary River Valley civilisations?
5. Among various factors mentioned as the causes of the destruction and disappearance of the Indus Valley civilisation mention any two which caused the destruction of some other contemporary civilisations as well.
6. Give any four principles of Asoka's Dhamma.
7. What explanation can you give of the fact that both the reformists, Buddha and Mahavira, belonged to the same social class?
8. Give any two principles common to both Buddhism and Jainism.
9. How the lack of patronage of the subsequent rulers became a cause for the decline of Buddhism?
10. What two important characteristics of the character of Buddha, if adopted today, can solve the problems of poverty and hunger in our country?
11. Explain why Buddhism declined in India but continued to exist in foreign countries.
12. Harsha had leanings towards Buddhism; at the same time he patronised Sanskrit literature. Give one example of such a king from earlier history.

13. Point out the difference between the penal system of Harsha and Guptas by giving examples.
14. "Harsha combines in himself some of the attributes and characteristics of both Samudragupta and Asoka." Prove the truth of the statement.
15. Mention one thing in the religious field which would have pained Hiuen Tsang, were he to come to life and visit modern India. Give reason also.
16. Give two examples to show that Mohammad Bin Tughlaq was a mixture of opposites.
17. Give two reasons for the failure of the system of token currency introduced by Mohammad Bin Tughlaq.
18. Give two reasons why Mohammad Bin Tughlaq though powerful and having great insight was not successful in most of his invasions.
19. Give an illustration to show that Mohammad Bin Tughlaq was a man with ideas far beyond his times.
20. Give two instances to support the view that Mohammad Bin Tughlaq was responsible for paving the way for the disintegration of the Delhi Sultanate.
21. Give the purpose of any three of the reforms which Mohammad Bin Tughlaq had in mind while introducing them and briefly describe the fate of any two of them.

Model Question Paper

CIVICS

Time Allowed: 3 Hours Maximum Marks: 100

General Instructions 1. All questions are to be attempted.

2. Marks for each question are indicated against it.

1. In what respect did the Moderates' concept of Swaraj differ from that of the Extremists? 15

Or

What was the initial reaction of the British Government to the Indian National Congress? Why did the British Government begin to regard it with suspicion and hostility? 7½ , 7½

2. "India is a Sovereign, Secular, Socialist, Democratic Republic" – Explain. 15

Or

Explain the following Fundamental Rights together with the respective restrictions thereon bringing out their scope.

(a) Right to Equality.

(b) Right to Freedom of Religion. 7½ , 7½

3. Which Directive Principles of State Policy reflect the country's economic goals? How far have they been implemented? 7, 8

Or

Explain the major features of Indian Federation. 15

4. Discuss the extent of the legislative powers of the Union Parliament and the State Legislatures as stipulated under articles 245-254. 15

Or

Discuss the composition and functions of the Parliament of India. 15

5. How is the President of India elected? 8

Or

How is the Union Council of Ministers formed? Discuss its functioning vis-a-vis the President and the Parliament. 4, 2, 2

6. Write short notes on any two of the following:

   (a) Powers of State Governors.

   (b) Judicial Review in India.

   (c) Planning Commission.

   (d) Preventive Detention. 4, 4

7. What is meant by Panchayati Raj? What are the main problems faced in its functioning? 4, 4

   Or

   Discuss the functions of a Municipal Corporation. 8

8. Give the policies and programme either of the Congress (I) or the Communist Party of India. 8

   Or

   What is meant by 'defection'? What are its effects on (a) Indian Political Parties and (b) Indian Democracy? 4, 2, 2

9. What are the basic principles of India's foreign policy? 8

   Or

   Discuss briefly India's relations with USA and USSR. 4, 4

QUESTIONS

1. "Present system of examination and evaluation in Social Studies fails to achieve its real objectives." Discuss this statement critically.

2. Give two illustrations of each of the following types of objective tests in-Social Studies.

(a) Matching Test.

(b) Completion Test.

(c) Classification Test.

(d) True/False Test.

(e) Multiple Test.

(f) Applica-tion Test.

3. Explain the need for including essay type questions in Social Studies paper.

4. Prepare a model test paper for any class you teach in Social Studies.

18

Societal Factors

Socialised recitation is an educational programme of the school which directly aims at the socialisation of the children by developing in them the traits of initiative and responsibility within a group membership and in harmony with group interests. Training children for democracy by giving them training in democracy is the all absorbing purpose of socialised class procedures. Co-operative enterprise is the 'keynote' of the method. According to Schorling, "The main purposes of the socialised recitation are to develop techniques useful in group work, to stimulate reflective thinking, to supplement previous knowledge, to encourage creative expression, to develop desirable social attitudes by providing practice in a large variety of socialised situations and above all, practice in the technique of co-operative thinking."

Yoakam and Simpson point out that in socialised recitation "Children are discussing, questioning, reporting, planning, working in natural ways. The teacher is a guide, counsellor, advisor, contributor and director in the best sense of the word, trying to get children discover things for themselves rather than to have them merely listening to them."

The Requirement

The traditional type of procedure of teaching does not provide for the active participation of the child in the learning-teaching process. It considers the child as a passive being. It does not provide sufficient opportunities for the child to express himself. Students usually learn by heart the subject-matter without understanding its meanings and significance. Ready-made knowledge is given to them. There is a lack of incentive for exercising imitative, originality and independent thinking. There is always the possibility that the child recites correctly and yet fails to comprehend the real meaning of what he has committed temporarily to memory.

Education for democracy is of recent origin. In the past the social aspect was not stressed. But now it is recognised that there must be a proper social setting and through education the child is to be prepared for social participation. Teaching as well as learning are seen in a social setting under the impact of sociological approach. Gandhiji said, "I value individual freedom but you must not forget that man is essentially a social being. He has risen to his present status by learning to adjust his individualism to the requirements of social progress." Child being a social animal should be prepared for 'social participation'. He is to be equipped with skills and abilities that would make him a better and useful member of the society. In the past such a conception of education was not taken into consideration in the educative process. Socialised recitation is one of the techniques of developing social understanding in children.

Purposes and Aims

1. To make teaching real, interesting and natural by increasing activity on the part of the pupils and by adopting the techniques of learning by doing.
2. To develop social consciousness among the students by providing opportunities to them to work together in a friendly and co-operative manner.
3. To give the students a training for social responsibility.

4. To reduce the social distance between the teacher and the taught by minimising the formalities.
5. To provide opportunities to the shy pupils to become more self-confident.
6. To give opportunities to students to understand each other in a better way.
7. To assist the students to express themselves freely and to develop the capacity to think clearly and in a concise way.
8. To assist the students to decide by collective discussions and to be benefited by each other's contribution and also share each other's experiences.

Various Kinds

(a) The informal group plan.

(b) The formal group plan and this may be further divided under the following heads:

  (i) The panel discussion.

  (ii) The symposium.

  (iii) The seminar plan.

  (iv) Workshop techniques.

The Informal Group Plan. The teacher and the taught talk about their experiences and problems in an informal manner. There is no ad-hoc agenda. Any member of the group may initiate a discussion. Every member of the group is at liberty to ask question, to ask for explanation and clarification.

Formal Group Techniques. Such techniques are organised on the pattern of a club, council, a senate or a committee. It becomes desirable to elect or nominate office-bearers of the group. Proper records of the minutes of the discussions are maintained. Such techniques impose heavy responsibilities and they must see that every pupil is provided opportunity to get chance to assume leadership.

Panel discussion. The panel usually consists of four to eight persons, a chairman and the audience. In a panel discussion, the representatives of the large group participate. The aim is to provide the features of a small group for the benefit of a large group.

A stage may be erected or a raised platform used for the panel personnel to sit. Seats may be arranged in a semicircular form to enable the audience to see and hear clearly the panel personnel. The discussion is opened by the chairman who explains the whole problem and co-ordinates the discussion and brings to a close the panel discussion by summarising the proceedings. The listeners should be given and opportunity to ask question and make contributions.

Long speeches and debates are not allowed in a panel discussion. The members of the panel should be fully prepared for the discussion.

Symposium. In a symposium two or more persons prepare their papers or speeches and present them to the audience. All the speakers talk about the various phases of the same problem and thus provide enough material to think about. Audience may be allowed to take part when the speeches or papers have been read. A chairman is also selected.

The Seminar. Generally advanced students who possess information at advanced and intellectual maturity can be greatly benefited through the seminar. A number of students investigate a problem and report their findings. The students may investigate problems individually or jointly. Reports are presented which are critically evaluated in the conference. The participants are free to ask for clarification of certain points. The teacher is the leader of the seminar. He must see that everyone gets some chance to contribute towards the seminar discussion.

The Workshop. It is a recent innovation. Many techniques are adopted in a workshop. Papers may be read, speeches may be made and discussions may be held. Practical work may be provided for the participants.

Merits of Socialised Techniques. Yoakam and Simpson give the following advantages of socialised techniques:

1. Pupils learn to plan activities.
2. Common interests and purposes are discovered.
3. Practice in leadership is gained.
4. Initiative is encouraged.
5. Independence of thought is achieved.
6. Training in courtesy is given.
7. Ability to report is developed.
8. Pupils learn how to take part in discussion.
9. Practice is developed in passing judgement.
10. Extensive experiences are made possible.
11. Self-confidence is gained.
12. Respect for others is developed.
13. Co-operation is learnt.
14. Teachers know pupils better.
15. Pupils have greater admiration and respect for teachers.
16. Learning is more highly motivated.

How to Make Socialised Recitation Effective?

(1) Topics to be discussed should be interesting and at the same time educative.

(2) Proper seating arrangements should be made.

(3) Adequate preparation on the part of the teacher is absolutely essential. He must find out ways and means to ensure total participation by pupils.

(4) The atmosphre of friendship should prevail. Every participant should realize that idea may be attacked and not people. Each child should be made to feel that his views are given their due recognition.

(5) The teacher is expected to play the role of a guide-cum-counsellor-cum-director-cum-contributor. It is his responsibility to see that the discussion is not off the track.

(6) The discussion must end with some conclusions. It should give the solution of a problem or a plan of action, the formulation of a policy, the evaluation of an issue or the acquisition of more knowledge about a topic.

(7) Reliance should be made on the interests, experiences and ability of the participants and should be supplemented by factual information supplied by teachers or leaders.

(8) Conversational tone is preferable to set speeches.

(9) All should be patient and tolerant of other's view-point.

(10) It should be used as a supplementary device.

What Socialised Classroom Technique Should not be?

1. It should never be used to propagate certain ideas.
2. Certain pupils should not be allowed to misuse their privilege by making it difficult for others to get to a fair dealing.
3. The group should not be forced to arrive at any definite decision at the time of discussion.
4. 'Heated' arguments for the purpose of overcoming one's opponent should not be allowed.

Teacher's Task

(1) He should enable the pupils to prepare themselves for class-room discussions by offering suggestions for reading or by questioning them.

(2) He must assume full control of the discussion and should also possess the ability 'to accept the position as one among the students' without surrendering his 'control'. He must acquire the art of making himself useful at the proper time.

(3) The teacher should ensure that the students go with right conclusion when the discussion is over.

(4) The teacher should assess the outcomes of the socialised techniques through devices like asking the students to summarise to draw charts map etc., of the principles of knowledge acquired through such techniques.

In the words of Yoakam and Simpson, "The teacher is a guide, counsellor, advisor, contributor and director in the best sense of the word, trying to get children discover things for themselves rather than to have them merely listening to him."

Demerits of Socialised Recitation. There are some drawbacks also as given below:

1. It is wasteful of time. It requires long periods of study.
2. It does not develop adequate mastery of the subject-matter.
3. There is a tendency of the class to wander from the subject.
4. It runs the risk of futile discussion.
5. In a socialised recitation there is always the danger that a few pupils will dominate the lesson.

Conveying the Ideas

Teacher: Today we are concerned with learning why we celebrate Gandhiji's birthday. What did you find out? Arun?

Arun: He gave us freedom.

Teacher: That is true. This fact gives us one clue to why we celebrate his birthday. Can anyone else think of another, Sohan?

Sohan: He was also the leader of the Indian National Congress.

Teacher: Another important clue. Is there another that we can bring to mind? Aslam?

Aslam: Gandhi promoted cottage and small-scale industries.

Teacher: Right. Another clue. What else did he do that we remember him? Harnam?

Harnam: He taught us truth and non-violence.

Teacher: Another important fact. Well, I think we have enough facts to work with. Boys and girls, we have a very special way of describing him, special names that we give him sometimes. Who will tell? Can you tell John?

John: He is described as Bapu.

Teacher: True. He was loved by all. There is another way of calling him. John, Can you describe?

John: Shakes his head in the negative.

Teacher: Can you tell Rohini?

Rohini: He is called the 'Father of the Nation'.

Teacher: Yes. Now let us do some careful thinking. We will be able to see how the facts we know tie in with our calling Gandhi, the Father of the Nation. Let us now concentrate on why he has been given the credit for being the 'Father of the Nation'. Let us think of what a good father does for his children.

(In this way the discussion continues)

A perusal of this form of discussion reveals the following:

1. The teacher is in complete control of the discussion.
2. He gives clarification of facts and ideas.
3. He keeps the discussion to the point and leads students from one fact to another.
4. He knows exactly where the discussion is to lead.
5. Students actively involve themselves in the development of the lesson.
6. Throughout the discussion the teacher provides an example how a leader guides the discussion. He represents the task clearly, listens to the discussion, encourages the clarification of statements and helps the members of the group to pull facts together into ideas.

Concluding.Remarks. The teacher leads them into thinking about and discussing these issues and often a tangible result in the form of a set of behavioural standards is produced. For example, the class may establish the following standards of leadership behaviour:

When I am a Leader. I give everyone a chance to speak,

I listen to others,

I help others decide what to do,

I ask others, in a nice way to do things,

I keep our work going.

The class may define followership behaviour in this way;

When I am in group. I wait my turn to speak,

I speak quietly,

I give ideas,

I listen to others, and

I work with the leader and other to get the job done.

QUESTIONS

1. Explain the meaning and purpose of socialised recitation in Social Studies.
2. Discuss the merits and limitations of socialised recitation.
3. Give an illustration of a communication between the teacher and students on any topic.

19

Community's Role

Community provides 'concrete', 'seeable', and 'tangible' resources which are extremely 'dynamic', 'interesting', and 'meaningful' for the teaching and learning of social studies. It is not enough for a child to have 'knowledge' about the factories, farms, council sessions, museums and social agencies etc. He must have the 'acquaintance with' all these. A community is a child's laboratory for having first hand learning about the ways of living. The community with its rich and varied resources can enrich and supplement learning in social studies. A well-planned programme can bring the school and the community quite close to each other. A school cannot remain an 'ivory tower'.

Important Community Resources. Ordinarily we include only those community resources which are within the 'walking distance'. Following are the important community resources:

Places of Civic Interest. These include the village panchayat. State legislature etc.

Place of Cultural Interest. These include art theatres, clubs, emporium galleries, Kala Kendras, museums, radio stations, T.V. centres. Zoos etc.

Places of Economic Interest. These include agricultural farms, banks, commercial centres, factories, telephone exchanges etc.

Places of Geographical Interest. These comprise dams, hills, lakes, rivers, river valley projects, rocks, springs, tea gardens, water falls etc.

Places of Historical Interest. These include caves, churches, excavations, forts, gurdwaras, inscriptions, mosques, pillars and temples etc.

Places of Scientific Interest. These consist of broadcasting stations, engineering institutes, thermal and hydro-power generating stations, television centres etc.

Government Buildings. These include fire stations, law courts, military installations, police stations, public libraries etc.

Forms of Social Control. These comprise attitudes, beliefs, customs, ceremonies, rituals, traditions etc.

Methods of Utilising Community Resources. These are basically two ways:

I. Taking the School to the Community.

II. Bringing the Community to the School.

Community Schools

Field Trips to places of civic, cultural, geographical, social and scientific places. These trips are very helpful in integrating classroom instruction stimulating imagination and learning by providing sensory perceptions, seeing life vividly, learning in the art of living with others and expanding emotional and intellectual horizons.

Community Service which includes cleanliness of the community, attending on the sick, social service in fairs, planting of trees, digging of manure pits, making of drains etc. All these activities help in developing a sense of dignity of labour, fellow-feeling etc.

Social Survey Clubs. Social survey clubs should be organised in schools which could undertake to investigate some of the crying needs and problems of the surrounding areas, e.g., the condition of roads, the percentage of literacy, the drainage of the village, street or town etc. The study of the community will help the child:

(a) to have a keener knowledge and understanding of social facts.

(b) to develop a more sympathetic attitude towards other people.

(c) to develop a desire to take more active part in community affairs.

(d) to have a recognition of certain forces that shape personal and social living.

(e) to have a greater sensitivity to the need for accepting social responsibility.

(f) to have a more intelligent concern for democratic institutions, their functions and contributions.

(g) to develop new interests in occupational fields.

(h) to understand the problems of the community in a better way.

(i) to appreciate that he must play an important role for the welfare of the community.

The study of the community will help the teacher:

(i) to correlate his teaching with the life of the community.

(ii) to utilise a rich source of instructional aids and material.

(iii) to fit the curriculum to the personal and social needs of pupils.

(iv) to develop better public relations.

(v) to co-operate with all other agencies engaged in school and community improvement.

Bringing the Community to the School. Following are the important means of bringing the community to the school:

Celebration of Festivals. Our festivals are the 'visible' embodiments of our culture. They form an integral part of community life. They can be exploited for purposes of education in schools. To quote T.S. Avinashilingam, "These days, far from being declared holidays with school closed, should be the days when school works in full strength not for the usual routine work, but for understanding the implications of the festivals and reliving them in the lives of children." Broadly speaking, we have six types of festivals:

(i) Religious festivals such as Shiva Ratri, Ganesh Chaudas, Durga Ashtmi, Anant Chaudas, Moharram, Easter, Christmas etc.

(ii) Seasonal festivals such as Basant Panchmi, Lohri, Baisakhi, Nirjala Ekadasi.

(iii) Days of national rejoicing accompanied by all kinds of fun, frolic, an and music such as Holi, Deepawali, Dussehra.

(iv) National festivals e.g. Independence Day, Republic Day, Mahatmaji's Birthday.

(v) Celebrations of the birthdays of national heroes e.g. Buddha, Shankaracharya, Guru Govind Singh, Guru Nanak, Guru Ravi Dass, Lala Lajpat Rai, Guru Teg Bahadur.

(vi) Literary festivals e.g. The Days of Tulsidas, Surdas, Tagore, Kalidas.

By organising the birthdays of the national heroes, the students may be inspired by high ideals by re-telling the stories of their lives, the dangers they faced, the tremendous odds they had to overcome and the efforts they had to make before attaining their objectives. It must be stressed upon the students that they must dedicate themselves to the service of the nation to which they belong.

National celebrations such as Independence Day may be used as occasion to focus attention on the various problems to be solved.

Celebration of the literary festivals like the days of Kalidas and Tulsidas help us to remember and study their great works.

Seasonal festivals help the children to understand the exhilarating effect of the change of seasons which the festivals indicate.

Attempt should be made to celebrate these festivals in the school premises so that the parents may also be brought into close contact with the activities of the school. Some of these festivals at which many people gather provide opportunities of social service to the students and teachers and thereby help in a good relationship between the school and community.

The School as a Social, Recreational and Cultural Centre. As most of the village schools are the only common meeting place in the villages, the cultural, physical and social activities in the villages should be planned, organised and held in the school with the joint co-operation of the public, the staff and the pupils. In this way, social service activities such as health and education weeks should be organised in the schools. Religious discourses, national celebrations, prachar sang programme attract members of the community to the school.

School grounds should also be made use of by village people for playing as they have no other properly maintained and marked grounds available for them. They may play after the regular scheduled games for the pupils of the school are played.

The older sections of the community may also use the school ground to spend their evenings and discuss problems of the day. Evening programme involving entertainment by magic lanterns, projectors or shows, radio programmes can be organised with no prejudices to school work.

District tournaments may be conducted in the schools where thousands of people meet on these occasions.

Adult Education Centre. The schools should become centres of adult education both in rural and in urban areas. They should conduct regular compaigns against illiteracy and educate the adults of the locality. Students should also be associated in this work.

School Library. Efforts should be made to extend the services of the library to the community and this may take many forms:

(i) Issuing of books to parents and others in the name and responsibility of the pupils.

(ii) Opening of school library for public use before and after school hours on holidays and during vacation.

(iii) Giving a room to a social service organisation in which to keep books and serve the community as a library.

(iv) Issuing of books to the Secretary of Old Students Association who may act as librarian to the old students and may be responsible for returning the books to the school.

Experience of the Members of the Public. Various "resource visitors" may be invited to the school to give out their life experience in various walks of life and increase the general knowledge of the pupils. "What we would like to see is a two-way traffic," thus observed the Secondary Education Commission. Interested members of the community engaged in various useful vocations and professions, will be invited to the school from time to time to talk about their particular work, to show its place and significance in the life of the community, to discuss its difficulties as well as its rewards. In this way, outside life will flow into the school and lower, if not knock down, the wall which at present isolates it from the currents of life operating outside.

Parent-teachers Association. There should be a parent-teachers association in the school which will help them to understand each other's point of view and will enable them to learn to co-operate in the common task for giving a better, more rational and more sympathetic deal to the children.

Exhibition. On occasions like the 'school day', an exhibition may be arranged for the benefit of the students and the public. This school exhibition may consist of the two sections:

(i) A United Nations Posters and Charts Exhibition consisting of UN posters and charts which are possessed by the School UN Association.

(ii) An arts and crafts exhibition consisting of paintings, drawings, collections of curious articles, stamps and coin collections etc. In this exhibition, the collections of parents may also be included.

Meeting with the Parents of Children of a Particular Class. The parents of children of one particular class at a time may be invited to have a general discussion with the teachers incharge of various subjects in that class. Discussion may centre around medical examination, projects undertaken by the class, progress of children and various other matters directly pertaining to the welfare of the children.

Inviting Parents to Witness talent Displayed by Children in Various Fields. Proficiency gained by a child at a particular game, or special aptitude shown at a particular co-curricular activity may be brought to the notice of the parent.

Participation by the Parents in School Programmes: (a) Some parents can lend a helping hand in raising funds for the school. Their help should be secured. This will develop in them 'sense of belongingness' to the school. These are the many ways through which the parents can help the school authorities i.e. by donating or lending books, giving stipends to the poor students, arranging mid-day meals for the poor etc.

(b) The school authorities should not hesitate to utilise the knowledge, skill and experience of the parents in supplementing class teaching. A doctor may be requested to give lectures on Hygiene and Physiology. Similarly, the services of the parents in other fields may be utilised.

Career Conferences. Career conferences may be organised and the parents asked to attend them. Specialists in different fields may be selected from amongst the parents and their talks arranged on the various aspects of their occupations.

Association of the Parents in the Management of the School. Parents may be associated with the managing committees of the schools. There can be no other person more interested in the school than the parents of the pupils.

Educational Conferences. Educational conferences should be organised in which parents, teachers and representatives of the education department participate. These conferences help exchange of thoughts, opinions, experiences, stock taking of the past and plan for the future.

Making the School as a Centre of Community Service. National, social and cultural functions should be organised in the school and the parents invited to attend them. School library may be thrown open to the parents. Labour weeks may be organised wherein students render them some social service to the community.

Celebrations of Parents' Days. It may be a full working day. The parents may be taken round the school so that they may see how the classes are held and where their children sit. Actual teaching done in the class may be shown to them. On the parents' day, activities such as debates, dramatics etc., may be organised. Children's work like calligraphy models, maps, charts etc., may be exhibited in one of the rooms of the school.

The parents may be taken to special rooms like the geography, history, science, craft etc. School sports may be organised on this day. It may take the form of Annual Prize distribution or School Annual Day. Adequate preparation should be made so as to give a good show of school activities. A light refreshment to the parents may be served if the funds permit.

Parent-Teacher Understanding

1. The teacher should show considerable patience and tact in dealing with parents.
2. He should not mind facing a rebuff or two at the hands of the parents.
3. He should allow the parents to talk voluntarily.
4. He should make a thorough study of the child's problems, his abilities, limitations and assets and discuss these with their parents.

5. He should not let the parent has the idea that the teacher is prejudiced against his child.
6. He should offer suggestions to the parents in a polite and convincing manner.
7. He should make the parents realize that he is sincerely interested in the welfare of the child.
8. He should impress upon the parents that he is also an active partner in the education of the child.
9. He should convince the parent that the school has the atmosphere and the apparatus to give the child an all-round instruction, make his life at school a profitable period and make him fit for life after school.

In view of the mass illiteracy in our country, the initiative for the home school cooperation rests upon the teachers. To quote S. Bala Krishna Joshi, "Parental cooperation cannot be had by learned disquisitions on the subject, or by periodical pamphlets posted to the parties. It cannot be created overnight. We cannot wake up one fine morning and find the parents pitchforked into cooperation. It is based on a series of silent acts of sincere service to children. It is the natural consummation of devoted deeds of dedication at the shrine of duty." All possible avenues should be explored to establish contacts with the parents.

In the end we may stress the importance of making the parents and the community interested in school work in these words, "The ordinary machinery for good school life," writes Thring, "is a thing of calculation and measurement but all discussion is in vain unless parents are interested."

QUESTIONS

1. Explain the use of community resources in the Social Studies teaching.
2. What do you understand by bringing community into school?

3. How can a teacher make use of community resources in making his teaching effective?
4. What are the difficulties in enlisting parents cooperation?
5. List any two community resources and explain their importance.

20

General Awareness

There is a general consensus among the educators that teaching of current affairs must form an integral part of social studies curiculum as current events increase the power of discrimination, comprehension, critical and constructive analysis—qualities needed for enlightened citizenship with which social studies are primarily concerned. Current affairs mostly fall within the social studies field. In fact, current affairs represent 'an extension' and 'exemplification' of the major topics in the curriculum of social studies. Teaching of social studies is likely to remain lifeless and meaningless without the study of current affairs.

Defining Current Affairs. R.S. Kimbal states, "It is a field, which is concerned with all these happenings, both domestic and international, social, political or economic, a knowledge, an understanding of which is necessary as a basis for citizenship, of loyalty and service." A close study of curriculum would reveal that these topics, by and large, come under the purview of social studies.

Current events are a living history and are part of the learning activities of 'social living' for the child. Only a well informed and well intentioned people can have a government which looks after the social and individual welfare of the people who make it.

Day to Day Knowledge

1. Expanding popular information.
2. Helping pupils to identify important problems and issues to see how these affect their lives and to sense what they can do about them.
3. Helping people recognise democratic values in reacting to problems and issues.
4. Encouraging pupils to develop habits of continued reading, listening, enquiring and observing ways of keeping well informed about current affairs.
5. Helping pupils acquire proficiency in locating, organising and evaluating information on important issues and in evaluating and analysing the judgement of others on these issues.
6. Helping pupils acquire the greatest possible proficiency in the skills needed for obtaining and using social information.
7. Helping pupils develop facility in the democratic discussion of issues, orally and in writing.
8. Helping pupils to see the importance of revising judgement in the light of new evidence.
9. Affording pupils a variety of opportunities for action to implement conclusions reached on important issues.
10. Promoting the ability of pupils to distinguish between more important and less important news items.
11. Promoting the ability of the pupils to take a position on controversial issues.
12. Developing the ability of the pupils to foretell the likely consequences in terms of present developments.
13. Helping the pupils relate school learning to life outside the school.

14. Promoting the critical appraisal of information obtained from the newspapers, magazine, radio, television etc.
15. Promoting discrimination in the choice of authors and sources of information.
16. Promoting understanding and tolerance.
17. Promoting national oneness and unity.
18. Promoting the cause of international understanding and world peace.

Broad Sphere

Current affairs in social studies include ideas, changes, movements and trends in parties and politics, election results, change in governments and government policies, defence, international relations and foreign policies etc. Reforms—cultural, economic, educational and social etc., amendments in the constitution, court discussion on election petitions and interpretations etc., all constitute current affairs in social studies.

Current affairs may be included in the following manner in school curriculum:

1. Teaching current affairs in addition to social studies.
2. Utilising current affairs for supplementing the teaching of social studies.
3. Utilising current affairs as a basis for social studies unit.

Nature of Current Affairs. There are broadly speaking four methods to use current affairs in social studies.

Current Affairs as a Subject. This implies including current affairs as a separate discipline of school curriculum. This approach is not very conducive as it will unnecessarily entail the study of additional subject and the students will treat it as an examination subject.

Current Affairs as a Resource. This view considers current affairs a "reservoir of illustrations which may be utilised to clarify the events, movements and topics described in the textbooks. Here, it is not obligatory on the part of the teacher to devote definite time from his daily schedule to the study of current affairs. He may do so occasionally.

Current Affairs as a Method. According to this view, current affairs should be used as a method or as a means or approach or procedure of simplifying difficult portions of the textbook and linking the present with the past. Elections to Parliament or State legislatures etc., may serve as starting points of a unit or a topic.

Current Affairs as a Means of Motivation. Children by nature are interested in what is happening now. They are interested in new inventions, new discoveries, elections, electricity projects etc. These topics can serve as motivation as this is the natural procedure of going from known to unknown, concrete to abstract, definite to indefinite and from immediate to distant.

Selection Rules

1. Continuity of the process of any cultural, economic, political and social event.
2. Consequence of the effects or results of a particular news or report in the press.
3. Nationality regarding the countries, groups and persons influencing events.
4. Recency of discoveries and inventions etc., groups and persons influencing events.
5. Reliability of sources, distinction between rumour and truth, fact and fiction.
6. Scope regarding the impact of an event—local, national or international.
7. Suitability regarding the age, ability, aptitude of the students.
8. Utility of events for students.

Illustrations of current affairs. Illustrations can be given as:

1. General Elections in democratic countries.
2. General Elections in non-democratic countries.
3. Elections of the President.
4. Space Travels.
5. Breaking out of hostilities between two countries.
6. International conferences and meetings and conferences sponsored by the UNO and other Agencies.
7. International Years like the child, women etc.
8. Interesting court cases and judgements.
9. Visits of a Foreign Dignitary.
10. Celebration of National or International Day.
11. Special Campaigns like literacy, Van Mahotsav, Prohibition, Cleanliness Drive, Family Welfare etc.
12. Inauguration of Special Projects.

Teaching Methods

1. Chart Making.
2. Debates on Broadcasting and T.V. Programmes.
3. Discussions.
4. Dramatising News Events.
5. Drawing Cartoons to illustrate events.
6. Map Drawing.
7. Youth Parliament.
8. Morning Assembly Talks.
9. News Bulletin Board and pinning clippings on it.
10. Preparation of Note-books and Files.
11. Quiz Competitions.
12. Round Table Discussion.

13. Talks of Experts.
14. Visits of Gram Panchayat, State Legislature and Parliament.
15. Wall of the World-depiction of current events on the wall of the social studies room through various types of visual material.

Teacher's Responsibilities

The role of a social studies teacher is that of a successful guide and a leader. For playing this role he must be wide awake, an active, enlightened and well informed person. He must listen to news-broadcasts and telecast, read current events, attend lectures and discussions, study and analyse reports and editorials, participate in school and community relations and see good newsreels and documentaries. R.S. Kimball has observed, "Current affairs can be taught successfully when a teacher is sufficiently interested himself. The varying degrees of success, however, seem to indicate that the ability of the teacher, rather than the quality of the medium or the method is the determining factor. Almost any device can be used effectively. The teacher's own interest, his own enthusiasm, his own understanding of what should be accomplished, are the matters which determine the failure or success of current events teaching. The best available media fail in their purpose when used by a class guided by a teacher unskilled in methods of current events instruction."

Other Issues

Teachers of social studies are under close scrutiny of the public as they form the core of the democratic action. It is widely believed that the standard of behaviour set by them in an out of the school stands examination and can be worthy of emulation by the impressionable youngsters who make up their student body. The teachers of social studies should have opinions but opinions derived in an objective manner from a weighing of evidence. The social studies teacher is expected to discuss issues that are considered controversial. Most of the current issues are controversial since they demand choice. If there is no ground for choice and, therefore, no problem of controversial treatment, the social studies teacher must be very careful to pursue his investigations with objectivity. The social studies teacher must operate within the limits set by his profession and the pursuit of truth. He should not air his views without any proportion.

Academic freedom implies that the social studies teachers should be willing to exercise good judgment, hold objectivity in high esteem and encourage reflective thought in themselves.

The teachers of social studies must also bear in mind that just as they are involved in academic freedom, students too equally and more importantly hope to learn to evaluate facts and human relationship for which they must have academic freedom to learn. Freedom of enquiry must be followed by free and objective instruction.

Academic freedom does not imply the right of indoctrination. James High of the University of California has explained this as "An opinion, derived by any means, if made the sole content of teaching and set up as the 'right' answer, constitutes indoctrination and cannot be countenanced under the guise of academic freedom." Schools are for the purpose of broadening the horizons of the students. Means employed must be objective and honest differences of opinion accepted. It is the duty of the school system to encourage reflective thought. Continued interest in the preservation of academic freedom throughout all ranks of society must stem originally from the schools. Reflection is the only unique and original tool man has. Reflected thought concentrated on the records of the human past results in wisdom of the exercise of human choice in the future. After reflecting, man does not always make the best choices, but without it any good choice would be totally accidental. Critical, constructive and tolerant attitude is a great part of adequate citizenship and all efforts have to be made in teaching of social studies to realize this objective. A social studies teacher has to perform this task very intelligently and skilfully.

One school of thought tends to hold the view that school is a temple of learning and its devotee i.e., children should be kept away from controversial issues. They point out that the conflicts of the real world must not enter into the portals of this temple and conflicting issues must not find their way in it. If they enier, they are likely to vitiate the classroom environment.

Rechard E. Servey points out that basically teaching acts comprise the following:

(1) Clarifying with the children the issue that lies at the heart of their concern.

(2) Guiding them in identifying the different choices possible for deciding the issues.

(3) Encouraging them to explore the facts and ideas which support the issues.

(4) Guiding them in an analysis of the facts and ideas to determine bases for opinions.

(5) Guiding them towards suspended judgment.

The social studies teacher should encourage the students to make their own choice, but to think more about it and to be on the alert for more pertinent information. The teacher should feel free to express his own favoured choice for action and to substantiate it but should point out that he too is limited in what he can do about making the final decision. He can somewhat assuage fears by suggesting that the other choices for action have strengths to be considered.

Regarding older pupils bringing up an issue unexpectedly not because they are particularly curious or frightened but because they are keen to know the reaction of the teacher, it may be observed that it will be advisable if the teacher responds by turning the issue addressing back to the questioner or by having the entire class respond to it. When the students have given their points of view, he should present his own in a 'most matter-of-fact way'. The teacher in no case should make provocative statements or make derogatory remarks directly or indirectly.

QUESTIONS

1. Define the term current affairs. What is their significance in the teaching of Social Studies?
2. Elucidate the role of a Social Studies teacher in the teaching of current affairs.
3. What are different methods of teaching current affairs?
4. Prepare a lesson plan on any one topic of current affairs.

21

Global Awareness

The key to the salvation of mankind lies in the reorientation of the minds of the people, or to speak in the language of the UNESCO preamble, 'in constructing the defence of peace in the minds of men.' And can there be any better base for raising the structure of lasting peace than the impressionable years of our young boys and girls in schools?

Role of United Nations

The signatories to the United Nations Charter have pledged "to live together in peace with one another as good neighbours, to take effective measures for the removal of areas of differences and to develop friendly relation among nations." It is understood that these ends cannot be achieved without education. This point is made explicit in the Universal Declaration of Human Rights in which it is declared:

"Education shall promote understanding, tolerance and friendship among all nations, racial or religious groups and shall further the activities of the United Nations in the maintenance of peace." One of the Resolutions of UNESCO reads:

"Member States of UNESCO in accepting its constitution have agreed that the purpose of the Organisation is to contribute to peace and security by promoting collaboration among the nations through education, science and culture in order to promote universal respect for justice, for the rule of law, for the human rights and fundamental freedoms."

Dr. Walter H.C. Lewis, a former Deputy Director General of UNESCO in his address to the American Association of Teacher Education in Chicago in 1956 stated, "... International understanding is the ability to observe critically and objectively and appraise the conduct of men everywhere to each other, irrespective of the nationality or culture to which they may belong. To do this one must be able to detach oneself from one's own particular cultural and national prejudices—and to observe men of all nationalities, cultures and races on equally important varieties of human beings inhabiting this earth."

Observations in the "Way of International Understanding."

1. *Physical Barriers.* People of different countries live in isolation.
2. *Political Barriers.* Narrow nationalism affecting understanding between nations and nations.
3. *Economic Barriers.* Restrictions on international trade, foreign exchange and currency.
4. *Religious Barriers.* Religious barriers leading to prejudices.
5. *Linguistic Barriers.* Differences of language not allowing people of different linguistic groups to come closer.
6. *Psychological Barriers.* Frustration and fear born of ignorance, selfishness and hostility leading to aggression and war.
7. *Educational Barriers.* Defective teaching of social studies leading to narrow nationalism and narrow loyalties.

Role of Education

'Education for International Understanding and Cooperation' reads that education should:

1. Make it clear that unless steps are taken to educate mankind for the world community it will be impossible to create an international society conceived in the spirit of the Charter of the United Nations.
2. Make clear that States, whatever their difference of creeds and ways of life, have both a duty to co-operate international organisations and interest in so doing.
3. Make clear that civilisation results from the contributions of many nations and that all nations depend very much on each other.
4. Make clear the underlying reasons which account for the varying ways of life of different peoples – both past and present – their traditions, their characteristics, their problems and the ways in which they have been resolved.
5. Make clear that throughout the ages, moral, intellectual and technical progress had gradually grown to constitute a common heritage for all mankind. Although the world is still divided by conflicting political interests and tensions, the inter-dependence of people becomes daily more evident on every side. A world international organisation is necessary and it is now also possible.
6. Make clear that the engagements freely entered with by the Member States of international organisations have force only in so far as they are actually and effectively supported by these peoples.
7. Arouse in the minds, particularly of young people a sense of responsibility to this community and to peace.
8. Encourage the development of healthy social attitudes in children so as to lay the foundations of improved international understanding and co-operation.

Programme Implementation

Our school programmes for international understanding should enable an individual.

1. To know and understand how peoples of other lands live.
2. To recognise the common humanity which underlines all differences in culture.
3. To work for a fair and just world.
4. To maintain interest in world affairs.
5. To recognise the importance of solving world problems according to democratic practices.
6. To appreciate the contribution of all peoples to the world citizenship.
7. To combine love of one's country with a broad social consciousness towards an inter-dependent community of nations.
8. To understand the economic, cultural and the like factors which make the world an inter-dependent community of nations.
9. To respect the dignity and worth of man by giving him equality of rights and opportunities.
10. To take world as one unit.
11. To realise that truth also triumphs and leads to human progress and prosperity.
12. To believe in common values and goals or the world community.
13. To understand that victories of peace are greater than victories of war.

Room for Education

Wrong Emphasis on 'My Country, Right or Wrong'. The Secondary Education Commission Report observes, "There is no more dangerous maxim in the world of today than, 'My country, right or wrong'. The whole world is now so intimately interrelated that no nation can or dare live alone without the development of a sense of world citizenship. In a very reach sense, therefore, patriotism is not enough and it must be supplemented by a lively realisation of the fact that we are all members of one world and must be prepared mentally and emotionally, to discharge the responsibilities which such membership implies." Nationalism should not be degenerate into nationalistic jingoism.

Adjustment of Human Consciousness. Dr. Radhakrishnan states, "We need today an adjustment of the human consciousness of the nuclear age in which we live. It is now conceivable that the human race may put an end to itself by nuclear warfare or preparations for it. This, if it happens, will be the result of the failure of man's consciousness to adjust to the technological revolution."

Progress in Art and Literature. K.G. Saiyidain writes, "There can neither be health, nor economic prosperity, nor the leisured pursuit of art and literature and culture in a world, that is either plunged in or overshadowed by war."

• ***More Interdependence and Intimate Relationship, in the World of Today.*** Modern scientific means of rapid communications—the radio, the television and the telephone—have conquered both space and time. K.G. Saiyidain rightly remarked, "A war starts in Europe and three million people die of famine in Bengal and millions more find themselves uprooted from their homeland, cut off from their national occupation and deprived of all that makes life pleasant, gracious, and meaningful."

In the words of P.E. James, "An industrial society by its essential nature, is global in its scope and international in its needs. If it is to survive, it must draw upon all the world's resources and all the world's people must share its benefits. Our way of living is dependent on the co-ordinated economic activities of distant people. This is the concept of one world—of one community of interdependent peoples."

Democratic Ideals. 'One World', 'One State' has taken the place of the slogan 'My country, right or wrong'. People have begun to realise that all men are equal and all the nations should strive for the betterment of the humanity so that all individuals get adequate opportunities to grow and develop.

Towards World Prosperity. The Vedic hymns speak of a world in which all people had a prosperous and happy life. India, true to her ancient traditions, rightly works for international understanding.

The Panchatantra states, "It is the thought of little-minded persons to inquire whether a man is one of ourselves or an alien."

Ways and Means of Creating World Understanding. Teaching for world understanding should pervade the whole educational programme – the attitudes of the members of the staff, curricular and co-curricular activities and experiences of the school. We have to fashion and plan our teaching and learning process in a way that the children can grow with world-mindedness. Social studies can be a very good means of promoting international understanding.

The Syllabus

Curriculum should enable our students:

(i) to learn that the earth is the home of man and other living things;

(ii) to learn the similarities and differences of the people of the world;

(iii) to learn the many ways of living on this planet and some of the reasons for the wide variety of modes of life;

(iv) to learn that world is a place of fun and beauty;

(v) to learn how to promote better understanding of the interdependence of the peoples of the world;

(vi) to learn about the division of the world into nations and culture and to make better adjustments;

(vii) to acquire an elementary knowledge of the major religions and the beliefs in the world today and to learn to respect persons whose views differ from their own;

(viii) to know something about the long struggle of mankind to replace conflict with co-operation;

(ix) to develop a desire and the simple skills to participate effectively in building a better world.

New Approaches

K.G. Saiyidain has said very lucidly that we should reorient our history teaching towards a higher and nobler objective and should bring through it re-education of people's ideas and emotions. The following points may be observed while teaching history:

(i) History of the countries should be taught objectively.

(ii) History should be taught with a cultural bias.

(iii) The impact of technological and scientific techniques on the lives of the different countries of the world should be stressed in the teaching of history.

(iv) The interdependence of different countries of the world should be explained in concrete terms.

(v) Selected stories from great personalities of the world like Gandhiji, Christ, Mohammed, Buddha, Alfred, etc., should be included.

(vi) Nothing should figure in the text book of history which may tend to spoil international harmony.

(vii) Students may be encouraged to read newspapers and magazines to increase their knowledge about the contemporary events.

(vii) Students should be told more and more about international agencies like the UNO and the UNESCO.

Geography: This enables an individual to have a vivid concept of the globe, where he can see all in parts in terms of the whole and where he can see his own country in inter-relationships. The students learn concretely how they depend upon others for the enrichment and happiness of their life. They come to know how geographical situations have affected the environment and course of history of different countries of the world. They are given a sense of space and location as affecting human actions.

Civics: A survey of certain countries' governments, economy, technology, family system, etc., would develop in children "an acceptance of differences and an appreciation of the reasons for cultural diversity." The students come to know that the modern civilisation is the result of the cumulative and cooperative effort of many people rather than the product of the genius of one people.

The Basis

The foundation of international understanding can be laid in the primary school. Indeed, it is especially important that effective work be done at this level, first because during these years children form fundamental attitudes which they carry with them into later stages of education and even into adult life, and second because most of the world's school children do not continue beyond primary stage.

"Most educators agree that one of the main tasks of the primary school should be to help children form healthy, well-balanced personalities. If they acquire respect for the rights of their fellows, a constructive approach to differences, a willingness to co-operate, and a sense of individual responsi-bility, they will be all the better prepared for the concepts of international understanding. Thus, the spirit of the school and the nature of the teacher-pupil relationship may be of most importance than the subject-matter taught."

"But direct teaching for international understanding is also possible. Many teachers believe that it should be undertaken with children from the age of 7 or 8 onwards. They can begin, for example, to learn something about other countries and their customs and about activities of the United Nations and its related agencies.

It is important, however, not to confront children with information or abstract ideas beyond their grasp."

Basic Level

(a) Stories of lives of great men and their main contribution to the world; i.e., those who have been fighters for freedom; who have moulded the destinies of a nation; great philosophers and saints and an effort should be made to emphasise their universal outlook, and love for humanity. In this could be included lives of Rama, Krishna, Buddha, Jesus, Mohammed, Kabir, Vivekananda, Dayanand, etc., as saints and religious reformers; Mahatma Gandhi, Nehru, Kennedy, Tolstoy, George Washington, Sun Yat Sen, Lenin as fighters for freedom.

(b) Lives of great scientists and mathematicians, e.g., Archimedes, Hevaclitus, Euclid, Pythagoras, Raman, Faraday, Addison, etc., may be taken up in simple story form and what they have contributed to mankind.

(c) Adventurers and explorers like Marcopolo, Scott, Magellan, Columbus, Vasco de Gama, etc.

Middle Level

(a) Teaching of social studies. It would be worthwhile if Social Studies is taught as an integrated subject. Different units may deal with topics on "Our Rights and Duties as Citizens" of free India (for class VI) and later of the world in class VIII or IX. The study and teaching of Human Rights would be possible in this context.

(b) Reading newspapers and books. This could very well be a topic for class VI and include the work done by UNESCO toward paper and print.

At this stage, it will also be possible to make a comparative study of the religions of the world. In class VIII common doctrines and tenets could be emphasised, e.g. the Ramayana, Gita, Bible, Qoran and Guru Granth Sahib along with Zoroastrianism and their Zend-Avesta and thus great personalities like Mahavira, Buddha, Shankaracharya, Nanak, Kabir, Ramananda, Chaitanya, Vivekananda, Swami Ram Tirath of India and in the same way of other countries could be introduced. Their unifying influence on society and in the removal of racial and other prejudices may be emphasised and a reference could be made to the aim of creating universal love for mankind – the cherished objective of the UNO.

High School Level

International understanding could be promoted through History and Geography too, but Civics and Economics provide an easier ground for pointedly teaching about the United Nations and its various agencies.

Topics like nationalism and internationalism invariably form part of the Civics syllabus as well as the UNO, the former League of Nations and so on.

Extra-curricular Activities

Following activities are suggested:

1. Reading materials based on:
   - (i) folk tales of different parts of India and of other countries;
   - (ii) Stories of children of other lands;
   - (iii) Fairy tales;
   - (iv) Simple stories based on epics and mythologies of other countries;
   - (v) Telling about famous men and women of India and of other countries, often in connection with anniversaries;
2. Dramatising stories from other lands.

3. Singing and performing action songs and dances from other lands;
4. Collecting pictures, handicrafts, household objects, dresses, etc., of other lands;
5. Organising exchanges at the school level of albums, toys, pictures, recorded music, children's books, children's paintings and drawings;
6. Field trips to museums, ports, markets, exhibitions and other educational institutions, wherever possible;
7. Establishing contacts between schools of different communities and nationalities located in the surrounding area. It might also be desirable for the city schools to develop contacts with sister-schools in the surrounding rural area. These contacts offer possibilities of promoting mutual understanding; and
8. Mutual exchange of children's games between schools of different regions.
9. Taking up such a project, the environment of the country, its historical background, lives of the people, social and religious organisations, lives of children, their hobbies, sports and games may be highlighted. Many similarities and differences between the country under study and India will come to the fore. Children should be led to appreciate the differences and the basic similarities of life, values and aspirations. In the planning of the projects, children's interests and their development needs should be given due consideration.

Programmes for Exchange

Exchange of different kinds of materials between schools inside the country and other countries could be profitably undertaken as an aid to promote international understanding. Such an exchange would include:

1. Exchange of outlines of different projects regarding the study of countries.
2. Exchange of outlines of different projects regarding the study of countries in return.
3. Helping students of one group to develop correspondence with children of the same age group in the country taken up for study. The correspondence could help children in collecting information about the varied aspects of the life of the people, description of daily life at home, in school, entertainments, games, food habits, dresses, occupations and products. Such correspondence may also result in exchange of posters, slides, tape-records, filmstrips, picture books, pictures of places of interest, art pictures, coins, toys, crafts, information about hobbies, songs, dramas, films and games.
4. Teaching and exhibition materials could also be exchanged. This would include:
   (i) Text-books, reference materials, children's magazine (manuscript and printed), scrap books, albums, newspapers, tape-records, folk songs, dramatic scripts, etc.
   (ii) Pictures and books of great men of science, arts, political life and leaders.
   (iii) Children's books, folk tales, explores, adventures, prophets, etc. (iv) National songs, festivals and procedures for celebrating.

Exchange of Teachers

1. The Indian National Commission for Cooperation with UNESCO and the Ministry of Human Resource Development should expand the programme of awarding fellowships to Indian teachers to enable them to study and work in schools in other countries.

2. Possibilities of school-to-school contacts for exchange of teachers in different parts of the country and between different teachers and between India and other countries should be explored. The Indian National Commission could help by preparing a list of such institutions which are interested in this type of programme.
3. The help of voluntary organisations like New Education Fellowship, Rotary Club, Lions Club, Experiment in International Living, World Confederation of Organisations of Teaching Profession, Indian Council for Cultural Relations, etc., could be sought with advantage in this connection.

Exchange of Students

1. There are great possibilities of promoting international understanding if educational authorities arrange short duration camps during holidays in which students from one region may live, study and work with students, of another region.
2. For the purpose of international exchange of students, the Scout Jamborees, the International Voluntary Work Camp Movement and such other projects may be exploited with advantage.

Use of Postage Stamps: The postage stamps can play a very vital role and provide many possibilities of enriching the curriculum work and co-curricular activities in the school particularly where a project on another country is being planned. The teachers can utilise the stamps to the maximum advantage of fulfilling the objectives of the project on understanding the country. In the study of great personalities of a country, the series of stamps on those personalities is a very handy tool to be used. Almost every country has brought out stamps on their poets, saints, scientists, great statesmen, pioneers, humanitarians, besides the flora, fauna and the beautiful landscape.

Role of Teachers

Teachers can develop attitudes favourable to international understanding among their students. Regarding the role of the teacher, CJF. Strong has observed, "He and the curriculum represent two vital formative factors for translating the aims and ideas of education into practice."

Teachers' Role outside the School. Outside the school, teachers can play their part as intelligent and educated adults. "It is for teachers, as people above average in training and in conscientiousness to find time for grown-ups as well as children, and to give all possible support to those organisations which are concerned with informing the mind and stirring the social conscience of the adult community."

Teachers' Role in Teaching Social Study. Teachers can and must do better work in this field. They can and must teach students to use their eyes and their ears with sufficient intelligence to distinguish fact from propaganda and to substitute comprehension for prejudice. They must develop a proper regard for the use of reason rather than force. This point has been stressed by Mr. Saiyidain in these words, "a first condition for the functioning of an educated and peaceful democracy is that people should regard loyalty to truth as more important than any other loyalty in life, whether to one's nation or race or country or community or anything else."

Teachers' Role in Understanding the Child. A UNESCO publication reads as follows: "We hold that in a very real sense: 'wars begin in the minds of men,' that war is a mental disorder strictly analogous with the psychological disease it sometimes cause. Therefore, we regard it as a matter of importance for social and international living that educators should be more concerned with the child, and the healthy development of his body and mind, than with the contents of the various subjects which go to make a school curricula'."

Research in International Concepts and Attitudes. Investigations may be made by the teachers in finding out methods whereby improved concepts and attitudes in the field of international understanding may be developed. At an early stage in the course, the staff should try to learn the attitudes of the students, the extent of training in international understanding which may be needed.

Visit to other Lands. Staff members should be encouraged, by leave of absence, financial aid, and by other means, to study and travel in other countries, and that exchange of staff members be arranged as frequently as possible.

Faith and Enthusiasm. Teachers should have faith and enthusiasm for the value of international understanding and co-operation and should possess the equipment to infuse this spirit in the minds of their students.

Emphasising the Value of International Understanding. While teaching various subjects the teachers should concentrate in helping students build up proper behaviour pattern and psychological dispositions impressing upon their minds that barriers of race, colour and distance do not stand in the way of uniting peoples of different countries.

Objective and Impartial Treatment. They should avoid indoctrinating the mind of the pupils. They should be impartial and highly objective in interpreting or describing facts. They should not be propagandists.

They should impress upon the students that, 'man' remains 'man' first and then he can be called a Jew, an Englishman, a German, Russian, Indian and American.

They should impress upon the students that there is no special merit or value in being born in one part or the other.

Awareness about World Situations. They should be well informed about the contemporary world science and its historical background, and concerned about improving the conditions of people everywhere and try to make students well informed.

Organisation of Activities in the School. They should organise the following types of activities in the school for developing an international outlook in the students.

(i) Organisation of UN Societies and international clubs.

(ii) Celebration of social days for heroes of peace and great men of all nations.

(iii) Displaying of dramas showing the horrors of war.

(iv) Encouraging students to collect stamps and develop pen-friendship between children of different countries.

(v) Organisation of debates, lectures and discussions on the working of the UNO.

We may close the topic with a quotation from Leonard S. Kenworthy that a world-minded teacher is an integrated individual, skilled in the science of human relations, and conscious of the wide variety of behaviour patterns in the world to which he may have to adjust—an intelligent participant in efforts to improve his own community and nation, mindful of their relationship to the world community, clear in his mind about the goals of education for international understanding.

UNESCO'S Contribution

Unesco is one of the specialised agencies of the United Nations. Its operation and structure are determined by its constitution which was drawn up by the members of the London Conference in 1945. This embodies the beliefs and hopes for the world of the Member States of the organisation. "Member States have accepted, among other principles, that a peace based exclusively upon the political and economic arrangements of Government would not be a peace which could secure the unanimous, lasting and sincere support of the people of the world, and that the peace must, therefore, be founded, if it is not to fail, upon the intellectual and moral solidarity of mankind." The Constitution declares that "the wide diffusion of culture, and the education of the humanity for justice and liberty and peace are indispensable to the dignity of man and constitute a sacred duty which all nations must fulfil in a spirit of mutual assistance and concern." It states that "ignorance of each other's ways and lives has been a common cause, throughout the history of mankind, of that suspicious and mistrust between the people of the world through which their differences have all too often broken into war." These are some of the ideas expressed in the document which determine the nature and purpose of the work of Unesco.

UNESCO'S Objectives

Article 1 of UNESCO's constitution states: "The purpose of the organisation is to contribute to peace and security by promoting collaboration among the nations through education, science and culture in order lo further universal respect for justice, for the rule of law and for human rights and fundamental freedoms which are for the people of the world, without distinction of race, sex, language or religion, by the charter of the United Nations." To achieve this broad aim three main fields of work are prescribed. The first is to "collaborate in the work of advancing the mutual knowledge and understanding of people, through all means of mass communication" and "to work towards the promotion of the free flow of ideas by word and image." The second is to "give fresh impulse to popular education and to the spread of culture." Finally, Unesco is to "maintain, increase and diffuse knowledge" by various means, including the conservation of the world inheritance of learning and culture and the encouragement of co-operation between countries in all branches of intellectual activity. These objectives are confirmed in the Universal Declaration of Human Rights, adopted by the General Assembly in 1948. Article 26 of the Declaration proclaims that "everyone has the right to education" and that "education shall be directed towards the full development of the human personality and to strengthening of respect of human rights and fundamental freedoms." Article 27 continues by declaring that "Everyone has the right freely to participate in the cultural life of the community, to enjoy the arts and to share in scientific advancement and its benefits."

Commissions on Education

The importance of the individual in the kind of the work undertaken by Unesco was recognised in the constitution. To make participation by the individual and by private bodies more direct, the constitution provides for the formation of national co-operation bodies, or National Commission, to integrate individual work in Member States with the work of the organisation. Most Member States have set up such Commissions. They are, broadly, representative of their respective governments and of the principal national bodies interested in work of an educational, scientific and cultural nature. These Commissions function as liaison agencies and sources of information in their own countries.

1. It tries to rehabilitate the devastated countries culturally.
2. It strives for world peace by taking the following steps:
   - (i) International exchange of teachers and students in order to remove racial prejudice.
   - (ii) The organisation of international camps where students of different nations will meet each other and exchange their views.
   - (iii) Organising tours of foreign countries so as to bring about understanding and goodwill.
   - (iv) Organisation of study circles with a view to studying the needs of other nations.
   - (v) Writing of history books with an international outlook.
   - (vi) Establishment of an international university so as to discuss common problems of all the nations.
   - (vii) Establishment of International Civil Service in due course that its employees may render service to the entire universe.
   - (viii) Reorganisation of the press, the radio and the cinema for international welfare.
   - (ix) The reduction of illiteracy especially in backward countries.

(x) Translating literary classics and significant contemporary works.

(xi) Organising art exhibitions.

(xii) Expansion of libraries and museums.

(xiii) Fostering international understanding through the improvement of curricula and experimental activities in teacher training institutions.

The Unesco has been doing a useful work for providing a proper environment for the success of UNO. Dr. Radhakrishnan has rightly stated:

"There is nothing national with regard to education. The different countries are provinces of a common republic of culture. There is no such thing as Proletarian Mathematics or Nazi Chemistry or Jewish Physics. Culture is international and science is cosmopolitan in its essence and reality."

Genesis. An interim Indian National Commission for Cooperation with Unesco was set up in 1949 by the Government of India, Ministry of Education. The Interim Commission was placed on permanent footing in 1951 in order to ensure a better implementation of Unesco's programme in the country.

The constitution of the Indian National Commission was revised in 1969.

The Actions

1. Dissemination of information about Unesco and other countries.
2. Celebration of UN Day, Human Rights Day and International Literacy year, Centenaries, Book years, etc.
3. Exchange of Persons.
4. Liaison with States and Universities.
5. Relations with other National Commissions.
6. Publications.

7. Associated School Projects.
8. Unesco International Coupon Scheme for assisting import of books.
9. Assisting Indian Exports to find Unesco jobs.
10. Unesco Clubs.

UNESCO associated school project. There are now over 800 schools and teacher training colleges in 61 countries participating in this programme. In 1953 when India joined the programme it started with six institutions which later increased to 38. These schools work on three main themes:

(a) Teaching about the United Nations and its Specialised Agencies,

(b) Teaching about the Human Rights and Fundamental Freedom, and

(c) Teaching about other countries.

UNESCO Clubs. The Indian Commission for Unesco has been encouraging the establishment of Unesco Clubs/Centres in different Universities. Public Libraries and other Educational/Cultural Organisations in India to function as the main clearing house to disseminate information about the purpose and programmes of Unesco, to enlist the support of individuals or groups interested in the fields of Education, Science, Culture and Mass Communication and to promote and popularise the work of Unesco.

At present we have about ' 300 Unesco Clubs/Centres which are functioning at different places in India. Sponsoring and setting up of Unesco Clubs/Centres is a significant trend in the efforts of the Indian National Commission for Unesco to obtain the support of maximum number or agencies for the Programme of Unesco.

QUESTIONS

1. Explain the meaning of education for international understanding. What are the hindrances in achieving this aim?

2. State the methods of promoting international understanding at the middle stage.
3. Why was UNESCO formed? Describe its role in the promotion of international understanding.
4. Outline the role of the Social Studies teacher in the promotion of international understanding among his students.
5. Write brief notes on the following:-
   (a) Indian National Commission for Cooperation with UNESCO.
   (b) UNESCO Clubs.
   (c) UNESCO Associated School Project.

22

Educating Citizens

An examination of social trends and emerging problems indicates that changes are necessary in the process of civic and social education within the schools and outside. The present political and economic conditions in India, the results of invention and technology and our relationships with the rest of the world require a serious study of the needs and possibilities of a suitable type of civic and social education. Never in the history of India has it been so necessary for the schools to readjust their work to accord with the social and economic changes that came with the dawn of the freedom of the country. Moreover, in a world in which the products of scientific inventiveness have so greatly outstripped their social and political controls, a varied and an intelligent programme of citizenship education must be adopted and carried through. Social Studies can play an active role in citizenship training.

The Concept

By education for citizenship we mean the development of the ideas, beliefs, habits, behaviour and attitudes of the individual so that he may become a useful member of the society and contribute his share for the uplift of the society.

Experiences and Situations	Learning Outcomes
1. *Student Council*. Sharing some of the functions of school administration with the students in the form of student council which may be responsible for making rules for discipline and work, organising games and sports, planning co-curricular activities, looking after school property, running cooperative store and a school canteen, preparing school handbook, looking after the school reading room, health and sanitation etc.	1. Students get practical experiences in the working of representative government, in choosing their representatives, in making and obeying laws made by them and others in formulating their judgement on matters of conduct and learn the necessity of having rules and regulations for our everyday behaviour in various groups and situations.
2. *Surveys*. Making surveys of the various needs of the locality.	2. The students develop the sense of belongingness to to the community and the part to be played by them.
3. *Social Service*. Social service to the school and locality by doing jobs like cleaning the school and surroundings, beautifying	3. The students develop a sense of responsibility and become acquainted with the social and civic problems and the need to tackle them.
4. *Visits to Legislatures*. Visits to legislatures i.e., Parliament, Assembly,	4. This helps children to acquire first hand information of the working of a democratic setup.
5. *Morning Assemble*. Holding regular morning assembly and congregational prayers.	5. This provides a good start for the daily routine of the school. Students develop qualities like God fearing and realise their responsibility to their fellows. They learn audience habits also. They are inspired to do noble deeds.

Contd.

Experiences and Situations	Learning Outcomes
6. *Debates.* Organising debates and discussions.	6. This enables the students to formulate their own judgement, and to develop habits of thinking independently, scientifically and creatively. Students learn to become good speakers and debaters.
7. *Clubs.* Having clubs for the organisation of musical and dramatic activities.	7. Students develop aesthetic sense.
8. *Educational tours.* Organising camps, excursions and educational tours.	8. Students develop a spirit of belongingness to a much large area, their mental horizons is widened. They learn to work together, pool their ideas and to adjust with each other by knowing the qualities or shortcomings of each other.
9. *Students' days.* Organising students' days in schools and assigning them the teaching work along with other school activities, students themselves acting as principals and teachers; the school personnel being busy with the task of guiding them in the staff room.	9. This is a very good method of impressing upon the students to learn virtues of self-discipline. The students working as teachers on that particular day learn how to control classes and develop qualities of leadership.
10. *Celebration of national days.* Celebrating National days. Community festivals and fairs.	10. Children become acquainted with the lives of great men and develop a sense of obligation to the heroes and mother-land and a sense of patriotism.

According to Payne, "Students come to school to learn to be healthy, to acquire civic practices, participate actively in home betterments, to learn to participate in groups, to properly utilise leisure and the like."

A Leslie Hutchinson observes that education is concerned with the whole man in a changing world which is the province of education for citizenship. Are we or are we not fitting our children to live wisely in the ever changing society?

It has been stated in a pamphlet entitled Citizens Growing Up, issued by the British Ministry of Education. "Man is primarily an individual soul with a personal destiny, a need for privacy and a solitude.... But this destiny is worked out and this personality is fulfilled largely through human relationships. It is these relationships public or political and private or personal that together constitute the background of citizenship."

In the words of the Mudaliar Commission, "Citizenship in a democracy is a very exacting and challenging responsibility for which every citizen has to be trained. It involves many intellectual, social and moral qualities."

Aims and Motives

Education for citizenship should enable an individual:

(a) To understand the social, economic and political forces that are shaping the face of the modern world.

(b) To be tolerant and broadminded.

(c) To think clearly and effectively without any kind of prejudice.

(d) To make decisions independently.

(e) To be a patriot in the true sense with a cosmopolitan outlook.

(f) To be a good leader and a follower.

(g) To be devoted to freedom.

(h) To admit his follies, if any.

(i) To understand his rights and responsibilities.
(j) To earn his livelihood in an honest way.
(k) To be firm against heavy odds.
(l) To utilise his leisure profitably.
(m) To act upon principles courageously.
(n) To maintain intergroup Understanding.
(o) To have faith in democratic ideals of life.
(p) To believe in the quality of man.
(q) To have a goal to make further progress.

Citizenship through Social Studies. The social studies teachers have to play an important role. They should utilise all the available opportunities to impart this training. The subject of social studies introduces the pupils to the political, economic and social life which they will enter after the school. As a matter of fact, the basic goal of social studies is education for citizenship. There are two important approaches for imparting training in citizenship.

The Exemplary Approach. Generally it is felt that example is better than precept. What may not be achieved by moralising, may be achieved through the examples of the members of the staff. The teachers of social studies set examples of ideal behaviour in their relations towards others and give an idea to their pupils about citizenship education.

Visits to legislatures may be organised and the students enabled to see how laws are framed by the elected members.

Providing experience. Experience is the best teacher. Opportunities for active and responsible participation should be given to the students both in the school and the community. Nobody can deny the fact that civic attitudes are learned and are the result of repetition and reinforcement. Group methods of teaching, class projects and group competition can help a great deal in this respect. A large number of activities should be provided which will train the students in citizenship and develop social interaction varying with the age and ability of the individual to participate and appreciate social experiences. Activities like student councils and parliament, organisation of play activities, the dramatics, the literary dramatic clubs may be undertaken.

Davis Valentine in *The Matter and Method of Modern Teaching* stresses the importance of providing direct experiences for developing understanding skills and attitudes which are basic to good citizenship and writes, that this will build up in the individual a strong and stable sentiment of loyalty to whole community and to varying interests expressed and embodied there ... It is that experience that is the real centre of the preparation for the larger loyalties of life.

Conclusion. By living and working in the school community, the young, people learn that rights involve responsibilities, freedom implies restraint and that the membership of the school community carries with it a sense of responsibility for the welfare and good reputation of the school as a whole.

Each letter of the word citizenship may be taken to denote as under:

C denotes	:	Clear thinking
		Common good
		Community feeling
		Consideration
		Constitutional respect
		Constructive thinking
		Cooperation
I denotes	:	Impartiality
		Individual's recognition
		Intelligent action
T denotes	:	Tolerance
Z denotes	:	Zeal
E denotes	:	Equal treatment

N denotes	:	National pride
S denotes	:	Self-discipline
H denotes	:	Social attitude
		Hard work
		Humility
I denotes	:	International outlook
P denotes	:	Patience
		Patriotism
		Public spirit
		Punctuality

Emotional Integration

It is a feeling of oneness which transcends all groups or cultural differences and synthesises the different castes, linguistic and religious communities emotionally into a compact whole. It is that cementing force that binds the citizens of a country in a unity. Emotional and national integration is the development of a mental climate that would help react in terms of oneness. It is an antidote to separatistic and divisive forces, narrow and fissiparous tendencies which sometimes tend to eat the vitals of national unity. National integration must inculcate pride and respect for the best in our cultural heritage and a wish to improve our country.

National Integration

This is required on account of the following reasons:

1. National unity is the primary requisite for national existence.
2. Country's progress in social, economic and political spheres depends upon the cooperation of all parts and all people of a country.
3. Loyalties such as one's own caste, community, race, religion or region stand in the way of national prosperity.

4. The ideals of democracy, secularism and socialism enshrined in our constitution can be realized only through emotional and national integration.

Jawaharlal Nehru stressed four aspects of national and emotional integration:

National Integration for the Creation of a Mighty Nation. The main thing we have to keep in mind is the emotional integration of India. We must guard against being swept away by momentary passion, whether it is religion misapplied to politics or communalism or provincialism or casteism. We have to build up this great country into a mighty nation, mighty not in the ordinary sense of the word, that is, having great armies and all that, but mighty in thought, mighty in action, mighty in culture and mighty in its peaceful service of humanity,

We should not become parochial, narrow-minded, provincial, communal and caste-minded, because we have a great mission to perform. Let us, the citizens of the Republic of India, stand up straight, with straight backs, and look up at the skies, keeping our feet firmly planted on the ground and bring about this synthesis, this integration of the Indian people. Political integration has already taken place to some extent, but what I am after is something much deeper that of an emotional integration of the Indian people so that we might be welded into one, and made into one strong national unit, maintaining at the same time all our wonderful diversity.

National Integration for the Success of Democracy and Socialism. Democracy, while it ensures free expression, and freedom of thinking, also demands something else. It demands unified action afterwards. It demands acceptance of decisions taken. Otherwise, there is a break-up. You are acquainted somewhat with the history of India. It has been our misfortune through long periods of history to be very factitious, to be liable to separatism, with the result that the great strength of India has been wasted in inner conflict, in inner argument and in fissiparous and separatist tendencies. Surely, we should learn something from the history of

India. We have produced great men in every field of human endeavour, in thought, in action, in art, in literature, in music. Yet we have failed to take advantage of this greatness because of the tendency amongst us to disrupt, to go our individual ways.

National Integration by Ending the Curse of Caste System. What will emerge from the labour and the tumults of the present generation? I cannot say what will tomorrow's India be like. I can only express my hopes and wishes. I want India to advance on the material plane to raise the standards of living of her vast population. I want the narrow conflicts of today in the name of religion or caste, language or province, to cease, and a classless and casteless society to be built up where every individual has full opportunity to grow according to his worth and ability. In particular, I hope that the curse of caste will be ended, for there cannot be either democracy or socialism on the basis of caste.

National Integration through Synthesising Religious Values. Four great religions have influenced India, two emerging from her own thought, Hinduism and Buddhism, and two coming from abroad but establishing themselves firmly in India, Christianity and Islam. Science today challenges the old concept of religion. But if religion deals not with dogmas and ceremonials, but rather with the higher things of life, there should be no conflict with Science or *inter se* between religions. It might be the high privilege of India to help in bringing about this synthesis. That would be in India's ancient tradition inscribed on Ashoka's Edicts.

Emotional Integration Committee (1961) on the Role of Social Studies in Emotional Integration

The Ministry of Education, Government of India, appointed the Committee on Emotional Integration under the Chairmanship of Dr. Sampurnanand in 1961. The Committee made valuable recommendations on the role of education in promoting the process of emotional integration programmes for youth in schools and colleges. The Committee laid special stress on the role of social studies. It observed, "The teaching of social studies at all levels i.e. the primary, secondary and University stages would impart knowledge of the geographical, historical and cultural background of the country and the world as a whole."

Suggestions. The Committee gave the following suggestions:

Re-orientation of the Curriculum. It is felt that the school and college curriculum should be reoriented to suit the needs of a secular state.

At the primary stage stories, poems, folklore and teaching of social studies, national anthem and other national songs, should find an important place.

At the secondary stage the curriculum should include, among other things, the study of language and literature, social studies, moral and religious instruction and co-curricular activities.

At the University level the study of different social sciences, languages and literature, culture and art and also the exchange of teachers and students should find place in the curriculum.

Co-curricular Activities. The place of co-curricular activities in the curriculum is considered to be very important. It is felt that participation in co-curricular activities helps in growth of a well balanced and well adjusted personality. It creates a group feeling of oneness and brotherhood, broadens the outlook and develops a catholicity of spirit and tolerance which are necessary for good citizenship. These activities include common observance and celebration of festivals and events of national importance, sports, educational excursions, tours and picnics, military training like the N.C.C., A.C.C., Scouts and Guides, Student Campus Debates, Symposia, dramatics and youth festivals. The use of audio-visual aids like films, pictures, radio and T.V. is very necessary.

Text Books. In order that the text-books play their legitimate role in strengthening emotional integration, it is necessary that they be reoriented and improved. In a preparation of history text-books special care needs to be taken to see that facts are not misrepresented, distorted or exaggerated to create prejudice. The get-up as well as the content of text-books require a change. At the primary level, the text-books writers should make a liberal use of pictures and illustrations so as to create interest in the child at the very outset.

Singing of National Anthem. Children should be taught to sing the National Anthem in unison and behave in a disciplined way when it is sung. They should also be taught the meaning of verses.

Reverence for the National Flag. Students should be told the history of the National Flag and taught at the very earliest stage to show reverence to the National Flag.

Celebrations of National Days. January 26, August 15 and October 2 should be celebrated in the schools with the full participation of the teachers, the students and the community.

Special Talks on the Unity and Oneness of the Country. Special meetings of the school assembly should be held from time to time and the speakers speak to the children on topics dealing with the unity and oneness of the country.

Taking Pledge. Students may be asked to repeat a pledge twice a year dedicating themselves to the service of their country and their countrymen. A draft of such a pledge in English is given below:

"India is my country, all Indians are my brothers and sisters.
I love my country, and I am proud of its rich and varied
heritage. I shall always strive to be worthy of it.
I shall give my parents, teachers and all elders respect and
treat everyone with courtesy. I shall be kind to animals.
To my country and my people, I pledge my devotion. In their
well being and prosperity alone lies my happiness."

Open Air Dramas. Open air dramas may be staged four times a year by every school. At last one play should be based upon a theme derived from the classics or from the history of ancient India. In predominant Hindu areas there should be some plays dealing with non-Hindu lives and vice versa.

Students Exchange and Tours. Such tours should be conducted from one State to another. The inter-State visits, if properly organised, should do much to acquaint both teacher and children with different parts of the country.

A network of youth hostels should be set up by all the States in selected places.

School Improvement. Students should be associated with the cleanliness of the school premises. This would not only increase their pride in it, and loyalty to the school but would also help in improving the school for future students.

Suitable Hand Books for Teachers. Suitable hand books for teachers in the social studies and languages should be published.

All India Award. An annual all India award for the best general essay on different States in India should be instituted.

Educational and Travel Documentaries. Educational and travel documentaries with particular emphasis on various aspects of Indian scenery, flora and fauna, on various developmental and reconstruction programmes should be produced for use in schools and these should form a regular feature of the schools.

School Projects. Schools may conduct several projects which improve their general knowledge of the country. For instance, a 'know your country' project can be undertaken during which children may share in your collection of information about a State in the Indian Union other than their own.

Exchange of Professors. Distinguished professors should also be deputed periodically to different universities so that a large number of student can benefit from their experience.

All India Youth Council. An All India Youth Council should be set up to coordinate all the youth programmes taken up by the Central and State Governments and also to help these various agencies to extend their efforts.

The emotional integration of the Indian people is a challenge that cannot be ignored charity and compassion must be practised if they are not to remain catchwords and empty phrases. Integration touches all points of national life and depends in the final analysis on our young people in schools and colleges. Of all the teachers of the educational institutions, teachers of social studies can play an important role in the field of national and emotional integration.

QUESTIONS

1. State the role of a teacher of Social Studies in developing and promoting values of emotional integration among students.
2. Elucidate the concept of emotional integration.
3. Explain the concept citizenship.
4. What steps should be taken to inculcate ideal of citizenship among students?